Jenni Keasden and Natalia Szarek

WORTH FIGHTING FOR
Bringing the Rojava revolution home

First published by Active Distribution in April 2023
This edition printed by Active Distribution in September 2023

Cover by Matt Bonner

Photo credits to the Rojava Information Center, YPJ Press Office, ANF, North Press Agency, Autonomous Administration of North and East Syria, and Hawzhin Azeez

ISBN 978 1 914567 21 6

www.activedistribution.org

*This book is dedicated to Anna Campbell
and to all those who have fallen in the fight for freedom*

ANKARA

TURKEY

BAKUR

ROJAVA

SYRIA

DAMASCUS

MAP OF
KURDISTAN

The distrubution of the Kurdish
population in the Middle East.

N

TURKEY

KOBANI

TEL ABYAD

AFRIN

ALEPPO

SYRIA

MAP OF
ROJAVA
Autonomous Administration of North and East Syria

Source: Rojava Information Centre, May 2020

QAMIŞLO

DERIK

SEREKANIYE

AL-HASAKAH

ROJAVA

IRAQ

QA

Areas within the Autonomous Administration of North and East Syria, emerging from the Rojava revolution

Occupied by Turkish army and Turkish backed mercenaries

Territories under Assad's Syrian regime

TABLE OF CONTENTS

PREFACE

Throughout our lives, we write to make sense of the world around us.

Sometimes it's love letters to friends in other cities. Sometimes it's poetry in the early hours of the morning, urgent blog posts and social media updates to tell people what's happening, journal entries of reflection and release.

Sometimes writing is uncompromising as it looks you in the eye, and sometimes the truth is subtle and sits between the lines.

But it's always stories, because stories are where we find strength in times of despair. Stories move us to **tears at the suffering of strangers. It's with stories that we send children off to dream.** If we want to know what's happening around the world, we can turn on the news. But if we want to imagine a new one, we need to tell stories.

In short, stories are powerful.

As we struggle to shape the future, we look to the social movements that have come before us to learn more about ourselves. Reflecting on her time in the Black Panther Party, militant Ericka Huggins uses a parable that comes from many traditional tales, one of men describing an elephant only by feel. One touches the elephant's side and says 'It's like a wall". Another the tusk and says 'It's like a spear" and another the trunk and says, 'It's like a snake" and so on. Huggins compares this to talking about the Black Panther Party: *"We knew the party we were in. Not the entire thing. We were making history, and it wasn't nice and clean. It wasn't easy, it was complex."* In the spirit that we are made up of our histories and not trying to be completely original, we would like to echo Huggins on this just as she was echoing age old tales. No one could sum up the Kurdistan Freedom Movement, or the revolution in North and East Syria. Especially not through a few peoples' experiences, especially not those of us who came from other places. We have no intention of trying. But we don't have to claim our perspectives are all-encompassing or objective to tell our stories. Stories are not just about remembering facts correctly- far from it. What we learn from our experiences – how we grow and who we become through living them - is just as important as the experiences themselves. When we learn something in one place that can be useful in another, we have a duty to try and share it as best we can.

We wanted to bring revolution home through stories of both the epic and the mundane, through day to day moments in all of their messiness and poetry. In a world where earnestness is looked down on, this book is where we give ourselves permission to fall in love with a revolution. This book is a product of shared moments with hundreds of comrades, of tales hundreds of years old, of the novels we read as children, of militant struggles old and new, and of an ongoing conversation that's happening right now. We didn't start it and we certainly aren't trying to finish it. But the more people contribute the richer we can build the future. This is what we are committed to be a part of.

It's impossible to summarise the complex history, geopolitics and ideologies that have shaped the Kurdistan Freedom Movement, and our experiences as internationalists within it. There's also the messy, imperfect, complex game of translation, both literal and cultural. We've included some key terms in the glossary on page 251, and tried to write in a way that assumes no background knowledge from readers, whilst not getting bogged down in definitions and context. The history and context is already far better explained in much more depth in other works and we have included some in the suggested reading on page 255.

BACKGROUND

Kurdistan is a land that has been divided. The British and French empires chopped up the region, and put sections under the control of Turkey, Iran, Iraq and Syria in the early 20th century. Kurdish resistance to oppression runs back even further and continues to this day. The Kurdish region of Syria (known as *Rojava*) caught the attention of the world after the uprisings across the Arab world in 2011. The Kurdistan Freedom Movement, which had been organising across all four parts of Kurdistan for decades, seized its chance. Autonomous regions in northern Syria were officially established in 2012, with people's councils driving out the Assad regime's forces and taking control of defence and governance. Though this was originally driven by Kurdish communities, the uprisings and the organisational structures that arose from it are explicit in its inclusion of all ethnic groups. Since the initial establishment of autonomous territory, the revolution has spread beyond Rojava (the predominantly Kurdish region), across a wide area of northeastern Syria.

The Kurdistan Freedom Movement is the social movement that has emerged out of Kurdistan's anti-colonial struggles of the 1960s and 70s. Its goal is to create a new kind of political and social system based on the pillars of grass-roots democracy, women's liberation, and ecology. With the weakening of the Syrian state, organisers within the Kurdistan Freedom Movement got the chance to really start putting this into practice within the autonomous regions of Rojava. When the Islamic State threatened to overrun the regions, they were ready to defend. The war against ISIS was a test of the self defence forces and drew a lot of international attention to Rojava, especially at the Battle of Kobane in 2014-15. Increasing numbers of international volunteers began to travel to North and East Syria to be involved in the movement and in its defence.

Bordering Syria to the north, Turkey has a long history of repression against the Kurdish population within its own borders. The Turkish state sees the autonomous region of Rojava to the south as a threat to its own authoritarian control. It has launched two major invasions of North and East Syria since 2013, consistently funded jihadist gangs in the region and engaged in constant low level aggression.

Despite the instability, North and East Syria continues to be an example of an extremely rare kind of politics. As such it is a magnet for radicals and revolutionaries from around the world.

Members of the HPC Jin Women's Civil Defence Forces

I. BEGINNING

Joining the Rojava Revolution
Jenni

Christmas day 2018 and I wake up in a massive old canvas tent under thick blankets. It's full of more than a hundred women, many still invisible under their own blanket mountains. Others are starting to move around, calling out to each other in a mix of Kurdish and Arabic. They smoke, wash, and bring strong tea and buckets of sugar. I stand up creakily, already fully dressed, and step outside. The border wall built by the Turkish state that divides North and West Kurdistan looms over us. A trio of flags fly on our side: of Kurdistan, of the YPG (People's Defence Units) and the YPJ (Women's Defence Units). They flutter bravely, only about three hundred metres away from the Turkish flag waving on the border wall. North Kurdistan is enclosed by Turkey's national borders and the indigenous Kurdish community struggles against extreme repression there. I'm standing on the other side of the wall, in the city of Serekaniye, in Rojava — the Kurdish name for West Kurdistan. Rojava is the home of a women's revolution, the people's revolution that has created an autonomous zone across North and East Syria. Those three hundred metres are a long, long way.

I check my watch, something I've already been grateful for many times over in my stay, as phone batteries die far from a charging point. It's 7.30am. It's cold, not as cold as a winter morning at home, but I can see my breath. The reason hundreds of us are here at the border wall in tents is very simple. The Turkish state has declared its imminent invasion of North and East Syria. And when you know even a little about the revolution in North and East Syria and the Kurdistan Freedom Movement, it's obvious that there's only one reasonable response to a threat like that. The incredibly strong organisational networks leap into action, bringing hundreds of people from all across society face to face with the Turkish army, to show their defiance, and to dance.

And dance we do. By the time I blink my way out of the tent the sun has not long risen but the dance is already going strong. Partly because of the cold. Inside the tents there are gas stoves, and a little away from the centre of the site there will be a fire later, but essentially the strong tea and the dancing are our main source of heating.

Kurdish dancing comes in long lines, everyone joining hands with anyone, men and women, young and old. There's never too many people, the spirals just get wider and wider to include everyone, spilling out of the site and round the back of the tents if they need to. Some people dance in leaps and bounds with flourishes, breaking and twisting away but always based on the same basic pattern. Some of us, mostly us newly arrived westerners, stumble through the basics. People come and go in shifts, but apart from breaks for speeches, chanting slogans, or welcoming the arrival of a new bus load of people organised by another municipality, the dance itself doesn't stop from morning until long into the night.

Some people here say we're a 'human shield' — one that is proudly standing between the enemy and our land and people. Of course, the YPG and YPJ have no intention of literally letting hundreds of civilians stand unprotected in the way of a military onslaught. These demonstrations are one part of a huge network of preparations — in military bases across the region the women and men of the self defence forces are getting ready to defend their communities with weapons. But in another sense, what we're doing here is anything but symbolic. The revolution, and the social movement that drives it, is fundamentally made up of the people. If it was not, it would have been extinguished years ago. The military forces alone could never resist the Turkish army, with its state of the art technology and the backing of NATO and Russia. The strength of the movement lies in how deeply rooted it is in people's everyday lives, all the day to day, unglamorous, human work and organising. Over the past decade, the movement has resolved community disputes, created economic possibilities, provided emergency accommodation and food to hundreds of thousands of displaced people, and made sure everyone can afford bread and fuel.

It can be hard to pin down exactly how to describe the movement, or even what to call it: the Rojava revolution, the people's autonomous democracy of North and East Syria, or the Kurdistan Freedom Movement more broadly. Whatever we call it, the movement is about so much more than military self defence. Self defence is essential to survive, but a revolution means a much deeper transformation. To say the people 'support' the movement doesn't even explain it; in a sense they are the movement and the movement is them. So when the people stand up to face the Turkish border wall and shout "We are here!", it's also a display of strength.

I am there as part of a small group of international volunteers, and we're still new in North and East Syria. Communication is a faltering game, and the mothers and grandmothers we sit with around stoves and cups of tea are endlessly patient with our stumbling attempts at conversation. For us it is worth every word, hearing how they organise in their communities, what life was like before and after the revolution, how they feel about the children they've lost in war. Before going, I felt hesitant about invading or imposing, getting in the way or trying to hijack their day. But when it feels like the whole world is lined up against you, and when all the dominant powers really are getting ready to either attack you in the front or sell you out from the back, it means the world that people travel thousands of miles to stand shoulder to shoulder with you, to dance, and chant and share together. Far from weird, it feels completely normal, completely right, like there's nowhere else we should be.

But how exactly did we get there? Where had we come from?

It's hard to know how far to rewind and where it started. Over a year and a half before, an old friend and comrade of mine and Natalia's, Anna Campbell, had picked up her bags and set out on the path so many of us would follow. She travelled to North and East Syria to join the women's defence forces of the YPJ. Before she left, I didn't know how internationalist the Kurdistan Women's Movement and Kurdistan Freedom Movement were. I didn't know we could be such a part of it, and even though I thought it was inspiring I didn't know quite how much it had to teach us. Anna's decision opened a door for me, and came at just the right time, as I was struggling to find direction and know how to channel my energy.

I wasn't alone in this. So many of the internationals who have become part of the Rojava revolution tell a story of searching for this direction. Organising in our cities and communities, we were still full of determination, need and rage. But we realised we were feeling a lack of clarity, hope and vision. Anna was searching for all these things, and so she went: not to save anyone, but to learn and grow. And she did, sending me breathless messages about the beauty of the revolution and how much she had changed. Of course, she did actually give a lot as well. Not by saving anyone, but by leaving her mark of warmth, power and revolutionary love everywhere she went.

After she'd been in North and East Syria almost a year, Anna went to the front lines to defend the region of Afrin as it faced invasion by the Turkish army in 2018. As I dance in Serekaniye, Afrin has been under occupation for months, and now the Turkish state is threatening to expand the same occupation and violence. Anna was killed in the Afrin war in a Turkish airstrike, becoming one of thousands of fighters and civilians killed defending the region against fascism and occupation, several of them internationalists like her. As the shock faded and the grief became part of life, I realised there was something else. If her coming to North and East Syria had opened a door, her death closed another one behind me. I could no longer ever turn away from the fight and decide to just give up. I didn't know what that would mean, I would be certain to make mistakes and take wrong turns, and it would doubtless change over time. But stepping back from struggle was no longer an option.

But my road to Kurdistan didn't just begin with Anna either. There's the question of when to start, but also where? There are many beginnings. One of them is when the spring of 2011 brought unrest and uprisings across much of the Middle East and North Africa: the 'Arab Spring' as Western news called it.

Rojava is the part of Kurdistan within the borders of the Syrian nation state, and when protests erupted across Syria and the government almost totally lost control, the people in the area of Syria that is Rojava Kurdistan were ready. They had been organizing in secret for years, despite violence, their language being banned, and the threat of every kind of repression, torture, or death. They had developed the capacity for self defence and were able to muster their own forces.

They had been bringing their communities together democratically and after only a short time were able to set up an autonomous region of self-government. The revolution was led by the Kurds of the region, but hastily established all peoples' right to organisation and a voice. Scanning through the membership lists of the administration's committees and assemblies shows how much they have achieved – Kurdish, Arabic, Chechen, Syriac-Assyrian, Armenian, Turkmen, Circassian and Ezidi delegates sit side by side making decisions together. Women had always been at the forefront of the resistance, organising against patriarchy in their communities at the same time as against the oppression of the Assad regime. Their example and leadership, as well as the heroic struggle the self-defence forces fought against the Islamic State, has made the revolution in the North and East of Syria stand out as something truly different. It's not a utopia. Far from it. What's special about it is precisely the opposite: that it's so firmly rooted in normal people's lives, with all our messes and imperfections. It struggles for nothing short of utopia, but it's committed to start right where we are now, with people as they are now, not in a fantasy ideal world. All this has drawn revolutionaries from all over the world, and it has lovingly opened its arms to us.

Another beginning was words set on a page in a claustrophobic isolation cell on a Turkish prison island. The ideology of Abdullah Öcalan, the imprisoned leader of the Kurdistan Workers' Party (PKK), is the beating heart of the movement in North and East Syria. In isolation, he chose to use his court hearings as an opportunity to speak to the world outside. Öcalan's *Defence Writings* are entire books: bold, unifying proposals for a new form of feminist, ecological, grass-roots democratic and loving socialism.

While the revolution was unfolding in Rojava, Anna, Natalia and I got to know each other a continent away, in another moment that I could call a beginning to this story. Back at home, it seemed that chaos had intensified and tensions were boiling over: riots on campuses, in poor neighbourhoods, in migrant camps along the borders. Along with hundreds of others we met each other whilst bracing against lines of police, climbing scaffold barricades, in small smoky rooms frantically scribbling paperwork or press releases, crouching on the ground in car parks painting banners, gathered round fires sharing stories. We battled and formed networks against evictions, education fees, climate destruction, cuts to benefits and services. We supported people while they fought for their status in

Europe and stood up to border police. We formed the strongest bonds, found and made beauty, took steps towards freedom, and even occasionally won a battle. At the same time, we got it wrong more often than not, and we got scarred and heartbroken by the problems, mistakes, failings, and hard lessons that we lived and played out.

When I was born at the end of the 80s, Britain had already seen almost a decade of Thatcherism, with its intensified attacks on community and resistance. We'd seen two hundred years of industrial capitalism, and it had infected our blood, while many thousands of years of patriarchy were written in our bones.

At that time, the Turkish government's brutal crackdown on left wing social movements claimed the lives of many and landed thousands of people in prison. On the streets of North Kurdistan, in guerrilla camps in the mountains and in the cells of Turkish state prisons, people were resisting the rising fascism of the Turkish state. The movement there would emerge from it like clay from a kiln; hard and purposed and stronger than ever. It was an all or nothing moment, and the movement emphatically chose all; to give all, demand all, live all and create all.

Meanwhile, anti-capitalist forces across the islands I'm from were reeling. A series of blows had hit hard: losses in workers' struggles in the 20th century, culminating with the defeats of strikes in the 70s and 80s; the brutal repression and internal conflicts of Irish resistance to British imperialism; the global exposure of the horrors of 'real' socialism and the exhausting material and psychological battle with neoliberalism. Resistance was scattered, but like seeds blown on the wind, scattered doesn't mean gone. Unseen and uncelebrated, normal people fought for their homes, for a decent quality of life, and for justice and dignity. Anti-globalisation protests would gain ground during my childhood, cross-pollinating with the peace movement and the environmentalist movement. When my generation took to the streets, pissed off for all our different reasons, ready for the fight and looking for people who felt the same, these were the legacies that we stepped into.

There's something like all of this and so much more in every story that brought someone to the Rojava revolution. In the movement in North and East Syria we're always encouraged to know our personal and social histories, to look deep into the past and forward to the future. Sometimes you can feel it all flowing through yourself, feel the millions of hands and shoulders lifting you up to where you are. Other times, you cannot help but fall back into the moment. And you need the moments too. Feet need to stay on the ground. On that day in Serekaniye they were firmly planted. Moving our feet to the steps of the dance, hauling sound systems around, firmly braced while reading a speech, staggering under the weight of heavy cooking pans that were brought out to feed several hundred people every day. Not everyone does all the same tasks. The revolution is by no means made up only of people with the privileges of full health and strength. It doesn't need to be, when care is knitted so completely into the fabric of life. The day to day, food and warmth and washing, the cleaning, the setting up and taking down, are every bit as important as any kind of revolutionary ideology. In fact, they both need each other.

Social movements against patriarchy, capitalism, the nation state, colonialism and all other forms of violence and oppression are gaining ground across the world. They are all the more powerful because they are politicising the day to day, making the most radical proposals of a whole new world, but based on the everyday moments of solidarity and liberation we already experience. On the cups of tea we make for each other to bring comfort and warmth. On the instinct to help our neighbours in the face of a pandemic, or the community networks that spring into action in the face of floods or fires. On the insistence of young people fighting for land to grow food on, and the elders teaching them how.

Of course, the forces stacked against our social movements are pushing back as well. Fascist and far-right movements are on the rise (either tacitly or openly supported by state powers); there's a misogynist and white-supremacist backlash. Rebellion is suppressed both with outright physical force, and with the more subtle but no less deadly attacks of liberal assimilation. A backlash shows we are doing something right, even though it doesn't make it easy. It shows we need to remember those radical demands, and what we have to insist on.

By the time my generation came of age, it wasn't a radical idea to say that everything was messed up, no matter where you were on the political spectrum and what you thought the solution might be. Students rioted over fees; basic services were being ripped apart; poor and working class communities were blamed for social problems, and faced renewed waves of aggression against their very existence. The ruling classes fuelled racism and other prejudices to distract from their crimes, and undermined communities or social justice movements covertly and overtly. Few people trusted capitalism, or thought the system was for us, or for justice, or for a future. The hopes of the 20th century were now viewed with either sadness or a cynical eye roll; whether that was the hopes of communism, of liberal democracy, or just of being able to get a secure job and live as well or better than your parents. There was little need to convince most people that we were living in deeply messed up times.

The radical bit, the bit that was very hard to convince ourselves or anyone else of, was that things could actually be different. Even within social movements claiming to fight for change it was hard to find real belief that change was possible. Many of us, from all different backgrounds and for all different reasons, held a part of ourselves aside from the fight. Outside of those movements, many people weren't against social change because they liked things the way they were. They just didn't have hope that it was possible to actually change the world for the better.

The Kurdistan Freedom Movement and the Kurdistan Women's Movement are an important part of the global fight. They have emerged from the history and people of Kurdistan, but they have thought globally from the beginning. The only road to true liberation for Kurdistan and the only way the revolution in North and East Syria can survive is a global revolution, a radical change in social structures worldwide.

Volunteers like us who have become part of the Kurdistan Freedom Movement came with our notebooks open, ready to learn, but found it was our hearts that changed the most. One of the most important and exciting things we can do is to connect the lessons, belief, energy and spirit of that movement with all the rebellions, organising and struggles in the places we come from. Our diversity is our richness, not a block to finding common ground. The more connected we are across distance, culture, or borders, the stronger we are.

This book was written by two internationalists who have spent time in North and East Syria organising with the movement there in various different ways. We want to tell the story of our time within the Rojava revolution. Some moments felt like the hardest times of our lives, and others were filled with joy, love and passion. In either case, we learnt a million lessons and could feel that we were part of something big.

So much of what we learnt so far away was really about home. We saw things in a new light, weaknesses but also amazing strengths we hadn't recognized before. The more we became submerged in the revolutionary political culture of Kurdistan, the more we could hear echoes of it in our histories, and the histories of the places we come from. We realised there was important work to do in trying to build bridges between the places, movements and worlds we were a part of.

There's a lot of translated concepts in this book, and translating is never an exact science. Things don't just map neatly into other languages, and we do our best to translate the spirit of the ideas, not just the words. That takes more time and more patience with each other, which is something we've promised ourselves to try and learn.

Similarly, this book isn't about copy and pasting a revolution. Of course, there are lessons to be learnt. But what the revolution in North and East Syria teaches us above all is more intangible; that there is hope. There simply has to be, and we make it ourselves when we come together, pick up every tool we have, and insist on building a real future.

***

A day later in Serekaniye and I've been firmly adopted by a joyful gaggle of women who arrived on a bus together from their city two hours away. I am genuinely sad to wish them all goodbye, wondering if we'll ever meet again. But three months later, on the 2019 International Women's Day celebrations, I hear my name cried out from the colourful mass of women in traditional dresses and pristine make up that's pouring off a battered old double decker. We embrace and shriek with laughter, and I find now I can at least hold down a short conversation. I'm learning that in this movement, you will find each other again, maybe when you least expect it. And by the 8th March 2019 the Turkish state still hasn't invaded.

For almost a year they carry on threatening. There's a constant sense that war might begin at any moment, a hovering threat. Diplomacy, campaigning, active resistance, knock on effects from global geopolitics, and at times sheer luck, keep it at bay.

That action at Serekaniye and others like it were of course full of press and media activists. International campaigning, showing the resistance in North and East Syria, and the solidarity actions across the world, were some of those thousands of efforts that held off the invasion for months. On the 9th of October 2019, in the shadow of even more serious threats, I go back to another mass mobilisation in Serekaniye.

Nine months have passed since that Christmas morning. By now I can speak passable Kurmanji Kurdish (the dialect of Kurdish spoken in Rojava), I have a job to do, and I understand the situation and context on a whole other level. There's a lot less dancing because this time the sun is beating down and the tents are for hiding from it. We sing and play songs instead. We don't stay the night this time, and after the mobilisation buses and minivans cart people away, still singing and chanting. A couple of us stay in the city, packing away our gear, weary and dusty. We buy falafel and cold drinks, and bring them to the house of some friends. We're sitting on the floor sharing the breeze from a wobbly electric fan, eating from greasy paper and talking about nothing in particular, when the *crump crump* of artillery shells exploding reaches us. We race outside and the trails of warplanes have scratched lines across the blue sky. War is really here.

YPJ fighter replacing the ISIS flag with the YPJ flag

2. BELIEVING

The Battle of Kobane
Natalia

Years before we arrived in Rojava, another war was raging in the region. Think back to where you were as 2014 drew to a close and we faced the uncertainties of a new year, the way we do every twelve months. I was in America, having just spent two days on a train travelling across the country and back to the Midwest. I was 'on my way home' in a double sense, planning to stop over for a few weeks with family in Cleveland, where I had grown up, before getting on a plane back to London, where I had built community and a sense of home as an adult. I watched the clock count down to midnight, bored and lonely, streaming a sports game on my computer, wondering what my friends – most of them in a time zone six hours ahead of me – were up to. I had no idea that another couple of time zones further, in a northern city in Syria called Kobane, strangers who I would come to refer to as friends were fighting for their lives in the cold, battered buildings of a war torn city in winter.

And so, five years before Jenni watched the Turkish shells start to fall on Serekaniye, the Kurdish people were yet again defending themselves from another invasion, this time with Islamic State threatening to overrun the city of Kobane. The battle of Kobane is like something out of a storybook, one of the most significant moments in the fight against fascism. As the forces of the Islamic

State (ISIS) devoured territory across Syria and Iraq, their self-declared caliphate clamped down on the lives of millions of people with a brutality and intolerance that beggar belief. Resistance felt futile: city after city, and village after village, were taken. The Islamic State had, secretly and not-so-secretly, the backing of many international forces, and support from a powerful neighbour, the Turkish state. They had money, weapons, and a powerful propaganda machine. The three regions of Rojava that had expelled the forces of the Assad regime in 2012 – Afrin, Kobane and Jazeera — were each surrounded by jihadist forces including the Islamic State, Al Nusra Front and others.

Late in 2014, ISIS launched an offensive on the region of Kobane and surrounded its principal city (also called Kobane). Against all odds, they were held back by a collection of local Kurdish-led forces and revolutionaries armed with vintage kalashnikovs and nerves of steel. These were the self defence forces that had grown out of the revolution: the YPG People's Defence Units and YPJ Women's Defence Units. For over six months the defenders hunkered down behind makeshift fortifications in empty buildings pockmarked with bullet holes, ducking behind colourful blankets that were hung across windows and doorways to hide from a sniper's line of sight. The units were backed further and further into a small corner of the city of Kobane, knowing every day might be the final stand. But as the New Year dawned, the defence forces were recapturing the city neighbourhood by neighbourhood – suffering heavy losses, but holding out. The new year brought rain and bitter cold to Kobane, and still ISIS couldn't take the city. The tide had turned. Realising that the Kurdish-led forces had a fighting chance, US airstrikes started to pepper ISIS-held sections of the city. By the end of January the city was reclaimed. Black ISIS flags were torn from rooftops and replaced with the bright colours of the YPG and YPJ. Fighters put down their guns and danced hand in hand, and civilians began to return and rebuild their city.

The battle was the beginning of the end of the Islamic State. And on a global scale, it brought the Rojava revolution to the attention of countless people around the world, at a time when we desperately needed an injection of hope and ambition in our social movements.

At least three thousand people lost their lives in the defence of Kobane. Men and women alike fought and fell as they took a stand against fascism. Many were teenagers, some were old enough to be grandparents. Some were seasoned fighters with many battles to their names, some had just signed up to defend their city. I came to Kobane five years after the start of the siege and was met with a bustling city decorated with billboards and memorials dedicated to those who died in the resistance. Hectic traffic, bustling markets and kids playing in the street make it a city like any other – until you come to the neighbourhood where the defence forces staged the final resistance against ISIS.

The neighbourhood has been left in the state it was in after the siege, street after street a life-sized memorial to the cost of war. It's referred to as a museum, an insistence on remembering the sacrifice that was given so that the people of Kobane – and the people of the whole world — could live free of ISIS.

We went around with a fighter who had taken part in the battle and now was responsible for welcoming visitors. He took us inside crumbling buildings, climbing up barely attached staircases and into the rooms where the YPG and YPJ units had fought and snatched brief moments of rest. He told us that the fighters who took part in the battle want to talk about it because they know it's so important – but sometimes they get paralysed by the memory, and they can't bring themselves to explain what it was like to lose so many friends, to see so much suffering, to fight for so long.

We pick our way past rusting cars riddled with bullet holes, the spent shells of thousands of bullets scattered on the ground and crunching beneath our feet. We step quietly into rooms where clothes are still hanging up, oil still in frying pans and packets from Indomie noodles scattered on the ground. We read the writing etched onto the wall with pencil and marker: *'Heval Dara li vir şehîd ket''* (Comrade Dara was martyred here); lists of the names of comrades and the fighting unit they were part of, some names crossed out – either wounded or dead. Quotes from Abdullah Öcalan (the central theorist behind the Kurdistan Freedom Movement); poetry; insistent declarations that 'we will be victorious'.

We walk past the fortifications thrown together from metal barrels full of rocks and sandbags, and I'm struck by the fact that the comrades who fought here kept going far past the point that most of the rest of the world believed that they could win. And not only that, but they didn't lose sight of what they fought for. There's nothing scrawled on the walls that speaks of hatred or cruelty, no exhortations to kill ISIS fighters or counts of numbers of jihadis killed. Only the love for their comrades and the world they are fighting for, the dignity of struggle, and the insistence on hope. Of course everyone is human and doubtless many fighters fell into times of darkness and motivations of vengeance. But not only was that not the overall narrative or energy, if there were moments of darkness it's just as certain that their comrades will have pulled them back and reminded them who they were. They knew what they believed in, and this gave them the strength to stay human.

Sometimes when we're involved in political struggle, it feels like we're waiting for a message from heaven to show up and say 'this is the big one". When we're faced with a particularly daunting or difficult resistance, we want some sort of guarantee – if not of success and survival, then at least of significance. With the benefit of hindsight, it's easy to say that the resistance of Kobane, no matter how painful the losses were, was 'worth it'. But at the time, the comrades on the front lines didn't know that their sacrifice would contribute to a victory that led millions of people around the world to stand in solidarity with the Rojava revolution.

With the battle of Kobane, the number of internationalists travelling to join the revolution increased from a trickle to a steady stream. It transformed a revolutionary project in a corner of the world that would normally be lumped under 'generic political upheaval' into the inspiration and hope for countless visionaries and organisers. But those who fought didn't know this. What they did know was that regardless of the outcome of the battle, they would be remembered by the loved ones and comrades who survived them. They knew what it looked like to live their beliefs. And that was enough.

While keeping that neighbourhood of Kobane as a museum is a powerful testament to a resistance that shook the world order, many of the people who used to live in the neighbourhood want to move back. In fact, many have, stringing up their laundry and creating life between the shattered shells of neighbours' houses. The movement has built a new neighbourhood for those whose houses were in the destroyed quarter, but due to the hasty rebuilding process, a lot of them aren't well built, and a lot of people still prefer to return to their old neighbourhood. Those responsible for housing have said that people whose houses are still more or less intact can move back, and they will receive materials and help with reconstruction, but those whose houses are completely destroyed cannot. It's one of the contradictions involved in working on such a big scale – decisions need to be made which some people will not be happy with. Mistakes are made and can't be undone, and a lot of people will experience the consequences. It's a constant juggling act between the principles of the movement, all the different things that the wider population wants, and simply what's possible at the end of the day.

The movement juggles lots of contradictions like this, for example the fundamental principle of decentralised democracy versus the need for centralised military structures for self defence. Another one is the necessity of ecological energy sources versus the immediate need for fossil fuels for daily life and income. I found myself asking – isn't that just a compromise? But I think there are some key differences between a compromise and a contradiction. A compromise is something you settle for, a mid point between two positions that is declared as 'good enough' and then becomes the status quo. A contradiction is a tension, a question you walk with, something that isn't good enough, but is at the same time a necessary part of the revolutionary process. A movement that avoids contradictions would slide into either dogmatism or co-optation, whereas holding contradictions is the art of walking that tightrope between revolutionary ideals and material reality.

Our social movements could learn a lot from the Kurdistan Freedom Movement about the art of living with tensions and contradictions — even while you try to overcome them. So many of our political movements have been either sucked into state and capitalist institutions, forced to play by the rules of a game rigged against us, or shrunk into stagnant political 'scenes' whose purism and dogmatism strangles how much we can achieve.

I wonder how we can let things be messy, imperfect and full of contradictions, but also more dynamic, diverse and impactful. I think that the answer lies at least in part from knowing what you believe in and having hope that it is possible. We often know what we're against, but we struggle to articulate what we're for. Without doubt the finer details of any radical social change will emerge through the process of struggle, but in order to fight for something you need to believe in it. It doesn't need to be perfect or proven in order for us to believe in it — when something's a work in progress, it needs our faith to help it grow.

That said, since returning I've seen lots of glimmers of an insistence on building and believing, of moving away from dogmatism. As it becomes all the more clear how much is at stake, I'm sure that our movements will rise to the challenge and paint a vision for the future as beautiful and compelling as the alternative is terrifying. Having a common political vision is the foundation on which we dare to hope, the balm that heals us when we lose a battle or a comrade, and the coordinates by which we navigate the messiness of building the world anew.

In the times I visited Kobane, a lot of people would tell stories about the resistance against ISIS over a glass of tea. One thing that people say when talking about the battle of Kobane is how at the start of the battle there were fewer women fighters, or they were in more supporting positions. But by the end of the battle, when the defence forces were squeezed into a tiny space in the city and often separated from ISIS by only a street (or in some cases, by a single wall) and people started to lose hope, it was the women fighters who were pushing forward on the front line. It was women – some not much older than girls, some mothers and grandmothers – who were fighting and defeating ISIS. Often the reaction to this is to express awe, to see it as an inspiration. But to me — in no way undermining how powerful and revolutionary an act it was– it's a reality that's almost cruel in its banality. Of course it was the women who didn't give up, who picked up the weapons of their fallen comrades, family members, friends, and fought to the bitter end. Because they had the most to lose. At the end they had a simple choice – fight, or be slaves.

When we look at the pictures of the martyrs of the battle of Kobane that line the streets, adorn billboards or fill up wall after wall of memorials and museums, we see faces serious with that knowledge. I read the date of birth next to a picture – 1999. Date of death – 2014. I find myself thinking — 'Girls that age should be in school, not in military forces'. The YPJ themselves don't recruit under the age of 18, but if you were in the city during the Kobane resistance, the line between civilian and fighter didn't mean much. This girl was 15 when she blockaded herself with her comrades inside a schoolhouse and fought against ISIS until their bullets ran out. With no bullets left, they all huddled around their final grenade and pulled the pin so they wouldn't be captured alive by the enemy.

We can't forget the thousands of Ezidi women and girls kidnapped and bound into sexual slavery by ISIS, how many years of hell they had already seen by their 15th birthdays. When they were freed, many took up arms to make sure that would never happen to another girl. When a young woman is liberated from her captors after years of being bought, sold, tortured, and then picks up a weapon and takes part in the liberation of Raqqa, who will tell her she is too young to fight? She fights to take back her humanity, to save others from what had been her living hell.

And we remember that it's not just desperation that drives her to it – it is also hope. The belief, the knowledge, that there could be something better. These amazing, determined women, they fight for a movement – for the women's revolution that has been unfolding across North and East Syria. We fight for the peoples' councils, the women's houses, the right for children to be taught in their own language, for the chance to build a home out of the shattered remnants of our cities.

At the time that these heroic women were fighting for a new world, I didn't have their hope and belief. I was bruised from too many lost political battles, too many social movements that swept me up in their euphoria only to dissolve months or a couple years later. I carried on politically organising because it was still a big part of who I was, but by the time images of the fierce women fighters of the YPJ popped up on social media, I don't think I really believed in it. I remember seeing a video clip of YPJ fighters dancing joyfully around a bonfire after the liberation of Kobane. I remember it being so beautiful, and powerful, and hopeful, that it brought tears to my eyes.

But then something inside me closed up again, and I kept scrolling through my feed. I couldn't bring myself to believe in anything so big, out of fear that it would come crashing down again and break my heart. I feel so lucky that I've been able to reconnect with the hope that drove me in those years when I plunged heart-first into political movements that declared "another world is possible". But this time it's not a hope based on youthfulness and infatuation with a new political scene. It's a love born from years of struggle, built on knowing what I believe in, that the path to get there will be rocky and imperfect, but choosing to walk it anyway. When we come down to the messy business of translating our politics into practice, the right thing will always have a lot of things wrong with it. Through these contradictions and imperfections, being one of millions around the world to hold the vision of the Kurdistan Freedom Movement is an anchor for me, helping me keep clarity and determination.

Five years after the Battle of Kobane, in 2019, I was sitting at a computer in a media centre in Rojava, writing press briefings while the Turkish army fired artillery from the other side of the border wall. I spent a lot of time choking on the superficial language that we needed to use when dealing with the mainstream media. Holding firmly to that anchor, I reminded myself that it was a necessary part of the resistance. However icky it felt, I didn't feel like I was compromising my politics by playing the media game.

In some ways I felt more removed from the struggle because I couldn't write exactly what I thought. I felt an itch to be more directly involved in the resistance — fighting with the YPJ or helping with humanitarian support. But even though I had to swap the language of anti-capitalist revolution for the language of humanitarian crisis and international conventions, I could trace an unbroken thread from the revolutionary ideals at the heart of the political movement we were defending, to the briefings and reports I was uploading onto the internet.

I knew that the people on the front lines, the people meeting with foreign diplomats and politicians, the people organising protests in Rojava and worldwide, and me writing reports on my laptop, were all fighting for the same things – not just *against* the Turkish invasion, but *for* women's liberation, for grass-roots democracy, for ecology. We were all pulling together, not against each other. And that's a feeling that I won't forget for the rest of my life. That feeling continues to drive me now – the memory of what it feels like to be one link in a solid chain of resistance.

This is the feeling that I want everyone in our social movements to have – from the direct action activist chaining themselves to machinery, to community organisers holding neighbourhood meetings, to campaigners sitting at meetings with government officials. It all needs to come out of, and be accountable to, a movement and the ideals that drive it. That way we don't get absorbed by the dominant paradigm – capitalism and liberalism – or break off into subcultures. We'll have the clarity to strategically use a diversity of tactics, but the integrity to be accountable to the grass-roots and our values. That way, political institutions are forced to engage with us not because we're palatable, but because we're powerful.

I spent the New Year's Eve following the October 2019 invasion in Amude, another Rojava border town that has seen its share of war. We had been invited to spend the holiday with the family of a young Kurdish woman who we worked with, so we piled into the van and drove to the house where her parents lived with her four sisters. For the whole evening, neighbours and relatives came and went, sitting on the cushions around the edge of the tiny sitting room and chatting, drinking tea and soda, and getting a kick out of the presence of a small group of internationalists. We made onion rings to share 'European culture' with our friend's family (which received a mixed reception), and met her four sisters who shared the family home with her parents, and the two brothers who had moved out.

At a few minutes to midnight we joined the sisters and brothers on the rooftop. We watched hundreds of bullets fired in celebration from rooftops – a hazardous tradition that local security forces try in vain to prohibit — shower down from the sky like flaming raindrops, before being ushered inside in case we were hit by a stray bullet. Just a few hours drive away — 150 miles as the crow flies – the city of Kobane also celebrated the arrival of 2020, without doubt also with illicit gunfire from the rooftops. It doesn't take much to visualise the bullet shells of celebration falling alongside those fired in war that are still scattered between the buildings of the destroyed quarter, the same way we walk through life with the memory of those we've lost beside us.

We continue to struggle for what we believe in, relying on each other and the strength we gain from believing in something bigger than any of us alone. This is the power that has made it possible for a movement as powerful as the Kurdistan Freedom Movement to not just survive, but to grow through decades of bitter struggle and come out stronger. It is what lets us keep fighting, so that the city of Kobane can rise new from the rubble, and so that its citizens – with the tenacity and ferocity of survivors – can hold remembrance and grief in one hand, and ambition and celebration in the other.

"You must believe, before everything else, that the revolution must come, that there is no other choice"

— *Abdullah Öcalan*

33

WE WANTED TO PLANT A GARDEN.

Natalia

We wanted to plant a garden.

I still have the seeds in my cupboard: lettuce, carrots, beetroot, cabbage. We had so many dreams and plans for this piece of ground. We had tilled the soil and composted our kitchen waste for months, hacked back purple thistles that grew above our heads and scraped our fingers raw, raked armloads of dry golden grass itchy in the heavy heat of summer.

When the brown hen decided to roost on her eggs even though we had no rooster, we walked around the village and traded her clutch with neighbours who had fertilised eggs. We snuck them into her nest and they hatched a few weeks later, a brood of chicks from a dozen different mothers and fathers. We watched her care for them as they grew.

When the attacks came the shells ripped through our neighbourhoods and tore open the earth. We had to abandon the garden. We gave the chickens away. We started putting coffins into the ground, instead of seeds.

This week it rained for the first time in months- the parched earth drank it in, we inhaled the smell of a new world. But we rejoiced not because the downpour would give our seedlings life, but because mud makes it harder for tanks to attack our villages and towns, because clouds provide cover from drones raining down missiles on our homes.

Now we watch the vultures of the world descend, ready to pick through rubble and shallow graves in their insatiable hunger. Ready to gorge themselves, even while the footsteps of our fallen comrades still echo in the streets of Serekaniye. I'm scared that the only thing that will be left to us when we're old is to look each other in the eye and say "remember when we were free?"

Hope has always been the hardest seed to grow. It feels too tender and fragile to exist in this world. Sometimes we smother it with fleece and netting, protecting it from the harshness of our surroundings. But in order for it to grow, it needs to be buffeted by wind so it can cross pollinate, it needs to learn how to defend itself against birds and grow strong roots so it can hold onto the earth. It will grow weathered and tough, it will lose leaves and branches.

But, my friends, when the summer comes, its fruit will be the sweetest of all.

Traditional leaders of Arabic clans take to the streets in protest alongside the Kurdish community

3. BELONGING

The people in resistance
Jenni

In October 2019, in the run up to the invasion of Serekaniye, I was living and working with a small group of women. We were putting in long days and half the night in campaigning and diplomacy. Basically we were furiously chipping away at the wall of silence and apathy the revolution was facing internationally. It wasn't the most fun assignment. Normally we were getting up to be faced with long hours at a computer screen in an office, but this morning was different.

After over a year of hinting and hedging, the USA had just announced they were actually pulling their soldiers out of their bases in North and East Syria. Not that they'd been standing bravely at the border, the finest military tech in the world poised to defend the people, anyway. The people in all of Kurdistan, and for that matter Syria, learned the hard way long ago that they have to defend themselves. American troops stayed faceless in their bases, or sealed away in armoured cars far from the dust, air and water of the region; far from the society itself and the fire that it carries so proudly. But their withdrawal was symbolic. It was an announcement that the US government and the system it represents was happy for the Turkish state to roll in and butcher, occupy, destroy.

So we were up earlier than usual, nervous excitement filling the small flat. Even those who normally didn't show their faces until the last possible minute at breakfast were bright eyed and ready to go, cameras and tripods slung over shoulders, ready to get out of the office and into the world. We were glad of the opportunity even as we were anxious about the near future.

A protest march had been called, and the morning showed every sign of the combination of chaos and purpose that is the beat the Rojava revolution marches to. We rushed, worried we were late, trying to disentangle conflicting directions... only to wait for ages. First, to pick up the others who were joining us in the car, women community organisers from the city. No way was the march going to prevent them from taking the time they needed to look smart and presentable. When they finally got in the car, they snapped selfies and giggled like schoolgirls, their gestures soft and loving. My companions from work were long term organisers, many of them ex-fighters from the self defence forces. Their faces are chiselled by the passing years into common lines of struggle, memory and hope. Though they also love a good selfie.

After another rush, we waited for a second time for all the buses to join the convoy. Bored, our team supervisor who was driving nipped our car out of the queue with a wicked grin and whizzed up the middle of the road to the next town for a cheeky espresso from a roadside pop up stall. Our drive took us past a lot of places where she fought in the war against ISIS, and she told me stories that were as matter of fact as they were heartfelt. It's in her character, she's direct, shows her feelings in a different way to many people that it takes a while to figure out. I wonder if she's like that because of the life she's lived, or if she was well suited to that life because of who she was in the first place. It doesn't really matter. Like all spectrums of human characteristics, what matters is there's a place for us all.

She pointed out spots where she had been surrounded, or had dug in and fought for days, or where a mine went off and took her close comrades from her or left them wounded for life. Now people sell ice cream, dogs and chickens potter at the entrance to villages, and kids traipse into schools. This is the society she fought for. Not every person in it shares all her ideals. You only have to go as far as the back seat of our car to find women who've chosen a very different life. But if we're not fighting for society, fighting to create enough breathing space for people to remember who we really are, then what are we fighting for?

I know society is a word that many, especially on the radical left, struggle to relate to. Many times we turn to words like 'community' or 'collective' instead.

I'm not against these terms, and I understand why people lean towards that. In one sense, you can call it what you like, and there's no perfect way to translate from other languages, we need to choose what's best in our context. What I'm talking about is humanity, as a whole and in the specific social forms we live in. But I use society here to imply the scale of the context we are connected to and should see ourselves in. I use it because even though there are plenty of problems with it, insistence on an alternative like 'community' can sometimes turn into just choosing to associate with a small circle that already agrees with us. I use it to push myself to see us as part of something much wider and more fundamental.

After our coffee we swung back out into the convoy. The people of North and East Syria were literally all around us. Another minivan slowed down next to us and honked obnoxiously. We saw our friends from the Syrian Women's Council, from the office upstairs to ours. The Council Coordinator leaned out of the window, waving her flag every bit as rowdily as the cluster of young men standing up on a flatbed truck in front of us. They were stomping, cheering and shouting, but their cockiness and egos deflated as the flatbed jerked forward and they toppled like a pile of dominoes. Our friend from the Syrian Women's Council did nothing to disguise her wicked cackle.

Minivans, buses, trucks, cars, and motorcycles leapfrogged their way to Serekaniye. No one knew exactly where we were going, but everyone was willing to follow the car in front and trust that there was order somewhere in the chaos. That trust made it true. After we arrived, sipping water to survive the heat, I greeted the friends and acquaintances that I'd come to know over the last year. You do start to recognise people just from demos and events, start to see the same faces. The scope of people at movement events is wide, don't get me wrong. It's a far bigger proportion of the population than any leftist or radical community I've ever come across in Europe. It's a truly popular movement. Still, not everyone in North and East Syria is totally sold on the revolution. There's plenty people who shrug and go along with it, some who've been disappointed by it, plenty who mistrust it, and then there's some who are downright against it. ISIS sleeper cells are still functioning. There's thousands of years of patriarchy to break through and that takes a lot more than the change of a flag.

It's good then that that's exactly what organisers are focused on. Women like our friend who was leaning out of the car (and was now up on a roof dancing about triumphantly with a flag tied round her neck, winking at me when she caught my eye) are the unsung heroes behind the images of heavy machine guns and clouds of smoke. The Syrian Women's Council, which mobilises women politically, and *Kongra Star* (the umbrella for grass-roots women's groups) are devoted to education, empowerment, and transformation with all the women of the region. Their work is long and unglamorous. The exact same goes for those plugging away organising the youth, or families, or trying to encourage workers' co-operatives and unions. I know their type from my home as well – quietly dedicated community organisers from all walks of life, building up community power brick by brick. The difference here is that they're connected to a system that supports them instead of blocking them, and to a programme for radical change. In short, to a revolution.

There's something deeply wrong in societies across the world. We need revolutions. But a revolution needs society even more. Without society behind it, any force will be an attack and not liberation. And where does a freedom fighter get their food, get sheltered on a dark night with enemy drones circling? Or cups of tea after hours of door-knocking, a safe haven when riot police crack down on protests? Much more than any of that, it's society itself, ourselves, that we have to understand, to nourish, to transform, to help become its fullest. A revolution is society, or it's nothing at all.

When was the Rojava revolution? Was it when the people of Syria took to the streets in 2011? When the region declared autonomy in 2012? Maybe it was years before, when women were still organised through Kongra Star but in secret, risking their lives. I think it's still going on. Revolution isn't just, or even mostly, dramatic moments of upheaval or political conflict. It's redesigning how we do the day to day. It's a process, it's every moment. It makes mistakes, it takes wrong turns. It still has a long, long way to go, starting with society in North and East Syria itself.

Patriarchal structures and attitudes still have a tight grip. The economy is a long way from being transformed into something collectively owned and run, not least because organisers are focussed on the long haul of education and discussion rather than trying to transform things with top-down declarations. The revolution may never be finished. The next generations are key. It happens in homes, in hearts, in our connections with each other.

I grew up into a political culture that was ready to reject society. Most of us had suffered pain from it. We were, quite rightfully, angry at being bought and sold, locked away or divided from each other and ourselves. We'd been presented with a framework for how to be and what to think that turned our stomachs. Our so-called opportunities consisted mostly of picking which kind of miserable or meaningless work we wanted to do. We had choice only in how we spent our money, and even that wasn't the case for everyone. We retreated angrily into various safe havens – be that a squat full of drop outs, a reformist workplace, self-referential university societies, an inward looking housing co-op, parties and raves or parties and ballot boxes. I don't want to point the finger at just one section of the left. I think a lack of trust in society runs across the board. Big unions often don't seem to trust the working class. Politicians don't trust their voters. Direct action activists don't trust anyone. Deep down, we've lost faith and so as soon as anyone lets us down or harms us we are ready to raise our hackles, hiss, and back away, caustically explaining why if only everyone was as smart as us it would be alright. Of course, there's nowhere to actually go. What none of us want to admit when we're mad at society is that we are society.

The Kurdistan Freedom Movement insists we push ourselves to remember this at every turn. We all carry the same poison from patriarchy, the state and capital. We are not pure. This already brings us back to eye level with society, makes us ready to engage. And where did we get all our revolutionary ideas anyway? They didn't fall like thunderbolts from the sky. Our histories, our communities, our societies, brought us that legacy as well.

The world view of the Kurdistan Freedom Movement envisages history as two rivers running alongside each other. Sometimes they cross, and mix, and make each other run clearer or murkier. One is the river of oppression, the state, and dominance. The other is the river of freedom, democracy, resistance. Society carries all of that. Where else can it be? We need to be able to find the good river in our society, offer ourselves to it. Democratic modernity, as the movement calls the alternative future we are building, is not about inventing something new. It's about washing away toxins, making breathing space, and trusting that under everything that's been heaped on it, society knows how to take care of itself. You can only do that if you love society. Love doesn't mean we can't be frustrated, or angry, or need to have a long and serious conversation. But without it, we don't

41

have the foundation to build anything on. We are right to be hurt and angry about oppression, and pain, and isolation. But we have to know our enemy and turn against the systems that have created this, not society itself.

Patriarchy, capitalism and the state live around us and inside us, yes, but we are so much more. These systems are parasites feeding on society. They could not survive without it because alone they can't create anything. The fact that we're all still here is proof that society is still alive underneath, and we just need to find it.

When we meet with and get to know the communities around us, we get to know their strength. And so we need to take action that always builds connection, brings us together. That's as important as any practical goal – any campaign we're trying to win or project we're trying to launch. We need to see ourselves in our societies and our societies in ourselves. As soon as we break with the binary of us and them we are all at once more complex, more humble, and more powerful.

***

On the day of the protest, I wasn't thinking that deeply about all of this as we started to flow out of the city, onto the main road that led to the next town. I was wondering what was going on. I asked around as I darted about with my camera, but no one seemed quite sure where we were going. Normally, similar demonstrations would stay within the city. As the heat took its toll I slowed down and fell into step in the women's block, which was at the front of the march. This is how it always is on demonstrations in the Kurdish movement, and this has become the norm across North and East Syria, which is much broader than just one ethnic group. Like much of the revolutionary ways of organising, it was a system developed by the Kurdish communities, but now women and men from Arabic, Aramaic, Armenian, and a dozen other backgrounds organise their marches this same way. It's a way of both showing and doing the principles of the revolution: that gender liberation goes front and centre.

But that day some things were different. First of all, right at the very front there was a small line of six or seven men. They wore the robes of the heads of *aşîrets* ('tribe' or 'clan', a federation of traditional kinship-based political and social structures), sporting the facial hair that leads to their nickname: 'white beards'.

The movement has a complicated relationship with these traditional structures. Sometimes their values and methods contradict each other, but the movement is willing to make some compromises to make it work. This is only partly because the *aşîrets* hold a lot of power. The movement also has a huge amount of respect for the strength of their communities and their steadfast refusal to accept external rule. At the same time it struggles against the reluctance to change, and finds it a long hard slog to build relationships that can start to talk about things like patriarchy in the context of the *aşîrets*.

Now, in the moment when Turkey was poised to invade, this sometimes uneasy alliance was at its strongest. No matter our differences, no one wanted the fascist armies of Erdogan to attack. The men at the head of the march that day would not have added their reputations, strength, people and considerable political weight to the force that was marching if they'd been expected to march at the back. And they were in an official role, representing their communities. They had a place. That's the kind of compromise the movement is willing to make.

For everyone else though, the custom still stood. Men had to march behind women. And many of the men on the march were more than used to this: they were happy and they cheered it on. But today, because the threat of an impending invasion brought in a wider range of people, there was a significant number of young men who were insulted and furious at the idea of not being able to lead if they wanted. The men and women of the neighbourhood defence forces who steward the marches were forced into a much more active role than normal. They linked arms and confronted the swaggering, shouting line of machismo facing them. Plenty of young men from the march itself also joined in, grabbing their peers round the waists, backing up the stewards, and insisting they stay in line, in the formation that is a physical representation of our values.

So we marched, all together in the face of external oppression, with our internal struggle raging and changing and developing as we went. It was the revolution walking. Just like the revolution, we went farther than a lot of people expected, and many of us didn't know quite where we were headed.

We arrived at an American military base. Apart from the 'white beards', everyone stayed well back. I found out later that we were told if we came closer they'd shoot. By coincidence, while we waited, four American armoured cars rolled into the base. The energy pulsing through the crowd was palpable. It parted, grudgingly, and silently. No one shouted angrily but no one waved or cheered either. You owe us, the crowd was saying. We are here. We deserve respect even if you don't know how to give it. Flags stirred in the listless wind – the flags of groups and parties that don't even always get on with each other. Men, women and children lined the sides of the road. Kurds, Arabs, Chechens, Assyrians, internationalists. All with age-old grievances, issues, complexities, memories, loves, bonds and loyalties between us. It's not a homogenous moment, but still it's a moment of unity.

After the demo at the base wrapped up, there was no sense of ending. My diary entry from that night says *'now we have work to do'*. I still didn't know just how fast that work would become a crisis: it was only a few days later that I would witness the first shells falling on Serekaniye.

No one out that day ever believed for a second that the imperialist forces were there to help us. We took the road outside the base partly because we couldn't let them leave without letting them know we knew what they were doing. But more than that, it was a time to come together in a moment of strength and mobilise society itself onwards from the protest, not to beg for help. It was the moment that we looked each other in the eye and grasped hands with the unspoken knowledge of what lies ahead. Now what the people had always known was writ large: that we have only ourselves to fall back on. Society is the greatest strength of the movement, and as war loomed heavy on the horizon it made sense to take care of our most powerful weapon. Let the enemy see it, just like at the protest camps at the border wall that had been so close by.

There was even greater chaos on the exit. The walk had been long and buses had rolled up to take us all back to the town where our vehicles were. Everyone knew we'd get back eventually and no one would be left behind, but the system for getting everyone on board was just jumping on whatever vehicle rolled slowly enough near you, pulled up by the hands of strangers, wedged behind someone's elbow. I rode back on the arm of my friend's chair, with a young girl I had never met before perched on my knee. Our bus held the young, the old, men, women, kids, the elated, the friendly, the grouchy, the shy, the swaggering. The driver peered through the cracks of the shattered windscreen and we lurched side to side over potholes causing the youths hanging halfway out of the doors to swing wildly out into space for a moment. I felt a sense of warmth, a generalised love for everyone around me. I didn't know most people on that bus and many of them I might not even get on with. But call it society, community, family, resistance, whatever you like, there was something holding us together.

This love and strength was the same thing that brought volunteers out in droves to house refugees in schools a few days later when the bombs started falling. It's what made many residents of Serekaniye refuse to evacuate, instead choosing to stand shoulder to shoulder with the fighters of the self defence forces, defending the city until the last possible moment. It's what makes Kurdish mothers welcome us like family. It's on all our streets and in our homes if we know where to look. It's exactly what we are all fighting for.

BEST LAID PLANS

Natalia, April 2019

Every day in Rojava is an exercise in unpredictability — just when I think I have my day planned, the plan changes. I don't like that. One morning I'm relaxing into the predictability of being on the rota for kitchen duty all day, making plans for what I'll cook for lunch, soaking chickpeas for dinner and getting the space ready. Suddenly, someone shows up and announces "We're gonna go drive to a nature reserve and take some cuttings of fruit trees for our tree nursery – we need you because you're on the garden committee". No space for negotiation, duty calls and besides "Don't you want to meet the lovely comrades at the nature reserve?"

I reluctantly find someone to swap in for kitchen duty and an hour later we're driving a minivan down a narrow track squeezed onto a ledge not much wider than the van itself, more pothole and mud pit than road. We're lost. After some nerve-racking manoeuvres the driver manages to turn the van around, and we rattle back down the same road in search of the elusive nature reserve. Eventually, we find it and pull up to the entrance – unannounced and unexpected – and are warmly welcomed by the guys on gate duty. They show us to the orchard and enthusiastically help us take armloads of cuttings from fruit and nut trees to take home and put in compost so they can take root. Who knows what else they were planning to be doing when we arrived, but not for a second do we feel like we shouldn't be there.

Just when I think we are safely on our way home, someone in the van calls out that they recognise the village we're driving past, so of course we take a detour to visit a family who live there. Once again we arrive unexpected and unannounced, and are warmly welcomed inside for hot sugary tea. We sit on cushions around the edges of the room as the elders of the family tell us stories of how in decades past Kurdish guerrilla fighters would stop over in the house during the day to seek shelter before continuing their journey by night. We push through the awkwardness of translation to drink in their stories about their family and the village they are a part of. They've outlasted decades of oppressive rule by the Assad regime, the arrival of brutal militias and the constant threat of invasion and occupation by the Turkish state.

The history they are part of, the warmth with which they greet strangers and the determination with which they face an uncertain future are what makes the revolution work. This is why Kurdish revolutionaries always say — "you need to know the people" — because no matter the continent, without their stories and their spirit, any political movement will be empty. And that is not something you can boil down into a strategy or action plan.

Resisting pressure to stay for dinner, we say goodbye warmly. As the sun sets we head off into the pitch black darkness, driving along the edge of a field and navigating by whim because we don't have a map, but also because we trust that whichever way we go will be the right way.

One of the many things internationalist volunteers in Rojava learn how to do is to trust. Trust forms the basis of our ability to live a collective rather than an individualistic life. We trust that whatever food there is will be distributed fairly, that the work that we're doing fits into a bigger picture, that when we need to get somewhere we'll get a lift. Getting from one place to another is equal parts chaotic and functional, as long as you trust the system. Whether it's walking down to the side of the road or the closest checkpoint to hitch a ride with strangers, or asking visiting comrades to squeeze up and bring you a bit closer to your desired destination, you get to where you're going- give or take a few days, and maybe with a few feet less of leg room.

It feels like half the time I'm in Rojava I'm driving around with 12 people crammed into an 8 person vehicle, dripping with sweat and passing around an increasingly warm bottle of water. Despite the heat, the crowding and the pain of my head cracking against the ceiling when the overloaded van heaves over a bump in the road, these are some of my favourite moments.

There is always music- what kind really depends on whose car you're in. In some cars it's back to back Kurdish revolutionary anthems, with a few ciao bellas or political European hip hop songs sprinkled in. If you're in slightly less traditional cars, it's anything from ABBA to Beyonce to Despacito. Or you might find yourself serenaded by Enrique Iglesias, or still listening to Despacito on repeat, with the occasional wild card like a pop metal remix of Jingle Bells or a traditional Kurdish instrumental version of My Heart Will Go On. Have I mentioned Despacito?

Why is this important? Because I've noticed that sometimes what we lack in trust in our political movements, we try to compensate with rules: either spoken or unspoken. Way too often this ends up stifling the diversity we need in our social movements, dictating how we express ourselves, the ways that we organise and what we bring into the space. On the surface of it, it might be implicit rules about what kind of music is the 'right' kind of music, the ways we express ourselves and who we hang out with. But deeper down, does it sometimes come out of a reluctance to commit to something unpredictable and unknowable, to take a leap of faith?

It's seen as pretty uncontroversial to insist on full information, consultation and transparency in any political movement that we are involved in. But looking at it through the lens of my experiences in Rojava, I wonder how much of that can come from a lack of trust in ourselves and each other. I want to be part of a political movement that is bigger and more complex than anything I — or any one person — can wrap my head around. So for my part, I've decided that I'm going to keep on working on letting go, and learning how to surf the chaos, the unknown and the unexpected.

YPJ recruitment banner asks "If not you, then who? If not now, when?"

4. TRANSFORMING

Change starts with the self
Jenni

"If not you, who?"

I was about 10 when I came across these words. I was in the caravan where we lived. Rain was pouring down the windows and the gas fire struggled against the cold air outside. I didn't really notice. A childhood spent between the draughty caravan and the fields it was parked on thickened my skin to wet and chill, and I was far more absorbed in whatever book I had hungrily dug out of the library this week. This one was a sci-fi children's book by the late Terry Pratchett. What the character is referring to is saving mankind. The child being asked the question has been playing a game, and it has become apparent that it isn't really a game. Not any more.

I lived easily half my childhood in the worlds created by story-tellers. As I grew up, stories were as real to me as reality. I'm not alone. Stories are how we make our own reality. Stories like justice, like ethics, like values and traditions. They're all the more real and precious for being something intangible. Clearly, we can come up with almost endless stories, endless options. This creation of our values, this making of a *choice*, seems to be a defining characteristic of humans. All that stuff about using tools, complex social structures, even language, it turns out we share those and more with loads of other beings on the planet. But our adaptability and creativity, the sheer variation of ways we have managed and manage to live, the scope of the stories we write by walking, seems to be both our greatest and most beautiful gift and a danger beyond all others.

The words *"Tu nebe, kı? Niha nebe, kengı?"* blaze across posters made by the self defence forces in North and East Syria: *"If not you, who? If not now, when?"* Speaking to a population left to stand alone against invaders, the meaning of the words is more starkly clear. You don't really need to put it on a poster. Thousands of young women are forced to confront this choice in a way I was shielded from, making my path much more wavering and jerky.

Somehow though, we found each other, me and some of those women. Twenty years later, under the meagre stars the city lights and hovering clouds of truck fumes allowed, we lay on thin mattresses in our yard in the city of Qamişlo in North East Syria. It was far too hot to sleep inside. Cacti and herbs in pots sweetened the air, which was disturbed by the distant rumble of trucks and the shuffling of my comrades, some snoring, some still typing towards a deadline as the night grew deeper. The concrete below me was still releasing the heat of the day. I was grudgingly covered by the thinnest possible sheet, because if I threw it off as I longed to, and allowed my body that had been raised on a rainy hillside to steam into the open air, the mosquitoes would make an immediate and skilled attack.

Not all my comrades were used to the heat either. One friend was from Afrin, the region to the west of us where altitude, rivers and olive trees meant the summer never got quite as intense. She's been organising since long before the revolution, back when she could have lost her life for it under the Assad regime. She's given her life to the fight, the physical battles of the military, and the more slow and subtle battles of heart and mind. Since the Turkish invasion of 2018, the same one where Anna lost her life, she can't return home. Somehow though, she and others from Afrin always manage to bring Afrin to us. I got to recognise not just the accent but the look and attitude of people, what in Kurdish you call the 'shape', of those from Afrin. A kind of groundedness, like they were just a bit more steady on their feet. A wry humour. A warmth and naturalness, and a love of strong coffee. I saw the same shape of my comrade in mothers and grandmothers across Afrini refugee neighbourhoods. She could have been living that life for years, growing trees and caring for the land in her village, raising a family, terrifying generations of young men into pulling their socks up. But she'd not been able to turn away from the other work that needed to be done, had asked herself, *who else?* Now she had the scars and shrapnel to show for it, meaning she always had to take the only actual bed we had, because that supported her injuries the best.

Never having got over my addiction to books and stories, I was reading until my eyes would close despite the heat. Having meant to for years, I had finally got to *The Parable of the Sower* by Octavia Butler while I was in Rojava. I felt guilty to be coming to such a classic (if you are a sci-fi nerd turned feminist, at least) so late in life. But I could not have been more wrong. It turned out to be exactly the right time.

"God," Butler writes, *"is change... All that you touch You Change. All that you Change Changes you. The only lasting truth Is Change."* Parable of the Sower is not a book about easy times. It's got post-apocalyptic tones, it's unforgiving, and it's real. The book is set in the mid and late 2020s, and in the year 2020 it read like a dark prophecy. But I closed the book more full of hope than when I opened it. And it does not tell us a story merely of people helplessly swept up in forces beyond their control. It tells us to be ready. It tells us to understand the world the way it is, to tap into the basic force of life, and to know that change is everything, so that if and when we can drive change, we are as powerful as any being. Human hearts and minds contain almost limitless possibilities, and we are both shaped by and shape the world.

The next morning, as normal, before the sun started punishing us again, I got up, shook the dust off my sheet and mattress, and joined my comrades for breakfast. I was the only international in our crew, one of the youngest, and by far the newest in the work we were doing. At times I felt like an idiot or an alien, but I was mostly treated the same as everyone else, for good and bad. Every day that we worked together, we were also supposed to be reflecting on, in fact criticising, each other.

One of the practices within the Kurdistan Freedom Movement that tends to raise the most eyebrows is the practice of *tekmil* — of criticism. With intense focus, analysis, insight and love, organisers within the movement critique each other and themselves according to the values they share, in order to learn from mistakes and challenges. Drawing on a long tradition of giving 'critic and self critic' in revolutionary movements around the world, the Kurdistan Freedom Movement sees the practice of tekmil as a crucial mechanism for accountability and feedback. Tekmil is incorporated into the daily revolutionary practice in the movement, so whenever we held a meeting, part of it was specifically dedicated to criticising each other's behaviour and attitudes. We would link the behaviour we were criticising to overarching social structures; but that was an explanation, never an excuse. You shape yourself, you drive change, and no matter who you are, you can take responsibility.

I never grew out of my taste in fantasy and sci-fi, and I carry inked on my skin the image of one of Terry Pratchett's characters. She's one of the witches, who stalk the edges: the edges of the world, of humanity, of good and bad. Where change lives. Like any self respecting feminist I appreciate a good witch. But on top of that, the role that Pratchett's witches play reminds me what it is to be a revolutionary. Being willing to take responsibility for their community; never leaving the tough decisions to someone else; knowing the darkness well enough to push the world towards the light; grounded in earthly, day to day humanity with no problem too small, but always seeing the big picture; and remaining in service, no matter what.

When the witches get together, there are so many strong personalities in the room that the walls creak under the strain. They all know their minds and they are on the same side but that doesn't mean they blindly agree with each other on everything. There's healthy debate and discussion among the Senior Witches, an earned hierarchy of experience and knowledge, a natural authority. And there's a rotating cast of Junior Witch characters who always have to make the tea.

I made the tea a lot in our house in Qamişlo. I had to find some way to feel useful. I certainly didn't have the perspectives of my comrades: the experience, the shrapnel, the natural authority of an Afrini grandmother. Other comrades were my age or even younger though, and even though I still felt that their experiences, personal and political, outweighed anything I had to contribute, they didn't act like that. When I screwed up, I was criticised. I was held to the same standards. It took a lot of adjusting to, to realise that this was a way of showing love to each other. No one was ever treated as less than a comrade.

It had been one thing to nervously gather myself to travel to Rojava. It was scary, but it was where my road led. It was a whole other kind of terrifying to learn that people were going to criticise me, lay out my faults, contextualise them with the big stories of our world, and expect me to rewrite myself. I had to rethink how I saw criticism, and that meant I could change how I gave it too. If we cannot even believe our comrades can change, how can we believe in broader social change? If we cannot listen and commit to improving ourselves, what right do we have to talk about anyone else doing so? If not you, who else?

Loving comradeship doesn't mean always affirming each other, or just accepting each other as we are. Instead, we should be in a constant, mutual, and supportive process of developing each other. Of course, no one is objective and everyone speaks from their own perspective. But what better measure to take of ourselves than our comrades' perspective on us? Criticism is not set in stone, but you should always listen and take what you can from it. I was also always invited to criticise my comrades – and, much as I lived in awe of them, none of them were perfect. When those imperfections, inconsistencies, or blind spots began to grate on me, at home I might have withdrawn or felt tension build. It was a whole new world to simply have a space where I didn't just have the option, but a duty to bring those points up.

In the early 2000s, Sakine Cansiz, one of the founding members of the PKK and one of the first women to take part in the Kurdistan Freedom Movement, reflected on the struggle she devoted her life to, saying that: *"The greatest achievement of this revolution is the work on developing the socialist personality."* Until she was assassinated by Turkish Intelligence in Paris in 2013, Cansiz lived and breathed revolution. She spent many years in Turkish prison for her work organising against patriarchy and colonialism, where she underwent every form of torture. She spent years waging guerilla warfare in the mountains of Kurdistan, and many more organising meetings, demonstrations, and actions. This was a woman who knew what revolution was about. What does this quote mean then, that personality development has been the greatest achievement? Perhaps it means, what makes the Kurdistan Freedom Movement stand out from many other revolutionary movements?

Change (which Octavia Butler calls the only lasting truth) is at least in part driven by decision, by choices. Social change is a long, uphill struggle. When we start to look more closely at history, beyond the glamorous moments of intensity, we can see that meaningful social change never comes about without some people completely committed to that change, taking the decision to work for it, with everything they have, way before they know what the outcome of their work will be.

"Shape change and you shape God", Butler goes on. Meaning, change is everything. It flows from the smallest level to the biggest and our task is (and always should be) to take responsibility for the changes we make. It's a hell of a task, of course. Do we think we're up to it? That's exactly why the Kurdistan Freedom Movement puts so much emphasis on developing ourselves. It's why my friend from Afrin didn't see any problem with giving her forthright opinion on how I spoke, what I thought, how I lived my values (though we did both eventually end up in a fit of giggles the day she, in true Senior Witch style, decided to take me to task on how I was slicing a watermelon). For her, it would have been unhelpful not to tell me what she thought, and she expected the same in return.

Still, I knew where we'd both been in the mid 90s. I was sitting about reading books, my main concerns in life brattish and petty with hindsight: youthful insecurity, family fights, or not being able to afford things I wanted. She was hiding in a tree for hours from squads sent out to kill her and her comrades, fighting for the survival of her people, starting to organise the resistance movements I would hear about in the news in years to come. That made any kind of critique pretty hard, and generally left me feeling like a fraud a lot of the time. But you can't do anything about where you come from. You can only choose what changes you want to make.

Peşengtî (pronounced *peh-sheng-tee*) is what the Kurdistan Freedom Movement calls on us to be when things get tough. When you break it down it means something like *being-in-front-ness*. It's usually translated as vanguard. It means you have a responsibility to model your values, to be an example, and to live in a way that can inspire other people to do better. It means, we recognise that first and foremost we learn from each other and our communities, and we should embrace that.

You don't get to decide if you are peşengtî. You'll find out later from the world around you, society will let you know. But you should strive to be. At first it annoyed me how much the women I lived with used to fuss over things like a little mark or tear in a pair of jeans, an unironed shirt, a chipped coffee mug when guests are coming, or food not being prepared exactly right. But after a while I started to think about what was behind it, and surprised myself by beginning to try to carry myself with dignity.

In the past I'd shied away from the idea of dignity. I used to worry that it would stop me laughing, loving, being grounded, being reachable. That was never true, whether I understood it or not. There's also a lot of different reasons why you might do something, and who you do it for. It's not about enforced respectability. It's about *respect*. Respect for our comrades, for people around us, and *pride*: in the work we do, and in what we are a part of.

Peşengtî isn't a matter of being in charge. If you feel like for any reason your experiences have left you ill equipped to tell anyone else what to do with their life, then remember that's not what we're here to do. Just because you are not needed to preach does not mean you're not needed at all. Speak up when you should, listen well when you need to, and be ready. If not you, who else?

Abdullah Öcalan famously said that only ten percent of the struggle was against the enemy, and ninety percent will be against ourselves. Less famously, a friend of mine once reflected that "you come all this way to Rojava and the first thing you're confronted with is yourself." The Kurdistan Freedom Movement has made a whole way of life out of unearthing and building up what's referred to as a 'militant personality': the version of yourself who relearns how to love, how to fight, and what you can achieve. A version of yourself that's always struggling to overcome the influence capitalism, the state and patriarchy has had on you. You'll never be finished. But that doesn't mean there's no point. You could say the same thing of any historical figure you've ever heard of and admired, or anyone in your life that you look up to. That is exactly what's so inspiring about it: if they were fundamentally special and different, it wouldn't be so amazing. We are all just people, but we can make choices. Us: these imperfect, messed up, battered, often misguided, insecure creatures, are all we've got. And while we'll never be perfect, we can make ourselves stronger, more open, clearer, cleaner of heart, more able to really love, more ready to be part of a big change.

This means, in part, actively seeking to learn from those who have something to teach us, and you don't have to go to Kurdistan to find them. Anti-racist educators, educators who understand class oppression, educators with a wealth of knowledge about all the different fault-lines of oppression we are wrestling with, are everywhere if we really decide to look. We should all be seeking anyone who has experience of struggle and resistance. And all those seemingly a-political learnings, from books and stories, our grandmas, our childhood friends, nature itself, that simply show us how to be.

It doesn't mean striving to become a soulless action man. If what you do doesn't warm people, if you don't know how to enjoy life and show love, no one will be interested in what you say or do. There's also plenty of space for people's different abilities and different ways of being. In Rojava I shared life with a huge range of different types of personality, of neurodivergence, of physical ability. The same words and understandings aren't used there as they are in Europe. Because of that, and because I'm not here to armchair diagnose anyone, it's difficult to draw exact parallels. All I know is that I was never once in a space where at least one person didn't have some kind of different ability or need, be it physical or mental. And that was just part of life- in fact, it was a good thing. Every person was expected to give everything we could, even to inspire others, but that doesn't have to look the same for everyone.

You might not know if you are peşengtî, but you know it when you see it in others around you, or you know who plays that role for you. For me, the best example is those women I used to live with. Yes, they are just people, full of flaws, as likely to be grumpy in the mornings as anyone else, but still, they made me want to be them with every word and gesture. They are hard as steel when they need to be, but ever loving, humble and full of humour. They are never too busy, even if what they're doing is preparing for a three-day seminar, or strategising international diplomacy, to ask how you are and really listen to the answer. They wake early and go to bed late, but they know how to enjoy life, from sweets to massages to comedy films. They share their wisdom, but they ask your opinion every time. They expect you to be the best version of yourself, and with never a word spoken, you promise them you will try.

When I was younger, I thought I rejected leadership in any form. Now I think we need it. In Kurmanji Kurdish the word used to describe revolutionary leader actually translates as something like *guide*, and the movement has worked hard to remember this. The point is that this isn't *ruling*. This is a leadership by example, by either literally or figuratively taking the front. One that relies on earned trust. One that isn't about you personally, it's about whether you know the way. And you might know one place but not another. A guide knows when to step in behind another and learn a new route. It opens the possibility for anyone to be a leader, even if you aren't 'in charge' — because there will always be others walking on the path with you.

The Kurdistan Freedom Movement takes embodying this kind of leadership seriously. It doesn't always succeed. While I was in North and East Syria, there were plenty of moments where I struggled when people made all the same mistakes, or fell into the same toxic patterns as my bosses back home. But at least this isn't just accepted as the way things have to be. Instead, we're expected to be constantly working on ourselves, and you're expected to call out bad leadership when you see it.

In certain crises, or fast moving situations, there isn't much time for discussion and explanation. But, as a friend once told me, those situations also rely on trust. "If you are authoritarian," she said, "you lose *authority*. If I shout at you every day, you will neither respect nor listen to me. If I am a good example, run a democratic space, empower my friends and comrades, listen well, and take responsibility, then on the day when I suddenly order you to act, I hope you would all know it meant it really was an emergency, and trust me in what needs to be done."

One of the more common nicknames for Abdullah Öcalan is Rêber Apo. *Reber* is this word that means guide. Apo is short for Abdullah but also means 'uncle'. This does a good job of conveying the warmth felt by so many people for the man who always appeared looking attentive and thoughtful, dressed neatly but in woolly jumpers more often than uniforms. Who smiles when he sees a bird, and gave pep talks to his people that would not be out of place in the final ring-corner scene of a boxing movie, but are referring to a life in search of freedom, rather than a knockout punch.

It can take people a time to understand the relationship of the Kurdistan Freedom Movement to Öcalan. It's taken me a while and I don't think I'm finished yet. I don't think I'll ever feel quite the same way about Öcalan as people from Kurdistan do, and that's ok. I can feel strongly in my own way, and respect and understand what he symbolises to other people. Because Öcalan stands for much more than just one person. For the Kurdistan Freedom Movement he represents all the influences on his life that brought him to his conclusions, the leadership that showed a people the road ahead, the organisation he created through sheer hard work and dedication, and the ideology that feeds their growth. It's not simply seeing him as an individual who is larger than life, but recognising that he has put himself completely in service to something that's bigger than all of us, and honouring that.

In the culture of political organising where I'm from, we can sometimes shy away from really owning the idea of putting ourselves in service, even if that's what we are trying to do.

This can be because of a very reasonable fear of appointing ourselves spokespeople or vanguards. A disdain for falling into the role of social engineers or claiming to have 'seen the light'. But whenever I raised these issues with comrades in North and East Syria they inevitably frowned and tutted and said that's not being a revolutionary. That's being arrogant, or power hungry, or dominant, or dangerous. Of course it's very important that we recognise these pitfalls and fight to avoid them. This is another reason we need to take our own personal development seriously. But just because that's hard doesn't mean that we should just turn away from the big questions. As Howard Zinn famously said (and I'm sure I could find a sci-fi novel to illustrate if you give me a minute): *"you can't be neutral on a moving train".* It's not possible to opt out when wider forces of capitalism, state violence and ecological destruction are in action.

And I think there's actually more to it than these legitimate concerns. Somewhere along the line we've become afraid to give ourselves wholly to the fight. We seem to think our well-being is a see-saw between struggle and health, and to live a life for social change is basically banging our head against a brick wall until the blood flows.

Instead we fall into a hopeless attempt to find a way to 'just live a good life' in the world in which we find ourselves. It doesn't work. Sometimes, not least when we're trying to live right in this wrong world, we can feel a weird division between what we think, feel, and do. An unsettling disconnection in the gut, a spinning head as we move from self to self and try desperately not to let the walls between them wear thin and expose the contradictions. In the small adobe house where I lived for a while in *Jinwar*, the women's village in Rojava, there was a Theodor Adorno quote on the wall over the cabinet where we'd grab a hairbrush or clip or packet of tissues. *"The right life cannot be lived in the wrong society. But the right struggle can be fought wherever systems of domination oppress the people."* These are more words I call on when I am struggling with a decision. It lifts a weight from my shoulders: the pressure to be living a blameless or completely ethical life. In the same motion it lays another one on there: the responsibility to fight for a world in which *everyone* can live ethically. *"Belief,"* writes Octavia Butler, *"initiates and guides action— Or it does nothing."*

Another friend I worked with for a long time tells her story as a logical expression of this. She was studying at university, and as she became more and more involved in politics, she was delving into her own Kurdish identity. The way she explains it, it sounds like it was just a one way street. As she came to certain understandings and beliefs, she had to take action. Not to do so would be to split herself in two, make her beliefs meaningless. She couldn't expect anyone to do it for her. Who else?

The years of fighting and organising, of the struggle, leave their marks. None of the comrades ever says it's easy. But easy is not the same thing as happy. Safe isn't the same thing as right. In doing the right thing, you do right by yourself. If you're deep in it when push comes to shove, you find out exactly who you are and why you're there.

I met comrades working with the movement from every kind of background. Whether it was the defence units, the women's village, diplomacy or education, there was always a mix of people. Some who'd come from student politics, some from quite wealthy, relatively privileged backgrounds. Others came from intense urban poverty, or villages where they walked two hours to go to school, and the whole family slept on the hearth in winter. Many women had left violent family situations. We learnt all of this and more about each other round the breakfast table, or in a session of critic and self critic. All of them agreed it's vital that everyone looks long and hard at where they are from, and the stamps it's left on their personality, and not just as individual reflection. It's an important task to map the world we live in within your personal history. To find yourself in the big picture and to find the big picture in you.

So many internationalists arrive in Rojava from Western countries ready to rush around feeling useful, and are more or less told that the best way we can *be* useful is to take some serious time to dismantle the orientalist, white supremacist, colonialist, Western-rationalist perspectives we've brought over with us — including the ones about what it means to be useful! This kind of thing is lifelong work and whilst we all have to do it, of course there's a special responsibility for those living the top side of an oppressive dynamic. But that privilege is not a reason not to commit yourself, whatever that means. I realised, looking back on a lot of moments at home, that we can use 'checking privilege' as a way out of a situation that makes us uncomfortable, or as a reason to give in. But going off to live our privilege is not actually checking it. Comrades from North and East Syria who are doctors, translators, programmers, engineers, professors, archaeologists, you name it, make themselves useful. For *change*. They work to change themselves as well, but they get to work. They don't get paralysed by guilt.

On the other hand, there's plenty of organisers with the movement who've been on the sharp end of everything their entire lives. Often they would share stories of things that nearly brought me to tears, holding back only out of respect for the fact they didn't seem to want that. When they didn't talk about it, you could fill in the blanks well enough yourself, able to guess what happens to women in prison under a regime that hardly bothers to pretend they don't torture and rape. I expected these stories to slow them down. Or define their interactions. Or at least give them some kind of trump card when discussing these issues. Instead, they only seemed interested in a collective response, a solution for the future, and saw their duties as no less and no more than anyone else. No one's going to do it for you: if not you, who else?

One night, after watering our plants and splashing the cold water over our hot, sticky feet, I made the tea. We opened a watermelon (just about managing to cut it well enough so that nobody started tutting). Some friends from other women's associations had dropped by. It was one of those rare nights when none of us was glued to our work, and we could share stories, and stretch our bodies out in the privacy of the high-walled yard. Sometimes those evenings people would casually tell mind blowing war stories, usually ending up chortling at a punchline of some ridiculous scenario that had emerged like when they fell in a river, the impressive part of the story almost slipping through the cracks (like, they'd walked for six hours with a comrade on their shoulders to get there). Other times people would spar and challenge each other on ideology or practice, ready to both listen and speak with conviction and the dignity that comes with believing it matters what you think. And the force of personality of Senior Witches that's got them through all these years.

That night, our guests started asking about me. They wanted to know about my family, send a silly video to my sister, quiz me on organising in Europe, ask me about love and relationships. I struggled to keep up with the rapid, casual Kurdish, and find what I felt had to be a balance between being polite but not acting like my story was as important to hear as theirs. But they wouldn't let it go, and it wasn't just idle curiosity. "We want to know how you got here," my supervisor explained, and she isn't a woman to say anything she doesn't mean. "You're a revolutionary too," she said, and it wasn't up for debate: much more a warning than a compliment. That means my story is also worth telling, and really honestly, not because it has anything particularly special in it but because we all need to tell our stories and hear each other's to understand how we can write the next chapter. How we can shape change.

Our history is full of people standing up to power despite their life already looking hard enough. It's also full of people who could have stayed in a comfortable life but who could never have found peace there, and so came to be what help they could. There's no stopping anyone asking ourselves: if not you, who else?

Do you know where you're going? Yes.
Do we know what awaits us? Yes.
Is it worth it? Yes.
Who can answer the previous three questions with a *yes* and remain still and do nothing, without feeling that something deep inside is tearing apart?
— *Zapatista communique, December 1994*

Movement flags and portraits of Öcalan adorn thousands of walls across Kurdistan

5. ORGANISING

A part of something bigger
Natalia

The month before I planned to leave for Rojava, I got down to the business of gathering all of the things that I thought I would need. The problem was, I had no idea what I was getting myself into, which made it hard to know what I should be packing. Would I need water purification tablets? Pyjamas? What's more likely to come in handy – a pair of running shoes, or a combat medic first aid kit? At some point in the stress of wrapping up jobs and projects, packing up my stuff and saying goodbyes, I became fixated on the idea that I needed to buy a sleeping bag. At no point was I told that I would need one, and in fact when I asked the people in Rojava who I was in touch with, they all said that a sleeping bag wouldn't be necessary. But I persisted in trawling through the online shops of outdoor equipment stores, reading reviews and comparing weight and warmth ratings. I couldn't imagine travelling somewhere where I didn't know where I was going to sleep, and not having a sleeping bag as some kind of safety net. Torn between these conflicting messages — people in Rojava saying not to bring a sleeping bag, and a lifetime of experience saying that I should — I bought a sleeping bag and then didn't pack it, opting instead to cram my rucksack with first aid supplies, spare socks and a small stash of energy bars.

Being able to pack light had been a point of pride for me, so although my outsize rucksack was filled to bursting, I felt that I had done okay considering I was travelling to a conflict-torn region for an indeterminate length of time. The rolled eyes and mutterings of the Kurdish revolutionaries who met us at arrival said otherwise. For them, travelling light meant fitting everything into a backpack the size of a corner shop plastic bag: the movement would take care of everything else. I hadn't yet mastered the knack of trust-falling into the arms of an organisation far bigger than I could see or understand, but it was something I had to pick up on the go.

From the moment of arrival, things became simultaneously predictable and unpredictable. I never knew exactly when I'd be picked up and transported to the next stage of my journey. I didn't know where I'd be staying each night, or how long I'd be staying for. I might be dropped off at a family's house, and spend the evening entertaining children with awkward attempts at communication. Or I might spend the night with a gaggle of teenage girls on a residential educational programme, waking up early in the morning to screeching and laughter. At the same time, some things are set in stone. I always had a place to stay the night. If there is food to eat, I would receive my share of it. I would be expected to help out if there was work to do, and to join in if there is a celebration of any kind.

During the first few days after my arrival, I applied the scant Kurdish I knew to asking a constant stream of questions – "where are we heading?", "when will we get there?", "how long will we stay?", "what comes next?" I never got a clear answer to any of my questions, but life slowly began to take on a routine that I came to understand. Every evening, wherever I was, we would lay out thin foam mattresses on the floor, spread out blankets in a range of wonderfully garish designs, and lay down to sleep. After only a few days of this routine I realised that I would never have needed the sleeping bag I had agonised over while packing — every family house, community centre or academy building would have a stack of extra mattresses and folded up blankets for whoever happened to be passing through. It took me a bit longer to realise that I didn't need to always know where we were headed next and how we were going to get there – I had to trust that the organisational structures of the movement would get me to where I needed to go.

Other details began to fall into place along with the stacks of folded blankets and relaxed attitudes of the Kurdish families whose homes we were dropped off at with seemingly no advance warning. Wherever we arrived we were greeted with a firm handshake by everyone in the room, and in most circumstances a glass of tea. As we were handed off between drivers, handfuls of tightly folded handwritten notes were also passed from driver to driver. They were notes written to loved ones active in the movement by friends and family based in different places, folded up and labelled with the person's name and the institution or place where they worked, sometimes with a distinguishing characteristic of the intended recipient to further narrow down the possible options. For internationalist volunteers it might be the country we're from, or 'the tall one' or 'with blonde hair'. Just like clueless internationalist volunteers, these notes would be transported down miles of road and passed across state borders, by countless people who didn't know where they had come from or what was written in them, only that they were helping them get to their final destination.

However random and opaque things seemed on the surface, everyone had exactly as much information as they needed to get done what they needed to get done. It just happened to be that the only information that I needed to play my part was that I had to be ready to leave exactly when it was time to go – no more and no less. As each day passed I understood more and more the breadth and depth of the revolutionary organisation I had come to work with. Reading about the scale of work being carried out by the movement in Rojava had already convinced me that our social movements had a lot to learn from the Kurdistan Freedom Movement. But being fully immersed in the complex and highly coordinated web of revolutionary organisation that harnessed the power of millions of people across time zones and state borders landed that understanding on a much deeper level.

After several days of stopping and starting, getting picked up and dropped off and picked up again, I finally arrived at the project where I would be living and working for the foreseeable future. It was dark by the time we pulled up the drive, and I could barely make out the shape of the single-storey concrete buildings connected by grey gravel paths. By now I knew more what to expect – I got out of the van, was greeted with smiles and handshakes, and was herded into a common room where I was served a cup of tea and scrambled to memorise the names of everyone I was introduced to. Eventually, I was shown to the women's house where I would be staying, easily fell into the routine of setting out the mattresses and blankets, and lay down, exhausted, in my new home.

From then on my days were framed by simple routines. The wake up call — usually a cheerfully loud *"rojbaş!"* ("good morning!" in Kurdish) accompanied by a rapping on the windows of each room — would rouse everyone at the project in the early morning. We would all climb out of our nest of blankets with varying levels of wakefulness, and take a few minutes to fold up the blankets and stack them in the wardrobe. The thin mattresses would be arranged around the edges of the room to serve as a seating area, or stashed out of the way leaning against the wall in the corner of the room. Being part of an organised movement that made sure you had somewhere to sleep also meant being organised: whether you were at your place or visiting, we neatly folded our blankets every morning and kept spaces far more clean and tidy than any collective spaces I had encountered back home.

There were plenty of blankets, mattresses and pillows, but if there were lots of guests staying then we pushed the mattresses together and shared blankets. Whether or not we shared a language with the comrades spending the night with us, we shared the work of laying out the beds and packing them back up again in the morning. Work was shared too. We took turns to clean the house, prepare breakfast and water the garden. We took on specific roles and responsibilities in the project, but when there was a big job to do everyone set aside their work to help out, whether it's moving a big pile of rocks to rebuild a wall, or recording a solidarity video to share online and send to comrades around the world.

This continued for a few months, including a term of education lasting several weeks. During this time, the wet, green spring weather withered into the dry, relentless heat of a Syrian summer. As temperatures increased, so did the likelihood of an imminent Turkish invasion. Rumours spread of Turkish troops gathering on the other side of the border wall in preparation to attack. Our daily routines continued, but alongside them preparations were being made for war. Across the region, tunnels and bunkers were dug out of the rocky ground as additional protection against bombings, and we were drilled mercilessly in emergency procedures so we knew what we would have to do if we had to evacuate. As part of these preparations, we were called in one by one to chat to our supervisors to discuss our work over the coming months.

The movement in Rojava is organised into different organisational structures (commonly referred to simply as 'structures') which sit within broader areas of the movement like the women's movement, the youth movement, diplomatic relations, economy and many others. If you're an internationalist volunteer, the structure within which you work – which might be an educational institution, an ecological cooperative, a health project or a women's initiative – is like your organisational home for your time in Rojava. This means that you are accountable to that structure and they are responsible for you. For example, you might be based at a women's academy, which sits more broadly within the structure of the women's movement. This means that your day to day life and work would be held by the academy — making sure that you have a place to stay, education and support to help you grow, and work to do — but if a more significant issue or conflict arose, you could go further up in the structure to get support beyond the academy where you were based.

Moving between structures isn't something that you can just do on a whim – the supervisors of your structure need to arrange it with the supervisors of the structure you want to work within. This means that the desires of each individual can be balanced with the needs and capacity of the structure where they want to work. After some months working within an ecological project, I was hoping to be able to arrange some work with the women's movement to learn more about what the revolution — and ecology — looks like within the autonomous women's structures. I was able to request some time 'on loan' with the women's movement in order to gain experience. I was expected to write a report of my time away from my structure in order to reflect on and feed back what I learned, and to arrange a discussion or seminar upon my return to share my experiences. As the possibility of war approached, we also discussed what my work placement would be in the eventuality of a Turkish invasion. As a computer literate native English speaker, it made sense for me to go to one of the many press centres in order to work on research and information distribution, which would play an important role in defending against an invasion. This decision took my personal preference into consideration, but balanced with where the work was needed and whether it would be a good fit for me.

I wondered if this was what it was like years ago in the months before the official start of the Rojava revolution. In the summer of 2012, a year into the seismic political upheavals across much of the Arab world that year, the people of Rojava rose up and expelled the brutal Assad regime's forces from the regions of Afrin, Kobane and Jazira. The actual moment when people took to the streets and surrounded the bases where Assad regime soldiers were based took place over a few days. But crucially, the Kurdistan Freedom Movement had been organising — both underground and openly — for decades. In the months before the uprising — just like I was experiencing seven years later — networks and systems of revolutionary organisation must have sparked and buzzed with communication and decisions that would build up to the flashpoint of resistance. People went from house to house with messages hidden in bags of bread. Weddings covered for clandestine meetings. They couldn't see the uprisings coming, but they were sure to be ready when they did.

From the outside, it was only that moment that was recognisable as 'revolution'. But no revolutionary moments are totally spontaneous, they come out of and are carried by revolutionary organisation that reach back into history as much as they stretch forward into the future. Recognising our place in these legacies of resistance is in itself a form of organisation – it allows us to learn from our mistakes and draw on the strength of being part of something bigger than us. Crucially, it also lays the foundation for planning into the future, rather than just existing in a moment that blossoms and wilts in the blink of an eye.

The reality of revolutionary history is one of organisation. Anarchists in early 20th century Spain, the rent strikes in Glasgow during WWI, Algeria's anti-colonial movement, the Irish War of Independence, the formation of neighbourhood councils in Bolivia were possible because people came together. Big and small, you name it. People have formed unions, groups, platforms or congresses. They're bound by collective decisions and follow a collective strategy, even if it's not always clear how the work they're doing fits into a bigger picture. And they've become organised *before* a crisis situation. That means having something solid that can keep itself going, ready when something does happen. Sensationalist western media coverage of events like the YPJ resistance against the Assad regime and Islamic State wants to paint a picture of magical spontaneity that turns the whole story into something that seems too good to be true; and that's because it is. If we buy these stories we will stand by wondering why things aren't springing up out of nowhere where we live. If we only start organising when an opportunity opens up, we will be too late.

Sitting down and talking through my options for the work I would do in the coming months wasn't just an exercise in seeing historic revolutionary organising from a new perspective. It was evidence of a social movement that was well organised enough to allocate skills and capacity to where it was most needed, across a wide range of institutions and locations. Having solid organisational structures means that no matter how many of us there are, and how much work is going on, we are all exactly where we need to be. Whether I was waking up early to water a newly planted orchard and nurture vegetable patches, or proofreading articles and formatting hundreds of footnotes on reports, I knew that I was playing my part.

At the same time, Jenni was coordinating education schedules, uploading videos, or getting sucked into the ins and outs of interpersonal disputes in one small corner of one small town. She spent countless days driving a minibus around to pick up other comrades, shopping or medicine or random bits and pieces. Although we were in different cities, working in different institutions and most of the time having no idea what the other one was doing, we were more connected in our political organising than we had ever been – even when we had previously been involved in the same small networks and organising around the same issues.

That feeling of connection wasn't just limited to the people I was close friends with, the people I spent my days with, or even the people who I had met at some point during my time in Rojava. I felt intensely connected with thousands of people across hundreds of miles, all of whom were preparing in countless ways for collective self defence. The most tedious of tasks took on the shine of being part of something bigger — the frontline became wherever there was work to do. Jenni described it like feeling that in Rojava, everything you do is part of a very long sentence, full of 'ands'. Instead of simply describing what you're doing as "we're working on getting a place up and running to organise mutual aid for people who are struggling in our area" you would describe your work as "defending the revolution on the front lines of the conflict, developing new restorative justice systems, writing books and articles, running educational initiatives, building the youth and women's organising... *and* we're, for example, working on a place for mutual aid."

During my time in grass-roots political organising at home, I often felt like I was 'firefighting' on one front or another, usually by doing work in response to an immediate crisis. Sometimes this was community work, responding to the needs of those most brutalised by the state or capitalism. Sometimes this meant organising protests and civil disobedience to put our bodies and voices in the way of crimes like fracking operations or deportation flights. Either way, this often left no space for organising — or even imagining — big picture change. This reactive work needs to happen, but it can wear you down. Something that gives us strength — both emotional and material — is knowing that you're not fighting this fire on your own. Being part of the immense organisational structures in Rojava meant that you knew that you had your corner to keep safe, but that you were part of a bigger resistance that forms, link by link, a chain that runs from frontline to frontline, forged together by the values we share and what we're fighting for.

Of course, on one level it's always like that whether we see it or not. We are in the struggle together, we are a part of the same web. And that connection, whether you call it heartfelt, spiritual, historical, or anything else, is a huge part of what keeps us going. But we must not be afraid to make it a concrete reality either. After returning home I felt dizzied by the absence of the organisational structures to connect me with the work of countless comrades, to help me decide where to put my energy in the face of overwhelming need for action. Mentally reaching back to comrades in Rojava, I reminded myself again and again that I was still connected, still part of the big picture even if I was no longer connected to the structures.

A few months later, Jenni was wrangling with the decision to leave Rojava and come home. She wrote to me about the old, wise, organiser from the women's movement who pulled her aside and told her: *'We think it's great that you'll go home and work for the revolution there. We need everyone to do that. And sometimes you'll be right and sometimes you'll be wrong, but don't leave yourself without organisation. You won't get anywhere without it.'* In the times we are living in, when our political and financial institutions are losing credibility, as our world is rocked by a series of crises — climate, economic, refugee and many more – this is the work we have before us. To build up our strength, to organise like we mean to win, to rise to the challenges we are facing.

The organisational structures that get built up to coordinate the work of the movement – committees, assemblies and reporting mechanisms – both feed off of and nurture the less concrete ways in which we are connected. Work reports get sent from all of the projects to the highest levels of movement coordination. People in positions of responsibility sit on coordinating committees which are responsible for sharing information and developing strategy across structures. But none of these would mean anything without the shared culture and emotional feeling of connection that we have with each other.

I was used to feeling this sense of connection – comradeship – with those who I had personally organised with, who I had known for years or spent countless hours with writing press releases or chopping veg at protest camps and community centres. During my time immersed in the political culture of the Kurdistan Freedom Movement, that sense of connection and love became something I felt with thousands of people I didn't know. They included those who I met fleetingly during visits to various projects across Rojava, and those whose faces I began to recognise at big gatherings and celebrations, but also those who I had never crossed paths with. Even though I knew that a lot of these people wouldn't be my top choice for someone to hang out with on a free evening, there was a basic assumption of respect and trust, an acknowledgement that we were bound together in some intangible and magnificent way. That trust extended beyond internationalist volunteers, beyond those who devoted their lives fully to the revolution, and outwards to all of the people around the world who are part of the movement for freedom and justice in every way possible. It was this trust that meant that wherever people who work with the movement go in Kurdistan, they will have a place to sleep, food to share, and work to do.

This feeling was generated and reinforced by the ways in which we lived and worked together. The fact that when you entered a room, every single person in the room would break off their conversation and stand up and shake your hand to welcome you into the space. The shared chants and slogans that we would shout on marches or when we lined up to see off comrades who were leaving our project to start work somewhere new. The expectation that when you found interactions with someone difficult, you would sit down and work through it respectfully and honestly, supported by your comrades. The insistence on remembering those who came before us by taking a minute's silence and making sure their memory lives on through the work we do and the path we walk.

Crucially, this political culture was rooted in a shared vision for what we were fighting for and an accountability to the organisational structures that were working towards this vision. Because if we're going to make sure that we're all pulling in the same direction, we need some clarity on where we're going. To even ask this question back home can expose how mixed up we are, how we lack proposals, goals, ideas for the future and articulation of our rage: in a word, ideology. For years, ideology was a dirty word for me. It brought up memories of tedious debates with dogmatic activists who used ideology as either as a stick to beat you with or to bore you to death. It seemed to me that ideology was something that existed on placards and behind podiums, but not as something that was alive, that not only shaped how we moved through the world, but did so with beauty.

The Kurdistan Freedom Movement in general, including the Rojava revolution in North and East Syria, has the ideology of Abdullah Öcalan at its core. It doesn't just exist as words in books and essays — the movement lives and breathes its ideology. It's part of who makes breakfast and how, it affects how you get dressed in the morning, and it stays with you until it guides where or how you sleep at night. It starts with the big picture — a world built on foundations of love, freedom, life and justice — and filters down to the smallest details: sharing out the blankets at night so everyone is warm. Standing up to greet people as they enter a room. Giving meaning and purpose in the work that you do, however small. Or, maybe it starts with the tiny details and builds up to the big picture. Either way, it's something that gives shape to the conversation between the world we want to live in, and the world that exists now. It's like someone you trust is always standing with you asking you about your motivations, or what you think the consequences of an action will be.

Often there are no simple answers, just an insistence on asking the right questions. Ideology becomes a way that we organise our minds and our values, so that we can embody our beliefs through the way we live our lives and treat each other. It's not a superficial idea either, or simply pragmatism. It's a value, a way of life and something that brings us together. A way to know, or at least trust, what each other is doing.

In October 2019, nine months after I arrived in Rojava, Turkey launched its long-threatened invasion. I had moved into my wartime work placement at the press centre some weeks before, and we sprung into action. Some of our collective grabbed cameras and car keys and headed off towards the front lines, and the rest of us stayed in our office to receive, organise and distribute information. It was second nature for us to organise ourselves to sleep in shifts so that someone was always awake and monitoring the situation. A few days after the first bombs were dropped, I shared this update with friends:

We are spread across North and East Syria but somehow everyone feels closer than ever.

When the threat of war was still hanging over our heads, I sent and received so many "how are you feeling?" messages, I felt held by these small communications and expressions of care. Now the air we breathe is so thick with comradeship and shared purpose that these messages would be superfluous. We have become an ecosystem — each of us playing our role in the resistance, knowing that the part we play is crucial — yet meaningless if taken out of the context of the whole.

It feels so powerful how our comrades across the world are part of this web too — protesting, blockading, boycotting, speaking to people. Hearing about the masses of mobilisations around the world brings tears to my eyes, and it feels like the most useful, hopeful thing we can be doing.

As we watched all of the international NGOs pack up their offices and evacuate staff to the border crossing with Iraq, we stood firm. We had built a foundation of collective purpose, connection and organisation, and it kept us full of not just purpose, but also hope. Our shared ideology kept us strong and reminded us how important the work we were doing was. We knew our history, and understood that we were one part of a long legacy of resistance, and that our choices would further shape that legacy. Our love for each other meant that we were willing to take risks to defend each other and the movement we were all part of. And our strong, well coordinated networks meant that we had the information and support we needed to be as effective and safe as possible. In the months before I had struggled with a way of working that meant I couldn't just unilaterally decide where I would go and what I would do when I got there. But when it came down to defending ourselves against the invasion, knowing that we were part of these well-organised structures was a weight off our backs and an injection of hope.

We all felt this foundation solidly beneath our feet during the resistance to the invasion of Serekaniye and Tel Abyad in 2019, but it played a crucial role even in times when the region wasn't under direct military attack. Time and time again, I saw the organisational structures and political culture of the movement hold a group of comrades while they moved through conflict, disagreement and crisis. I was part of many hard conversations trying to resolve conflict between people who had fallen out, or as a response to someone behaving inappropriately. I wrote reports evaluating challenging situations and shared them with those responsible for the organisational structures I was working within. I got over my instinct to smooth over disagreement and instead stood up in meetings to deliver clear and honest criticism of comrades whose behaviour I was struggling with. Faced with no other option, I learned to be patient, and saw change happen in both big and small ways. The change usually took longer than I wanted it to, and almost always longer than I would have stuck around for at home. Throughout the most challenging periods, our ability to continue to work, learn and overcome obstacles together was held by the strength of our organisation.

We'll never be completely happy with everything that a wider group of people does because we're not carbon copies of each other. We can constructively criticise and support each other, change, grow and move forward. But at some point we will probably be associated with something that we don't think is ideal. This is all part of building something bigger than ourselves. We ourselves are not pure either, and will make mistakes that we will — hopefully — learn from and become better versions of ourselves. But still all around me I see people only working with groups so small that they can manage to agree on everything. Which can create a lot of amazing things, but a social movement is not one of them.

An organised movement doesn't mean a homogenous one. It is an ecology, a forest with a deeply woven web of elements and relationships that push and pull on each other. It is interdependence and wholeness – one tree out of a forest of a thousand trees isn't on its own one thousandth of a forest. The trees need each other (and the countless other beings and substances they are connected with) to become a forest. And just as within a forest there are trees, and insects, and fungal networks and birds and moisture, different people occupy different spaces within a movement. If a movement is well organised, it provides accountability for leadership and a path for it to follow. At the same time, it supports people to be fully part of it in lots of different ways – whether that means doing political work alongside raising a family, as someone organising within their workplace or as someone who puts their life fully in service to political struggle.

Those who take the decision to become full-time revolutionaries within the Kurdistan Freedom Movement take a sideways step on this path that places them in a slightly different position, but they are still walking in the same direction as everyone else. From when they make their decision, they put themselves in service of the movement, choosing political work over family, career and personal gain.

Because full-time revolutionaries give up a normal home and family does not mean they live without love or connection. Far from it. Being a full time revolutionary means that we try to really live what we believe: a love that is not wrapped up in domination or possession, a love that multiplies infinitely instead of closing in tightly. It is seen as their duty to try and embody these values and be a living example.

Stories of Kurdish revolutionaries risking their lives to rescue each other or giving their lives for each other in an instant are uncountable. A youth organiser I knew once stayed in a cave in the mountains for weeks, risking discovery by the Turkish state, because she was nursing a comrade who'd broken his ankle and couldn't get around. The love between comrades who owe each other their lives is tangible.

Through offering yourself in service you become entwined in a web of care. When you are sick, you are looked after. There's a whole network of homes to take care of the many thousands of comrades permanently injured, in war or elsewhere. Where you can still contribute, you do. Where you can't, you still have the same value as anyone else.

Like international volunteers in Rojava – but not just for a limited period of time – the work that the full time organisers do is guided by the needs of the movement. Wherever they are sent they will have a place to sleep, food to eat and funds for basic needs, but no private property and no separation between their private lives and their lives as revolutionaries. They play a crucial role in the ecology of the movement, but not one that can exist without all of the other elements.

The whole ecology includes artists and professionals, families and students — there are as many different ways of being part of the revolution as there are people.

A lot of people think that committing to struggle above all else means that you automatically become disconnected from society and live in a weird bubble. And perhaps this is because when we make that commitment here, we tend to do it as individuals. Then we run the risk of disconnection much more, as we lack accountability and organisation. But we have to believe we can do better. Not everyone can or should make organising their lives. But someone should. It should not mean separating from society; it should mean diving deeper and deeper in.

After only a few months in Rojava I lost track of how many family homes, community centres and institutions we had been welcomed into, staying for tea, a meal, or spending the night. Big families squeezed into tiny homes still devoted precious space to keep a stack of extra mattress pads and blankets for guests, the hospitality culture of the Middle East interwoven with the comradeship and trust built up by the Kurdistan Freedom Movement, over decades of organising.

Once we were inside, friendships and personal connections were built through shared meals, laughter and mutual support. But it was the organisational links forged by the movement that opened the door in the first place. Soon the memory of my fixation on bringing a sleeping bag seemed ridiculous; the knowledge that I would always have somewhere to stay was as deeply embedded in my life as the political vision that I was working for. So when a newly-arrived internationalist volunteer showed up at our project, carrying a sleeping bag and tentatively asking 'can I sleep here tonight?' I almost laughed out loud at the thought that he would even need to ask in the first place. When I packed my bag to leave Rojava and head back home, I had mastered the art of travelling light even by Kurdish revolutionary standards, and I boarded the plane with my bag half empty.

In the West, even within our movements for collective liberation we are used to finding individual solutions for how we live and how we support ourselves while doing the political work we feel called to do. A well organised movement like the Kurdistan Freedom Movement is able to generate collective solutions to these questions, enabling revolutionaries regardless of their class backgrounds, employability or access to different forms of privilege to live – with plenty of hard work and minimal luxury – for revolution. Of course this doesn't eradicate the impact of class and privilege on our movements. But it at least goes some ways towards equalising the effects. It means that people don't disappear from political organising because of precariousness and poverty on the one hand, or into high-powered careers and home ownership on the other. We have a long way to go before we will have the scale of autonomous movement economy that the Kurdistan Freedom Movement has. But we need to work towards creating collective resources that make sure everyone gets what they need.

We are deeply connected with everyone who is working to build a different kind of world. That connection exists whether or not it's reinforced through organisational structures, collective political culture or shared ideology. But organisation makes us greater than the sum of our parts, it takes all of our diversity and all of our differences and forges them into strength. We are part of something so much bigger than any of us alone, and that makes us powerful – that means we have the potential to shake the foundations on which capitalism rests.

Make no mistake — capitalism and the state are organised. And if we ourselves are not organised, we don't stand a chance. So we'd do well to remember the advice of the revolutionary women in Rojava who have learned to wield political organisation as a form of self defence: our resistance is only as strong as our organisation.

The mother of Hevrin Xalaf prepares to meet Turkish Army tanks with an armful of stones

6. FIGHTING BACK

A woman's place is in the revolution
Jenni

As we come marching, marching, un-numbered women dead
Go crying through our singing their ancient call for bread,
Small art and love and beauty their trudging spirits knew
Yes, it is bread we fight for, but we fight for roses, too.

— From 'Bread and Roses', a song of women's labour struggles

There's four of us there on the porch watching the sunset. Two of us from Europe, trying to drink in everything we see, and our hosts, two middle aged unmarried sisters from Rojava. It's still summer, warm enough that you can smell the hot stones under the water that was sloshed across them, and they're already dry five minutes later. It's a magical moment, the way the golden light is falling, the reality of where we are somehow utterly, undeniably real as earth, and delicate and precious as glass. The house is set back in a big, uphill-sloping yard, and if you look past the chicken house and the fig tree and over the wall you can see the whole village.

It's just the right season for figs, but we aren't really eating them fresh. Instead, with every meal, the sisters bring out last year's fig jam. Dark cocoa brown, rich and thick, the whole figs softened within it taste somewhere between mild alcohol and chocolate- like Christmas. It's almost as addictively wonderful as the stories they tell us. The big L-shaped house is the one they grew up in, where both their parents died (the father a long time ago and the mother more recently). The other siblings have all married and left, but neither of them wanted to. It's not hard to understand why not. Kurdish freedom fighters have been coming and going from this house since before I was born. Back when the whole family could have been killed for it. Back when people used to walk across the border to North Kurdistan to work the harvest. When these then-young women did it, their boots were packed full of bullets for the guerrilla fighters.

They're warm, and strict, and set in their ways, browned and wrinkled from years of sun, wind, piercing glares, and broad smiles. We stayed with them for several days and they became one of the families that I went to visit whenever I could. We were always as excited as kids to hear their stories and they oblige. What with that and the jam, we were determined to find something we can share to give them something back. Luckily, I had discovered not so long before that the mothers and grandmothers of Kurdistan (in fact, this probably goes the world over) are permanently, critically in need of a back massage. As soon as women here are old enough to stand up by themselves, they start carrying their younger siblings around. They learn to cook and make tea, to clean. As they get older, they only do more. They get up before everyone else, to scrub and chop and heat and sweep and fetch and carry. Village women go out to the fields, bullets or no bullets in their boots. When they come home they do it all over again, whilst changing clothes and drying tears and playing and putting to sleep. At pretty much no point do they rest, receive anything like the care they give, or think about themselves and their bodies until they have a problem. So by the time they reach the age of these revolutionary sisters, the years are written in a thick, heavy script in their muscles and joints. That these friends of ours have made the decision to remain child- and husbandless takes some weight off. However, this decision (slightly, but not drastically unusual) adds pressure in other ways as money becomes more of a stress, and the entire responsibility for a property lies with them.

I used to play on a sports team, so I speak the language of muscle kinks and crunches pretty well. Unlike help in the kitchen or on the grounds, a massage is something these women will accept from a guest. As I work on their shoulders, the sun sets, we slap the odd mosquito, and I wonder what it means that we're here. I find my mind drifting down a wormhole of questions. How can we support each other? What does it mean to be part of a movement? What does it mean to defend ourselves and who are we defending? What do we have in common? Where are we different? How do all the small moments like this one, however intimate or quiet, infinite moments of experience, add up to something meaningful, something we can share? Somewhere down there, at the root of it all, my fingers still softening an old, rigid knot under a shoulder blade, I realise I'm asking familiar things. Familiar partly because they are so big they seem small, so fundamental they seem obvious, but are usually anything but. And familiar because we've heard about them when women from the Kurdistan Freedom Movement tell us what they were talking about when they made the movement what it is today.

Women in the Kurdistan Freedom Movement have been asking questions since the movement first started to take shape. A while ago (but within my lifetime), they made space and time while they were fighting a war to ask themselves why they were fighting. But that wasn't all they were asking. Two of the biggest questions, the ones so big you can hardly see them, the ones that drive revolutionaries to fight in the first place, were *'Who are we?'* and *'How should we live?'*

When you spend time with women who have been organising with the movement for a long time, you can really *feel* how those questions are behind everything we do in struggle. A collective identity, outside of the system, and a search for how you should be living. The answers are under attack. The answers are many things for many people, but to find them in practice we need self defence.

A part of me will always be sitting on that porch in the sunset, hearing the stories, breathing in the air, and anticipating the jam. But this is the Rojava revolution and these women aren't just a romantic image that young militants come to visit and honour before they get back out there to do politics. They have just as much work to do themselves. They're both active in their local commune, the most local unit of the democratic system set up by the movement after the region was declared autonomous. That means they're running the fledgling grass-roots democratic system at its most important level. They hold leadership positions, come to every demonstration and event, and mediate conflicts in their local community. They are part of autonomous women's organising through Kongra Star, the women's movement umbrella organisation for all of Rojava. They host visiting organisers and guests. They have complicated, nuanced opinions fed by their culture, their religion, and all those years of experience, their roots firmly planted in their childhood yard. They're part of lively debate and disagreement about how to run their community. Them, and thousands of other women, among them many older women and mothers. This is where we start, says the Kurdistan Women's Movement. This is who we should be listening to, and empowering, and trusting, as we build our future.

It was also these kinds of women who were some of the first out waiting for the Turkish tanks to roll past when the USA and Russia started escorting the Turkish army on patrols through the areas it had just bombed and occupied, in late 2019. They sat by the side of the road in their long dresses, looking like they were gathering fruit or herbs up in their aprons. But this time the bulge was rocks, which they hurled as vehemently as any of the youths gathered with them, at the passing tanks and armoured cars. Among them, often leading them, were the mothers and grandmothers of those who had died in the defence of the region. When foreign powers left pathetic packets of food, they got thrown right back too. We don't want your pity or charity, the mothers of Kurdistan cried. We want our land, and we want you out. You've brought war, so we will fight to the end.

The mothers of those who have fallen in struggle sometimes feel like the glue that holds the movement together in North and East Syria. Perhaps their children fell to bombs like the portraits of the young men and women who smile down proudly in their uniforms from far, far too many walls in every town and village. Perhaps they were assassinated for peaceful, civil work like Hevrîn Xalaf, a well known politician who the Turkish state had killed by mercenaries. Her mother, like so many others, stands up proud under her picture and turns her pain of loss into a revolutionary flame.

For many people across the world, even just the word 'Rojava' conjures up images of the young Kurdish women fighters of the YPJ, the Women's Defence Units. The almost unique nature of the force, their history and presence, and the role they played in the fight against the Islamic State is a huge part of what brought the attention of the world to the revolution in North and East Syria. The YPJ is an all female force, established in 2013 as an autonomous organisation linked to the mixed-gender YPG People's Defence Units. And it's more than that.

The women's army doesn't even try to be like a traditional, men's, state army. Why would they want to?

Ask any YPJ fighter and they'll tell you that they're acutely proud of the qualities traditionally dismissed as 'feminine' (and therefore weak) that they have honed to make them a force to be reckoned with: the meticulous, gentle delicacy needed as a sniper, the sensitivity to shoot just one precise bullet at a time from a heavy machine gun. The emotional awareness and embodied connection that keeps a commander in touch with every member of her team. The multi-level perception and plain gut intuition that can guide tactics and keep you safe. Bravery and strength that comes from a will to protect, defend; the courage not to commit violence but to stand your ground, to refuse to leave (by all accounts often until the men stay with you out of sheer embarrassment).

Any YPJ fighter you talk to is likely to be proud of a few other things as well. Maybe how well she can braid her comrades' hair. Maybe her spotless novelty cartoon character socks. Definitely her home, and her people.

Fighters in the YPJ are deeply rooted in their identity, history, and land. Not because they don't see themselves and their struggle as international (and plenty of international volunteers, Anna among them, have arrived and found a place for their own home and history in the ranks). It's because the most important thing about the YPJ is not what they're against, but what they're fighting *for*. They *mean it when they say "If we had all the power in the world, we would not attack anyone. But if all the world attacks us, we will defend ourselves."*

Without self defence, nothing can survive. Roses and gorse have their thorns. A hedgehog its spines, a deer its speed. The YPJ are a part of the self defence of the Rojava revolution. But what sensationalist Western news reports often fail to cover is that the women of the YPJ, these often young and always impressive, beautiful, strong women, have to be understood as part of a political and cultural ecosystem, one that needs every part to survive, defend itself, and thrive. This ecosystem includes YPJ fighters; old women on their porches making jam; all the civil and political organisers; the educators; the artists; the diplomats; the story tellers; the journalists; the mothers; young girls claiming their right to their language, bodies, and learning; the mediators, all these thousands of women have organised themselves into the vanguard — the peşengtî — of the revolution.

Since the setting up of the PKK in the 70s, the Kurdistan Freedom Movement was always questioning what had up until then been considered a-political: women's position in society, the family, personal relationships. Women such as Sakine Cansiz worked from the beginning to put 'women's issues' front and centre. As Abdullah Öcalan continued to develop the ideology of the PKK, he was watching the struggle and resistance of women around him closely, discussing with his female comrades and supporting them however he could. He saw connections with the lives of the women from his village. He looked at the Soviet Union's attempts at socialism in the 20th century and felt that there must be some reason they were falling back into violence and authoritarian state mentality- could it be that they weren't willing to centre the struggle against patriarchy?

The movement started to take a long hard look at things like family structures, men and women's relationships, marriage, and other things that were often just taken for granted as natural. Just like feminist movements across the world, the Kurdistan Women's Movement also decided they were far from natural. In fact, they were a frontline of struggle. If they didn't fight on that frontline, their other efforts might be wasted. On the other hand, if they could change women's situation, they'd be making a truly deep, fundamental change. "We saw women as the most oppressed," one friend explained to us in a seminar on the women's movement. "By colonialism, capitalism and the state, just like men, but then even again within their own homes and families. If you empower the weakest element, you can flip the whole system on its head. That's a huge part of why we focus on that."

In Kurdish, the word for '*woman*' shares a common root with the word '*life*'. The movement is determined to rediscover this connection. They've made a commitment to show that a struggle for and by women is a struggle for life, and society.

In the mid 90s, the women's army and women's party were founded as part of the PKK, but independent and autonomously organised. This gave the women in the party unprecedented strength to fight for equality. To fight, they had to know who they were. This was the first step to self defence, to a strong base. They were fighting for the right to live in line with their values. It turned out the only way to do that was to transform the whole world.

Because Abdullah Öcalan crystallised these experiences into a written manifesto, they've spread across the whole of Kurdistan and beyond. It is the same ideology that is the basis of the revolution in North and East Syria. In short, it says that women's freedom is essential for society's freedom. Patriarchy is the root of oppression. Not only because it came along first, but because patriarchy kills empathy and connection. Patriarchy allows relationships between people to be based on exploitation or violence, making the horrors of capitalism and the state possible. It says that only a world in which patriarchy is defeated can be a truly democratic world. This is one of the reasons so many of us have flocked to North and East Syria. We too had been asking, '*Who are we?*' and '*How to live?*' Questions of identity, and of making the right choice, had driven my life for years.

I got a lesson in who I was years ago when Anna, Natalia and people in our community suggested we have meetings without the men. I didn't see the point beforehand. Then I saw how different we all were when we were in that space, including me. It was a small step but it's exactly the kind of small step the Kurdistan Women's Movement had started by taking.

Many men in the Kurdistan Freedom Movement were happy to declare themselves socialists in search of freedom but not actually change the way they related to their female comrades. "You were a lover, a sister or a mother, they couldn't see beyond that.", a Kurdish comrade shared with me. When internationalists hear this story, many of us might wish it wasn't so familiar. Twenty years later and halfway across the world, the friendship group Natalia, Anna and I were part of were trying to find words for very similar problems. Where did our personal relationships fall back along typical lines of who did the work and care, who took the blame, who had a voice and who didn't? Why did our so-called comrades treat us differently? Why did we, as women, struggle to trust and support each other?

This last one was bigger than I wanted to admit. The truth was that I hadn't always seen the need for women's or feminist organising to happen separately. I might have said that was partly because I was questioning of the whole social construction of gender, or womanhood, and my place in it. I think those conversations have a lot to give us and are important. For some people, they're part of a path to becoming more themselves, whatever that means for them. It's important to have space to question our gender and identities, for a lot of reasons. But for me personally, if I'm honest, it wasn't the whole story.

Since I was a kid, I wanted to be independently strong and tough, rejecting whatever I felt was an attempt to label me as weak. I wanted to be in 'the Boys' Club', and I censored myself to get there. I was dismissive of anyone less willing to play the game.

Years later, after starting to question these attitudes in myself, I looked at the women organisers around me in Kurdistan, feeling deeply humble. They were rebels against any oppressive gender stereotype, but always focussed on each other first and foremost. I was surprised when I heard one of them tell almost the same story as me. 'I didn't really like women," she said. 'I found it easier to get on with men. I had internalised a lot of bad things about women, and about myself. If you don't like yourself, how can you defend yourself?"

For her, it was her time with her comrades when they were all imprisoned that changed things. Locked away with other women organisers, she faced herself. Despite the best efforts of the Turkish state, the Kurdistan Freedom Movement had by that time managed to organise within prisons, turning them into what they commonly call their 'university' for revolutionaries. This huge effort of collective organising stood its ground in front of the relentless assaults of the prison system, and kept hundreds of comrades from falling apart and being broken. The movement organising structures in the prison were no different to the ones outside, and there was an insistence that comrades were always working on themselves, developing, and facing hard truths. In her case, what she had to realise about herself was harder, she said, than anything the prison did to them. Locked away with only her women comrades, she realised she didn't want her comrades' care because it made her feel weak. She didn't trust them fully. She didn't value their respect as much as that of men. But she also realised she could change all of this.

Things had changed for me as well. I was lucky enough to meet the right people. My friends who were fighting the immigration system. Women who didn't have the luxury of capitalising on privileges other than gender the way I did. People clawing their way out of abusive relationships. My stubborn, gentle comrades who pointed out to me the ways we were all treated by the men who supposedly saw us all as equal. Plenty of comrades could see more clearly than me the need for all of us who were dealt a rough hand by patriarchy to stick together against it. I started to let myself think and feel things that I had pushed away before. I was beginning to feel like we were under attack as well.

We couldn't always connect our own lives to the big picture, to the structure. But we'd all been hurt, ripped off and exploited. I started to see that the small was the big. The anxieties and fear I had around men were not my fault, or just my problem. The family planning centre that helped me when I was a teenager was closed now, along with dozens of other services. I couldn't safely hold hands with another woman in the street. And there was a deeper grief, for something lost or never had in our lifetimes, that we didn't yet have words for. Some way that meaning and love had been stripped out of life.

What was our self defence? It could be the hot food and shared head scratching over jobcentre forms at the women's group in the tower blocks down the road from where I lived. It could be the feminist sports team I played on for years, that taught me how to massage out those kinks, and how to feel strong and together. It could be scooping up friends more times than I'd like to remember from partners turned violent, controlling or unsafe, and friends who checked on me when it looked like I could be headed that way too. It could be wrangling with Home Office casework and red tape, til two in the morning if that's what it took. It could be repurposing that intimate and defining female habit of travelling in packs to the loo, to make sure our trans friends never had to go to the toilet alone in a club. It could be babysitting while someone raced off to work, make an application, or just get a chance for five minutes peace. It could be all the times someone got me home. It could just be taking the dance floor back.

I couldn't necessarily sum up what it was that brought all those things together, what they had in common. They were like different worlds in some ways. But something did, and in big and small ways, from demos to kitchens to the computer, we'd been organising too. So when images of YPJ fighters, Kurdish mothers in colourful scarves, councils hundreds of women strong started filling our screens, it lit something up in us. A women's revolution, a movement actually in control of a territory, that was putting the fight against patriarchy front and centre. Was it too good to be true?

Any extended stay in North and East Syria leaves you in no doubt that people are absolutely sincere and passionate about women's freedom being key. It's no cynical branding ploy (and if it was, they could have thought up something better to get global sympathy than proposing we overthrow patriarchy, which is still not that popular an idea). But that doesn't mean the work is done. Patriarchy is alive and kicking in North and East Syria. This includes inside the minds and hearts of those fighting hardest against it. As everyone struggling against patriarchy across the world knows, we haven't picked an easy fight.

Back in that same little village, the women's movement is working in a dozen different ways, and all on the different fronts that even one small town holds. The local council is run by the 'co-chair' system, meaning there has to be both a man and a woman in any decision making role. Not long after this was brought in across the budding democratic institutions of North and East Syria, in reality a lot of men were bypassing or tokenizing their female co-chairs. So then a rule was also brought in that documents needed to be stamped or signed by both chairs. If the woman in the role hasn't agreed, it doesn't go ahead: from making sure everyone has fuel and bread, to maintaining the roads and communal spaces, and decisions on education, resources, arts and culture. These decisions affect economic issues, diversity, security, the present and the future.

I got to know the woman co-chair of the village. She always managed to be everywhere at once, present for everyone, and at the end of the day when her male counterpart went back to find his dinner waiting for him, she was cooking for her family. Another woman from the village was almost as busy in grass-roots organising whilst also taking care of her severely disabled son. She was fighting for recognition and support, material and emotional, and struggling against stigma even while organising local women, for example in the *Mala Jin*, the Women's Houses.

The Mala Jin in this region (and across North and East Syria) show more than anything both how many problems there still are, and also just how much beautiful work is being done and what huge steps have been taken. The Mala Jin are community conflict resolution and justice centres that focus especially on domestic violence, abuse, and problems in the home. They are run by experienced women from within the local communities. No one knows better how to deal with their problems than those who have lived it themselves, who have spent their lives struggling against this alone and now have the chance to struggle together.

While women from the village have an independent say in the general mixed-gender council, they also have their own separate associations. Across North and East Syria, *Kongra Star* is the umbrella organisation for women's civil organising. It's made up entirely of volunteers who empower and organise women in their own communities, and build up a network. Kongra Star organisers were working for years before the revolution gave them status and made their work visible and safe. They risked imprisonment, torture and death for it. Still, there was no replacement for bringing the women of their communities together to talk and organise, and they pushed on against all odds. I once translated for an interview with the Kongra Star chairwoman for all of North and East Syria and when the interviewer asked 'How do you communicate with the public?" she genuinely didn't understand the question. Who is 'the public' here, if not normal women in their homes? So there isn't really a question about how to communicate with them – we *are* them.

In every town and village you'll also see the neighbourhood defence forces. They're men and women who volunteer to keep their community safe. The women, of course, are autonomously structured. The *HPC-Jin* (Women's Division of the Society Defence Forces) are part conflict resolution, part community mediator, part everyone's agony aunt, part traffic warden, part firefighter. They're all mums and grannies, brown tabards over their colourful dresses, AK-47s slung across their backs and faces wreathed in smiles, (when they're not firmly directing young men around with the kind of authority only weathered mothers can wield). In the war, these were the women who cooked for the fighters on the frontline. But while making dinner, they also kept their guns with them — just in case.

It's complicated and messy, but all these efforts are not just for show. They're to meaningfully and concretely transfer power and resources to women on a practical level, whilst simultaneously educating and organising them. This is to redress thousands of years of oppression, and to pull society out of the mess we're in. It's not just about placing individual women in positions of power. It's about the very core of self defence: our collective organised force.

Identity is deeply important in the Kurdistan Women's Movement, but it's always a collective one. I was pushed to look closely at my personal history, but always in a context. Without '*who are we?*' there can be no '*who am I?*'

It's not that everyone is the same. The questions I had around, '*what even is a woman anyway?*' didn't get any neat or simple answers in Kurdistan. There's worlds of difference. Even within Rojava, for now, some women are university educated and others can't read or write. Some have ten kids, some none, some work the fields all day, others grew up in the city. There's different ethnicities, religions, languages, ages. Everything you can think of. Start thinking about that on an international scale and it boggles my mind. There's enough different women, people the world thinks are women, and women fighting to be recognised as women, in just my home town. To try and flatten those differences, just make sweeping statements that 'womanhood' is this category that makes millions of us the same, and that we experience the same, is dangerous territory. It can ignore class, white supremacy, colonialism... things we ignore at our peril if we want to connect our movements.

The Kurdistan Women's movement has been an anti-colonial one from the start. Out of both principle and necessity. It can't be lifted out of that context and softened. It should challenge us all to think about how we can be part of anti-colonial struggle. It challenges us all to ask if our movements, our feminism, our perspectives, are also anti-capitalist and militant. If not, can they really be a basis for global solidarity between women, between anyone? Is any women's movement that doesn't focus on material conditions, class, race and resources, fit for purpose?

The Kurdistan Women's Movement, like the movement as a whole, focuses a lot on education. One question asked over and over again is, *what is a free woman?* Yes, we found some answers. But never just one. I started to think the process of asking was more the point. Where you start to walk when you ask that, and who you walk with. For me the question of women's struggle is the same. I'm not going to pretend I understand the experiences of a mother of ten from a village in Kurdistan, any more than I do those of even half the women from my country. The things that oppress us wear different masks in different times and places. So our struggles have been different.

So, I make an active choice to find what common ground we do have, to always listen, and to fight for and with each other. Difference is strength. It's a huge thing to try and connect when we are so diverse – and it's a huge thing we are trying to achieve. If we can manage it, we will flip the system. What the Kurdistan Women's Movement has already achieved is amazing, and its ambition is still nothing less than the same for everyone in the world.

Sometimes I found what at first glance looked most different the most in common. I'd spent years as a queer feminist questioning the relationship of heteronormativity, capitalism and the state. I was critical of those power structures, but I was also in love with the possibilities of queer life and freedom, convinced they were about so much more than just who I was intimate with (though of course that mattered). I arrived in Kurdistan expecting that part of me to be shut away, braced to have to go along with gender politics that in some ways grated on me. I was willing to, because I felt it was worth it, but I felt it would be a trade off, a compromise.

At first, and at a superficial glance, that's exactly what happened. At times, I and other queer internationalists often found ourselves struggling, feeling a push back of a different kind to what we did at home. After one evening where I was quizzed by some rather stern mothers, starting with what gender I was and moving swiftly onto to whether I was married, or had been behaving ways I shouldn't if I wasn't married, I came back to our academy angry and miserable. 'It's just so hard to be queer here," I complained to the other internationalist comrades I lived with. I was expecting sympathy from one friend who came from a background of lesbian feminism herself but had been with the Kurdish movement many years. She wasn't unkind, but she gently redirected my point. "Yes," she said, 'but not really as much for *us*. And maybe in ways we can't even understand."

It took me some time to understand what she was getting it. It meant once again starting to see things a whole different way, realise that just because struggle doesn't come in the forms I'm used to doesn't mean it isn't there. I was used to sexuality as a headline theme of liberation, or a battleground in itself. Here, that energy was channelled into a wider struggle for women's liberation: for a revolutionary rewriting of gender roles and a shaking up of traditional models of family and romantic love. Discussions on the nature of gender, though widespread, came in a really different form to what I was used to. But they were still centrally important. I began to feel that when you dug deep, we were actually talking about a lot of the same things. Even more than that, I realised that when I was around organisers of the movement, I was living among people who had built a life outside of the nuclear family in order to fight capitalism, the state and patriarchy. They'd given their lives, and sometimes their deaths for it. If I couldn't find myself here, what did these politics of mine even mean?

Returning home, I came back to the feminist circles I'd been a part of before. Just right when I got back, a right-wing populist party in Scotland had become the latest of conservative forces to jump on the transphobic bandwagon and try and weaponise the language of women's safety to spread hate and fear. Much more heartbreakingly, the feminist movement I grew up in has over the last few years turned on itself, splitting bitterly along several lines, one of the most highly charged being trans inclusivity. People who should be struggling together against patriarchy and towards revolution are taking reactionary, defensive positions and allowing that hate and fear to turn us against each other. A lot of the conflict stems from wanting to make sure that our political action is in line with our values: that the movements we build value each other's humanity and right to exist. So it's understandable that people care and are willing to draw lines in the sand. The Kurdistan Women's Movement in Europe has decided to work with women's organisations from many different sides of this division. Building towards a vision of a global movement of women's movements, they are always asking what it would take for different groups to work together. Because this is rarely done in our current political context, I find myself often pressed to pin down and explain the movement's stance on trans women and trans issues.

It's vital that we examine all of our political organising to see whether it moves us towards our values, or away from them. At the same time, I think that often these questions are more about our own struggles at home than anything else. It's here that we have got into this mess, and demanding that struggles from a completely different context agree to draw the same lines as us and weigh fully into our debates is not going to get us out of it. I also hear hints of prejudice and orientalism – the assumption that the Middle East is a more backward place than we are. It's the same perspective I carried when I arrived in Rojava, thinking that because I am a queer woman I was some kind of front line of queer liberation. I also come from a totally different context, from a region that has built empire and wealth by tearing resources from land and communities around the world – including the Middle East. So really, I'm not the frontline. Queer and trans folk from the Middle East are defining their own terms, struggles, priorities and perspectives. Many of their organisations work with the Kurdistan Freedom Movement, and many individuals who are part of the movement also have what I would call queerness in their identity, though they might well have completely different words for and understandings of it than I do.

Meanwhile, women's and anti-patriarchal struggles are divided across many different lines, all of which are important conversations. The beauty and power of the Kurdish Women's Movement's example is that we're always pushed to build something bigger and better beyond all of that – instead of excluding people now, we bring each other in to fight for the world we believe we can get to if we can unite against patriarchy.

I have known queer and trans internationalists to have bad experiences in Kurdistan and in the movement. Just like I've known us to have bad experiences at home. I also know many queer and trans internationalists who have found freedom and power in the anti patriarchal struggle of the movement and been welcomed by it with open arms. Just like we also find joy and power in our struggles at home. I know people from Kurdistan and other parts of the Middle East who are in the struggle in all the different identities they hold, whatever we call them, in the good times and the bad. That so many of them have been able to join in asking "what is a free woman?" is made all the more powerful by the fact there is no one simple answer.

The movement is also always asking, *"what is a free man?"* Yes, women's freedom is essential if people in general are going to be free. That's the way things are at the moment. But men are just as trapped by patriarchy, perhaps even more so. The 'Boys' Club' I'd envied so much when I was young isn't given by nature, and it's often not even a nice place to be.

Despite a fierce insistence on autonomous organising and an uncompromising critique of patriarchal behaviour, the Kurdistan Women's Movement doesn't take an antagonistic position to their male comrades or to men in general. The idea is to collectively be so independent and so strong that we are able to work with men politically, as comrades, because the lines of accountability and standards of behaviour are in place and we know what we're doing. We're better able to love across gender if we can do so as comrades.

Interestingly for me, I found that there the line was that we absolutely *must* engage in the education of men. To 'kill and transform the dominant male' is a whole theme of education and discussion. Despite the widespread presence of guns, no, it's not literal. It's about reflecting on patriarchal relationships and patterns that we've internalised and unlearning them. It's the responsibility of the women's movement (collectively, not individually) to guide men in that process. It's the responsibility of men to do the individual and collective work it takes to follow that guidance.

Back home, I'd often got sucked into friendships with my male comrades where I was supporting them, or helping them learn and move through things. It takes a lot of energy when it's one person and not a collective force, and it's possible to get into unhealthy dynamics. The alternative seemed to be to give up on them completely, which I went through phases of doing but also somehow always felt unsatisfying. Becoming part of a collective force that could support us *all* to break away from patriarchy, whilst also keeping us strong and not letting men lean on individual women, was a revelation.

More than that, 'killing the dominant male' is for everyone: women, men, all genders. Long term, experienced women's organisers would be the first to say they have not yet finished that work themselves. I saw the ugly reality of it in people I respected In Kurdistan just like at home. I was let down by women who should have been an example, behaving as dominantly and patriarchally as any man. I see it in myself. Learning not to always want to be in that 'Boys' Club' was only the beginning. The movement knows patriarchal masculinity and femininity are not neatly separated by sex or gender, and the fight starts within ourselves.

Collective strength takes work. You might always have twice as much work as the men. When you're with the movement, you always organise autonomously as women. There only has to be two of you in a space (though ideally there will always be more!) for you to take collective decisions, answer to each other first and foremost, and show a united front to the men. You don't show them any division that they could exploit to divide you, intentionally or not. You critique each other in private but not in front of them.

I got a short sharp lesson in how deeply this runs one day when the women I worked with were furious with me. And rightly so. I'd gone off by myself, a stupid thing to do in the first place, and then managed to get lost, take hours to get home, and have half a village out looking for me. My friend's face was full of that particular rage that only comes right after you've stopped panicking that someone was dead, her jaw clenched tight to restrain her emotions. I was tearful, exhausted and desperate to explain and excuse myself. I turned to her and started to speak but she just raised a hand and said quietly "not in front of the men." Right. We'll talk later. Even in a moment when she probably really wanted to speak her mind, she shelved it because it wasn't appropriate. However much I'd screwed up, our organising was bigger than both of our feelings.

We need autonomous spaces to organise against patriarchy in whatever we do. Yes, we are all different, but we need to make space to learn about each other, understand each other to build the bigger picture and be able to support each other. We need that space, to strengthen ourselves. But there's a reason why we're doing it. It's not to attack anyone else, it's to emerge strong enough to, as the friend put it, 'flip the whole system on its head". To make a better world for everyone.

'Who are we?' 'How should we live?'

The answers to those questions are bottomless — we could spend lifetimes answering them. I certainly wasn't going to get anywhere that evening we spent with the sisters on their porch. There were tea glasses to wash up, there were shoulders to rub. But I keep those questions with me.

We realise soon enough that we can't answer these questions if we can't defend ourselves. We can't answer if we're turned against each other. But if we really take the questions seriously, we're going to change everything. And they aren't just for the women's movement. As we would find out in Rojava, a revolution has to question everything. There was still so much to learn.

SEASONS

Natalia, Autumn 2019

As the year turns, each month is marked by an influx of creatures, descending onto the land like Old Testament plagues. A wet spring means we watch our step when we go outside to avoid trampling the frogs emerging from under leaves and stones and furniture, filling the night with a deafening chorus of croaks. Gently warming breezes carry thousands of yellow butterflies through the air, and hundreds of swifts criss-cross the dusk-glow sky.

The weather turns dry, and each morning we check our shoes for scorpions and tread softly as we listen for the slither of snakes through the grasses. The sound of midsummer is the smack of giant crickets crashing into the windows and doors of our buildings, their DNA code still programmed to the wide open Middle Eastern flatlands before the arrival of concrete walls. Camel spiders skitter across rooms in search of shadow, and giant wasp-like insects try to build nests in the exposed light sockets dangling from the ceiling. As the heat grows unbearable, giant black flies buzz heavily indoors and out, landing on eyes and mouths and food, swapping places with a plague of mosquitoes and sand flies as the sun goes down.

Finally, as the summer wanes, mantises creep into our rooms, perching motionless on furniture, quizzical and menacing, until they lash out lighting-fast to snatch at passing insects. The waves of creatures descending on the land feel biblical — like I've been transported to a time when this land between two rivers cradled early human civilisation, when people lived on more equal footing with the beasts we share this earth with.

We look back at that era in political education sessions, learning that it was here, in Mesopotamia, where humans first learned to dominate nature rather than living as part of it. With that exchange of stewardship for extraction, men also began to dominate women, signalling a shift from the matrilineal society that had existed up through Neolithic times. Since then, we've lived in the patriarchal system that drives extractive capitalism. We trace the exploitation of natural resources to the exploitation of women, and learn that to look for the answer to one is to find the solution for the other. It is here, in the lands where the Islamic State caliphate unleashed a terrible brutality against women, that the oil wells flow like arteries from the earth, unable to quench the thirst of Western states for more. The links between environmental and misogynistic violence run deep throughout our history. In Europe, women were burned at the stake as witches as our land was torn from community ownership and into the private property of the privileged few.

The revolutionaries we meet in Kurdistan often tell us, "you look for something in the place where you lost it". So it's here, between the Tigris and the Euphrates rivers, that we look for the seeds that were scattered by our foremothers as they waged the resistance of survival. These seeds connect us to a time before, whispering of a moment where legacy meets possibility.

Members of a village commune meet as part of the democratic confederalist system of Rojava

7. TRUSTING

The state within us
Natalia

As the brutal Syrian summer gentled into autumn, the invasion we were all bracing for arrived. The Turkish army and its mercenaries gathered at the border while airstrikes and artillery pounded the neighbourhoods and villages of Rojava, and we were all called to our work to defend against the attacks. Jenni was pulled out of the village, away from elderly friends and fig jam and back to snapping photos for twitter and badgering campaign NGOs. I sat in a draughty flat above a car dealership in the city of Qamişlo, writing press summaries and articles for one of the many media centres that had sprung up to meet the increased demand for information about the invasion. The withdrawal of American troops from the border had opened the door for the launch of attacks by the Turkish army and Turkish backed mercenaries all along the border. The crash of artillery shells ripping into buildings across the city would jerk my attention away from my screen for a moment — *'Where did it hit? Is someone going out with the camera?'* — before getting pulled back into the rapid-fire typing that was our role in defending the revolution that we had become part of. I knew that by staying where I was I was taking risks, and there were times that I felt scared. I also knew that I was playing out the worst nightmares of friends and family back home — war had broken out and I had put my chips down on resistance, knowing that this made survival a riskier gamble. But although I felt fear, and guilt at hurting those I cared about, I felt like I was exactly where I needed to be.

This wasn't the first time I felt this way. Eight years earlier – almost to the day – I sat in a car with a computer on my lap, extension cable hooked up to a trailer parked up in the largest Traveller site in Europe. Earlier that year, a group of us had arrived at the Dale Farm Irish Traveller site in Essex and set up a protest camp. Unlike some of the county's residents, we weren't protesting the existence of the site and calling for an eviction based on violation of planning regulations: a very British form of ethnic cleansing. Instead, we were there on the invitation of the Traveller community who lived in the trailers and chalets on the site, supporting the community's intention to resist the eviction that the local council was threatening. The planned eviction would force 100 families from the land that they had bought years ago, making them homeless and leaving them with nowhere but the roadside to park up on. Over the course of many months, activists joined forces with the Dale Farm Irish Traveller community, building up trust, a high profile solidarity campaign, friendships, and lots of barricades.

While holding down a part time job at a community garden and settling into a new home in London, most of my extra time and head-space was sucked up by the Save Dale Farm campaign. Some nights I slept at the site, then cycled to the station as the sun rose to jump onto an early morning train from Essex and into London to arrive in time for work. As the eviction date approached, my job, an increasingly rocky relationship and a good night's sleep all fell further down my list of priorities. Despite the tireless work of countless members of the community and a committed crew of solidarity activists, the date of the eviction was set.

The night before the Dale Farm eviction, I still couldn't quite believe that it would go ahead. The courts had stalled the eviction process before, and on some level I trusted that it would happen again. On a logical level I knew that it was unlikely, but in some corner of my brain I still thought that governments were bound by the same moral instincts as we were. I spent the night sleeping in the back seat of the car which would serve as the media team office for the day. I woke up before dawn, cold and stiff, and waited to see what the day would bring.

Instead of a last minute reprieve from the courts, the eviction began before the sun had a chance to take the edge off a bitterly cold October night. The dawn brought rows of black clad riot police to the gates of the Dale Farm community. They carried shields and batons and tasers, and ripped open the brick wall around the site with sledgehammers so they could swarm past caravans and chalets as whole families looked on in horror.

In the following hours I sent out press releases and gave interviews while watching riot police terrorise families, assault and arrest my friends (both Travellers and non-Travellers), and destroy a community. The news kept trickling in to where I sat with my computer: one of the mums on site was injured and had to be rushed to hospital, friends were arrested, someone was tasered. A column of smoke rose into the air as a caravan caught fire in the chaos.

I kept on writing press releases and ringing news desks. We turned down a slot on Newsnight: the formidable trio of sisters who were the spokespeople for the community needed to re-gather and be with loved ones. It was too much to ask for them to broadcast the story of their loss to millions of voyeuristic viewers. As I watched the bailiffs tear down the homes that the state had deemed illegal, destroy the community it had declared an eyesore, I promised myself that I would never allow the state an ounce of trust, that with the passing of years I wouldn't forget that the state is an instrument of violence.

When the Turkish army invaded Rojava eight years later I once again witnessed the violence of the state against communities – this time the columns of smoke I could see from the window came from bombed neighbourhoods and not a burning caravan, and we were bracing for the advance of Turkish-backed mercenaries rather than riot police. I was still doing media work, still fighting the battle of information from behind a computer screen. Still gritting my teeth as I distilled the lives of people I care about into facts and sound-bites that the media could absorb.

I couldn't help but feel that history was repeating itself in more than one way. Not just that at political crunch points I always end up in front of a computer, proofreading and uploading, but that the whole world was watching while a fascist leader commits ethnic cleansing and a land grab. The world watches, does nothing, and says 'maybe after this he will stop." It wasn't the first time since arriving in Rojava that I traced a line into my past, from the war-torn Poland of my family's history, to the wreckage of the Dale Farm community, to the war-battered buildings of Syrian neighbourhoods. In different decades, and different countries, those with power sit around a table in their suits, sip their glasses of mineral water and betray humanity.

I realised that, on some level, I was still waiting for a government body of some kind to step in and make it stop. Whether it would be the UN or NATO or the Arab League, the Americans or the Russians, in the back of my head I was still trusting that someone with the 'real' power would put a stop to this.

They didn't and they won't.

As bombs rained down on North and East Syria, America issued a statement that amounted to: 'well, the Turkish army is here now, so they might as well stay'. Families who had fed me and given me a place to sleep were driven out of their homes by the Turkish-armed militias that streamed across the border. For days, the roads were packed with people seeking refuge, carrying food, children and a few possessions on their backs or squeezed into cars. And then the cities and towns fell eerily quiet as those who remained stayed indoors and waited to see what would come.

The United Nations Security Council met twice to talk about the situation, but did nothing except 'express concern". In Serekaniye, where the mercenaries had crossed the border from Turkey to surround the city, my friends and comrades were shot at, bombed and burned. The overseas NGOs left, evacuating their international staff and leaving behind empty offices and local employees. And on top of all that, four months later the UN closed the only crossing where humanitarian aid had been getting into the region.

Britain said 'we won't give Turkey new weapons contracts, but they can keep the ones they have'. One year later they signed a new free trade deal with Turkey and continued to export military equipment.

Today, the occupation of Serekaniye and Tel Abyad continues, and the families driven out of their homes hunker down for another cold winter in refugee camps.

Even more surprising than the failure of state powers to intervene on behalf of people was the small part of my brain that was trusting them to do the right thing. I was unsettled to find that there was still part of me that gave the state a moral credibility that it simply doesn't deserve, and I had to ask myself, 'who do I put my trust in, and why?". Perhaps this lingering trust in the state is not so surprising after all — I grew up white and middle class in America, a society where the violence of the state is mostly aimed at people of colour and the poor and working classes. Although I had come face to face with police brutality at protests and developed anti-state politics from years within the direct action climate movement, I still held the ability to opt out of resistance — and the resulting state violence — more often than not.

Of course it's in the interests of the state for me to believe that the state is on my side. And to an extent, it will be, in its divide and conquer strategies to secure my compliance at the expense of others. By offering some people legitimate forms of 'resistance' within capitalism, while criminalising the existence of those who don't fit within certain parameters, the state invites us to throw other struggles under the bus.

But a freedom that is based on the oppression of others isn't truly freedom. This is why countless revolutionaries, from the Zapatistas to Audre Lorde, have argued that a crucial step towards collective liberation is recognising that our struggles are linked. The challenge we face is to find ways to wage resistance – both in acts of collective self defence, and inside our own heads. If we don't get rid of the state inside our heads, we'll lose sight of how interconnected our fights are, and we'll sell each other out.

***

In many ways the Dale Farm eviction resistance was the third and final blow of a series of failures in political organising that I experienced in quick succession over the year leading up to it. First was the implosion of Climate Camp — a powerful network of anti-capitalist groups that mobilised against climate change using militant, direct action tactics — due to a crisis of vision and internal conflicts. Arguably, the beginning of the end was the failure of the 2009 COP15 UN climate talks to produce a meaningful global climate agreement. Despite its proclaimed lack of trust in state-solutions to climate change, Climate Camp participated in a massive mobilisation that geared itself towards intervening in national and international decision making processes. Although the outcome of the COP15 talks affirmed our low expectations, it seemed like a lot of us just lost steam in the face of the feeble agreements produced by the summit. When we give everything that we've got and those in power still fail us, what's left to do?

After the 2009 COP15 summit, the Climate Camp network staggered and lost momentum, and was eventually ripped apart by conflict and exhaustion.

The second movement collapse that had a big impact on me was the militant anti-fees students' movement of 2010. Protests, walk outs, occupations and direct action spread like wildfire across universities, colleges, secondary and even primary schools as tens of thousands of students expressed their outrage at the proposed tripling of University fees. After months of student revolts, the Liberal Democrats (widely backed by students due to their election pledge to oppose an increase in fees) buckled and Parliament voted in the fees increase. A few half-hearted demonstrations in early 2011 petered out as students turned back to their studies to claw back hours of work lost to political meetings and occupations. What would it have looked like if we had refused to back down? Did we stop fighting because despite our moral outrage, government decisions had too much legitimacy for us to reject them?

After the losses of Climate Camp, the student movement and the Dale Farm eviction, I stumbled along, keeping a toe dipped into the world of radical politics, but never so deep that I couldn't pull it out. I found a sense of purpose and community in growing vegetables and joining a sports team. I drifted away from Traveller solidarity organising after a year. I started to limit my political involvement to delivering trainings on media work and facilitation, and showing up to the odd demo or participating in one-off projects and events.

Looking back on the years where I held my relationship with political organising tentatively, I can see all the different ways in which I was trying to avoid caring about something too much and then getting hurt. I increasingly wore my political beliefs as an identity rather than something that was expressed through action. At the time, the only way I could express my sense of fragility and fear was through the language of boundaries and self care, which worked as a form of individual self protection even if it didn't challenge the root causes of my fear and fragility. I learned to laugh at the starry eyed idealism of my youth, because it was easier to imagine myself naive than to face the question of what it would take to try again. I didn't realise it at the time, but the state had successfully defined the parameters of what I thought was possible, of what I could bear to imagine. Without realising it, I learned to enforce the mentality of 'there is no alternative' onto myself and others. I didn't learn to balance the patience of long term struggle with the insistence, the militance, of 'this isn't good enough'.

I know I'm not the only one to have entered a social movement full of love and idealism, and withdraw in pain and cynicism. I would see old comrades on the street sometimes at big mobilisations, moments where we would heave ourselves out of our lethargy, let ourselves experience a glimmer of hope, a reminder of what we can accomplish when we work together. But mostly, having failed too many times before, we couldn't even imagine what victory would look like.

In those years, I missed being totally absorbed in something, and I ached for the unwavering faith that I was doing something that was right, that my life followed the line of my beliefs. But I was also so scared of feeling the crushing despair and loss of hope that followed the collapse of Climate Camp, the failure of the anti-fees student movement, and the eviction of Dale Farm.

All of these events produced a huge number of people committed to a cause and convinced of the corruption of the system. We shared a perspective on what was wrong and we'd started to build networks of trust and action. But it seems to me that those of us who were immersed in the radical political movements of the 2000s and 2010s weren't quite able to take the next steps and build a movement that could withstand the loss of individual battles and continue fighting the war. Yet so many of us were and are ready to do so – we just hadn't quite found the way.

While many of us continued to seek ways of changing the world, many of us also lost some of the boldness and ambition with which we used to throw ourselves into political organising. Having experienced the deception of infiltration by undercover police officers or the crushing betrayal of harmful behaviour from comrades, we found it hard to keep on trusting each other. Most of us had been hurt in one way or another by our political organising – whether by the state or by our comrades — and we turned to spaces outside of our movements to heal and soothe us. Some of us had families, and found that many of our social movements are geared towards those without children. Others built walls of cynicism around ourselves as protection from hurt and heartbreak, or approached political organising with the desperation of addiction, self destructive and isolated. Some of us grappled with mental health crises, homelessness, substance abuse and criminalisation, and turned to survival. Others found ways to make the struggle less hard, confining it into smaller and smaller parts of our lives and keeping it at arm's length from our hearts. Or we let ourselves be absorbed by the system – or built systems out of movements to access security and stability, a pay cheque and a sense of progress. Although our coping mechanisms and levels of involvement in political organising varied, it felt like we were all doing our best not to get hurt, finding individual ways to protect ourselves rather than building forms of collective self defence.

The way the state pressures us to scale back our resistance is shaped by our position in relation to the state. It was easier for me to pick and choose how to engage with activism because the security afforded me by my middle class background, university degree and white privilege. At the same time, as an immigrant certain kinds of direct action carried more of a legal risk for me with the threat of deportation. But at the end of the day, I could always fall back on an NGO job — embellishing my CV with my activist exploits — and be seen as the edgy political friend who attends protests on weekends and wins debates at house parties. Or I could launch myself back into full-on political activism, aware that my experience of state oppression would be buffered by my social, financial and legal safety net. Neither of these options — which felt like the only two available to me — felt like they were building a social movement that was driven by those most impacted by the violence of the state and capitalism. A movement with a powerful and principled commitment to self defence, so that those at the sharp end of the state and capitalism don't risk the most through resisting.

During my time in Rojava, I was pushed by revolutionaries within the movement to ask myself lots of questions that I wasn't sure I knew — or wanted to know — the answers to. Deep down, do I believe that a state is an inevitability? Do I think that what I'm fighting for is possible? Has the idea of a state become so entrenched in my mind that however militant the tactics I use are, I am simply lobbying the state in more confrontational ways than a petition? If I truly believed that our communities and social movements, and not the state, are the key to radical social change, what political work would I be doing? If I really believed that we could win, how would I be living my life differently? Do I moderate my resistance to forms that still allow me to successfully navigate life under capitalism?

I don't think I'm the only one to have traded the ambitious dreaming of my youth for the slightly jaded and tired pragmatism of political maturity. But I'm intensely grateful that the folks I met in Rojava insisted that we don't confuse complexity and nuance with cynicism and resignation, that we don't use 'sustainability' as shorthand for selling out. I can't speak for everyone, but I know that my hope and trust in our social movements was ground down by what felt like our powerlessness compared to the state, and by our own failure to stand by each other in collective struggle. In Rojava I learned to link these two things together and open the door to rebuilding my sense of belief in radical social change.

In the Kurdistan Freedom Movement, the term 'state mentality' refers to how we internalise the state in our perspectives and behaviours. This includes both our acceptance of the state as an inevitability, but also how we replicate the power relations of the state in our relationships to others. Becoming aware of our tendency towards state mentality is an important step towards freeing our minds from the internalised state. A lot of anti-oppression movements focus on how we internalise white supremacy and patriarchy and unconsciously reproduce it through our actions and attitudes. In the same way, because the Kurdistan Freedom Movement sees the state as another relationship of domination, being able to challenge this mentality within ourselves is an important part of dismantling it on a systemic level. This is an important concept in the movement itself, not just for internationalists coming in. This means everyone in the movement is on some level still fighting the state within, fighting state-like thinking. It might take the rest of our lives, but the important thing is to keep working on it.

State mentality is how we reproduce systems of domination. It can show up as being a bit of a control freak, as trying to impose 'revolutionary values' from the top down rather than inviting and convincing people to adopt them. It can show up as assuming that people, especially people from groups the state has marginalised, can't be trusted. When we see these tendencies as an example of state mentality, we can analyse them politically and bring our personal change into conversation with system change. State mentality can show up in non-hierarchical groups as much as in top-down ones. If we see hierarchy only as a structure rather than a mentality we won't be able to challenge it. However it shows up, it creates distance between us and stops us from trusting each other. When we let go of personal control, we open the door to building collective power.

This isn't saying that dominant political institutions don't play an undeniable role in how political battles play out. They do, and any effective social change strategy will include intervening in and defending ourselves from these systems, or taking their resources back when the time is right. But anything states and state-based institutions give up will only be hard won by social movements around the world applying pressure. This will happen through boycott and blockade, building up alternatives and putting ourselves on the front lines. And what we win from the state can only ever be part of the battle. We also have to build a new world on our own terms.

The Rojava revolution shows us that if people are organised and determined, the only limits to what we can achieve are those that we place on ourselves. If we fundamentally believe – however deep down – in the ultimate power of the state, we will never overcome it. On the other hand, if we truly believe in the power of society, and strengthen that belief in others, we can build a new world.

***

In Rojava, I came head to head with my own state mentality from pretty much the moment I arrived. Just showing up to join the movement demanded that I handed over a level of control over my life that would have previously been unthinkable. With a scant few words of Kurdish and virtually no knowledge of social etiquette and expectations, upon arrival a fellow internationalist volunteer and I were handed off from pickup truck to pickup truck like a baton in a relay race with no information about what might happen next. We had to swap control and information for trust and adaptability, a theme that continued throughout my time in Rojava.

Back home, I had perfected my ability to plan. I was proud of it. Effective political action boiled down to planning: nailing down your theory of change, your action plan, your comms strategy. At first I mistook the chaos of everyday life in Rojava as bad organisation and bad planning. It didn't take too long for me to check myself and exercise a bit more humility. Obviously the movement in Rojava is capable of planning and executing immense organisational tasks with precision and punctuality — from front line military tactics to housing and feeding hundreds of thousands of people displaced by war.

The sometimes haphazard approach to making decisions and plans wasn't down to a lack of organisation, it was a manifestation of a different way of organising. One that centres human relationships and trust building over formal systems and policies. One that is organic and emergent — not trying to fit things into boxes and binaries, but seeing what grows out of the complex web of people, place and time. It was a way of organising that has stood the test of time and produced a huge social movement capable of adapting while staying true to its values. It was a way of organising that I found incredibly difficult, and regularly pushed me way out of my comfort zone.

Life in Rojava is full of all sorts of twists and turns, scattered with long periods of waiting for something to happen (sometimes I knew what I was waiting for, usually I didn't) and making plans that don't happen because something else happens instead. Being out of control became something I practised every day, and slowly it started to feel more comfortable. I came to recognise that often my desire for control (including feeling like I have control because I have access to information) comes from a sort of state mentality. But the opposite of that grasping for control is not powerlessness. It's trust. And trust makes you powerful.

The state teaches us that the unknown is scary, and so we control ourselves through limiting what we dream is possible. The state doesn't trust the people, and it cements its power by making sure that we don't trust each other. For revolution, we need trust. When we let go of state mentality, we swap having all the information for having shared values, we build trust rather than control. If we keep clutching at control, things will only be as big as we can hold in our hands. But by letting go the world around us opens up to its revolutionary potential, and becomes so much bigger than any one of us.

***

We made a lot of mistakes during and after the Dale Farm eviction resistance which have weighed heavily on me for years. But a lot of things still bring me hope when I think back on them. How a group of activists, including lots of youthfully militant anarchists, and a traditional Irish Traveller community learned to work together, live together, and love each other. How the impeccably dressed site residents, confused about why we were always so dirty and scruffy, would generously bring us clothes from the boot sales they would visit. This continued for weeks, with us awkwardly refusing the brightly coloured and glittery tops. After observing that most of us only wore black, the residents started bringing us rhinestone-studded black tops and sequin-adorned black hoodies, and from then on they became Dale Farm protest camp fashion, a fusion of two worlds. We learned that it was important to not just give solidarity, but to receive.

At Dale Farm, we wrangled with the tensions between a non-hierarchical and meeting-heavy style of activist organising and a community decision making process that was based on natural leadership and chats over tea in caravans. We learned to adapt, and that what felt right for us wasn't necessarily right for everyone. When we're open to learning different ways of seeing the world, we chip away at the state mentality we hold in ourselves. We begin to imagine new horizons and ways to get there that we weren't able to see before. We become more free.

We didn't manage to prevent the eviction of the Dale Farm Traveller site. Amongst its shortcomings and failures, and the pain and heartbreak it caused, the eviction resistance at Dale Farm had a beauty to it because it was a moment in which we chose to stand together. I learned a lot about the violence of the state from the Dale Farm eviction resistance. But more importantly, I learned how powerful people can be when they stand together. I learned about the strength of women, and that the deepest understandings of oppression come not from the people who study it, but those who live it. I learned these lessons again and again in Rojava, and in re-learning them I deepened my understanding of why the community at Dale Farm, and the resistance to the eviction, posed such a threat to the British state.

The night before the Dale Farm eviction, a few of the women from the community burst into the small chalet that had become our media centre, where the press team was furiously writing social media posts and last minute appeals to the public. They swaggered past our laptops in their stilettos, raucous and dressed to the nines as always, and insisted on distracting us with hysterical laughter and handstands. We couldn't stay serious in the face of their antics, and we laughed together while blog posts and press releases sat unfinished on our screens. From them we learned that sometimes the most important work is not part of the action plan, but it's strengthening human connections, and giving value to the friendships that we had built through living and struggling side by side.

Every system finds ways to maintain itself, but when we learn to recognise it we can fight it. They may build the cages that contain us, but way too often we throw away the keys ourselves. Still, life always finds a way – the vines clambering over fences, the seeds taking root in the unlikeliest of places, and the trees shattering concrete with unstoppable strength. Throughout history humans have turned towards freedom the way sunflowers turn towards the sun. The impulse for justice and solidarity, for humanity and beauty, runs strong in our veins, we just need to trust it.

HOLIDAYS

Jenni, December 2018

I've been in every single house in the two small villages near our old academy. For Eid, or Ezidi New Year, or half a dozen other holidays, we'd down tools, be that a spade or a laptop, dress nice, and head out door to door. At every house, we were pulled inside, to shake hands and kiss cheeks. Then it was sweet tea or eye watering coffee, and handfuls of sugary sweets. I'd always barely swallowed my hot drink and managed a greeting before it was up again and on to the next house. By the end of the day we were high as hell: on caffeine and sugar, but also the rush of being welcomed so easily into so many homes and spaces. So many smiles, no less genuine for coming out a hundred times that day for whoever comes to the door. No, we didn't exactly get to know anyone deeply in these moments but it's a way of staying connected, valuing ritual as a moment of touching-base. If you work within the movement – including internationalist volunteers — you go as the movement, not just as yourself. The movement holds these traditions just as dearly as society.

What was funny for me was that sitting there cross legged on the packed-earth floor of village homes, or on brightly coloured cushions at the top of the stairs in an apartment in the city, I remembered we actually have the exact same thing where I grew up. For those who don't know, it's traditional in Scotland to visit your neighbours on New Year's Day. It's called First Footing. You sit on a chair, not the floor, and you drink a dram of whiskey instead of a glass of tea, but that's just dressing. The principle is the same. I think about radical political movements spreading out on the first of January throughout homes and neighbourhoods in Scotland, acknowledging the tradition whilst showing ourselves present for society, ready to hear what's really going on with people, no matter who they are. I wonder what it will take to make this a reality. I know it or something like it is coming, and that many others are thinking along the same lines. The only question is, where do we start?

YPG and YPJ fighters dance in celebration in Kobane on its liberation

8. FINDING HOME

Loving where you come from
Natalia

If you can't give meaning to a grain of wheat then you can't give meaning
to a sheaf of wheat.
If you can't give meaning to a sheaf, then you can't give meaning to a field.
If you can't give meaning to a field you can't give meaning to your land.
And if you can't give meaning to your land, you can't defend it.

— Kurdistan Freedom Movement saying

In 2004, the George W Bush vs John Kerry presidential campaign raged as I was deciding my next steps after high school. I told myself – and anyone else who would listen – that if George W Bush got re-elected, I would leave the US. That kind of chat was pretty common in leftie circles: a collective eye roll about the stupidity of the American public, and idle browsing of Canadian immigration websites. My family came to America from Poland when I was young, and being a citizen of Poland made it easier for me to consider crossing back over the Atlantic to study. In November, as the election results rolled in, I found myself having to either follow through or eat my words. Bush rode a wave of patriotism — actually thinly veiled racism and imperialism — into a second term in the White House. As Bush celebrated his victory, conservatives in Ohio celebrated another success, having passed a law that banned gay marriage – or anything close to it – within the state. As a queer teenager who was out of the closet more from a sense of defiance than self-love, it was a mutual rejection – if Ohio hated me, then I hated Ohio and America and I needed to get out.

I had grown up in a Polish immigrant household, raised by a mother who was isolated, unhappy and unstable – and blamed it all on living in America. From an early age I was taught to scorn the country I lived in, and this easily slipped into a left-wing anti-Americanness as I became politicised. As a teenager, the nationalism and jingoism of American patriotism grated against my budding political sensibilities, and my response was total rejection. I was able to reel off a shopping list of American crimes at home and overseas (the Kent State Massacre of anti-war protestors by the National Guard, the backing of Pinochet's coup in Chile, COINTELPRO's decimation of American black liberation movements), but I struggled to find language to explain why stories of resistance and mass mobilisation (the Montgomery Bus Boycott, or the Stonewall uprising) would always bring me to tears. When I learned about these moments in history, I felt awe and pride, and somehow that I belonged to this part of American heritage in some vast, unnamable way. But it wasn't enough to keep me there – I sent off my applications and decided to go to university in England, even though I had never stepped foot on British soil in my life.

I don't know if it was by instinct or luck, but by coming to England to study I gave myself enough distance from a dysfunctional political system and my dysfunctional family that I could start to figure out not just what I was rejecting, but who I was. Years later while in Rojava I dug even deeper into that understanding of identity, trying to piece together lots of moments in my life which shaped who I was and where I belonged. Kurdish revolutionaries focus as much on huge sweeping social transformation as they do on deep, personal change. The movement puts a huge amount of emphasis on understanding yourself, and building a sense of identity that isn't rooted in the capitalist, patriarchal system.

Unsurprisingly for a movement that was born out of the anti-colonial movements of the 1960s and 70s, a crucial part of that identity has to do with where you come from: the culture, land and history that bears witness to our insistence on survival and resistance in the face of genocide and occupation. But the Kurdistan Freedom Movement doesn't just see itself as a movement for peoples colonised by foreign states — it sees itself as a global movement, and offers its analysis, practices and ethics to everyone fighting for a more just, free world. This means that the emphasis on knowing who you are and feeling strong in that applies to everyone, whether you come from Rojava or from the 'heart of empire'.

Moving to England as a teenager, I didn't think further than the fact that I was escaping from America, the capitalist, petrol-guzzling, gun-toting global empire. I naively assumed that the National Healthcare System and the (at the time) affordable university tuition fees somehow meant I'd moved to a progressive place, and didn't come with the same baggage as the all-guns-blazing, flag-waving 'US of A'. Predictably, my illusions were quickly shattered. In my first months at university I learned about the deeply entrenched class system of the British state from working class friends, realising that what I had assumed were outdated stereotypes in BBC period dramas still existed, albeit in different outfits. From friends whose families came from anywhere outside the South of England, I learned about struggles to keep language and culture alive, while experiencing the sharp end of economic deprivation and marginalisation.

As I learned more over pints and in shared kitchens than I ever learned from my sociology lectures, I threw myself into political organising both in student societies and outside of the uni. Somehow slipping between the cracks of Amnesty International and the Socialist Workers' Party, I stumbled upon radical political organising, and tumbled headlong into love with the eco-anarchist movement in the upswing of Climate Camp, Plane Stupid and other direct action groups. Through protest camps, blockades, arrests, workshops and endless meetings, I learned to trust myself and other people, and to defend my community and my home.

I walked a good long way down the path of building my sense of self and sense of home in England, but it felt like there was always a crisis of belonging hovering in my peripheral vision. I didn't know how committed I could be to the long, hard road to radical social change if I was from somewhere else. I sometimes felt like a fraud — trying to make the place I was living better, while having abandoned the country I grew up in because it felt like a hopeless cause.

Years after moving to England, I started to feel homesick for America. I felt like I had unfinished business there — I was haunted by the identity and home I had rejected when I was 18, by the person I could have become had I stayed in the Midwest. So nine years after I had arrived in England, bright-eyed and naive, I got rid of half my possessions and packed up the rest, and bought a plane ticket to Ohio.

The plane took off in the grey drizzle of a London winter and landed in a sparkling white polar vortex – a winter so cold that schools had to close and slabs of ice metres thick jutted out onto the shores of Lake Erie. The world around me was familiar and foreign at the same time. As I trudged alone through the snow to comfort myself with books from the library or waffles from the diner, I felt painfully far away from the people that I cared most about. I tried to focus on the things in front of me: healing my relationship with my mother, and volunteering at urban farms taking over vacant lots in the city. I built up some friendships and experienced moments of joy and possibility. I could hear the way I spoke getting more American again — but people still asked me where I was from, my accent unplaceable.

As the months passed, I had to come to terms with the realisation that the States didn't feel like my home any more, or at least that England had become more of a home. Home is about history and roots, but it's also about people, energy, and time. I had put nearly a decade of work into putting down roots in England – developing friendships and building a chosen family, throwing myself into political organising to make it better, planting seeds and watching them grow. I was always going to be a little bit 'in between', but without realising I was doing it, I had made some kind of commitment in my years across the ocean. So the following winter, I packed up my stuff again and flew back over the ocean. This time, it didn't feel like I was running away from something. It felt like coming home.

***

In the summer of 2016 the Brexit referendum took place. Just like we did when faced with the prospect of Bush, we rolled our eyes and shook our heads at the state of the world. I didn't stay up to watch the results come in, I shrugged on another layer of cynicism, and told myself that I was ready for anything. I wasn't the teenager who fell head over heels in love with radical politics any more. I had experienced the devastation that comes from losing major political battles, and the isolation that follows groups falling apart because of internal conflicts and weaknesses.

I woke unexpectedly in the early hours of the morning from an unsettled night of sleep, and blearily checked the news on my phone. 52% of voters had decided to leave the EU off the back of a campaign that whipped up xenophobic sentiment and promised anti-migrant action. Half asleep, I grappled with this shift towards fascism, what it meant for me and for the place that I called home. My partner – also an EU citizen – slept on next to me. I wasn't sure whether to wake them or not. It affected me more than I'd thought it would, my blood memory calling up echoes of Poland under Nazi occupation, of displacement and death and loss. Two months later, Arkadiusz Jozwik – a Polish man living in Essex – was killed in a hate crime by a group of young men who had overheard him speaking Polish. I was hit hard emotionally, especially because it seemed like nobody on the left noticed or said anything. It all started to feel a bit closer to the skin, but also bigger, like one of the political moments that always took my breath away when I read history books as a teenager. The moments when normal people see the ugliness in the world, and rather than burying their heads in the sand they square their shoulders and get ready for the struggle ahead.

The Brexit referendum pushed me another step back into politics. I knew what side of history I wanted to be on, so I took a leap of faith and joined a group fighting for grass-roots power for communities in London. After four years of being scared to commit to a political collective, I stepped into being a political organiser again. I re-connected with the joy of collective struggle, and was nurtured by the care and wisdom held by the other organisers in the collective.

When I had returned to England from my year back in America in 2015, I had decided that this was my home. A bit over a year later, the Brexit campaign told me that I wasn't welcome. But this time I wasn't going to reject it and run off looking for somewhere else to call home. It reminded me that I couldn't take things like 'home' for granted, that to belong to a place you had to fight for it, and for everyone living there.

As a gardener, I think a lot about roots, and soil. In order to grow, a plant needs to take root, it needs to be nourished by the soil it's grounded in even as it grows upwards. As humans, we also draw on the places we are from as we grow. By going back to America, to see if I could pick up the pieces of my past and build myself a future, I was learning more about where I was from and how it shaped me. By choosing to fight for my right to call post-Brexit Britain home, I was putting down new, deeper roots. In a lot of ways the passports I hold could allow me to glibly call myself a 'citizen of the world', but to do so ignores not only the reality of power and privilege, but also the importance of being able to call a place 'home'. I was finding out that we can't separate out who we are from where we come from.

When I decided to go to Rojava a few years later, I felt deeply settled in England, and so I saw it more as a trip than a move. Still, as someone not prone to homesickness, I was surprised by how intensely I missed England during my first months in Rojava. Although it felt like the right place for me to be, I didn't feel like I fit there. I found myself jealous of those internationalists – often the younger ones – who arrived in Rojava with a sense of homecoming. They took to different ways of doing things and new experiences with enthusiasm bordering on euphoria, reminding me of myself a decade before. It seemed to me like they felt at home from the day they arrived, whereas I had already put down roots in a place far away, and the process of yanking them out of the ground was jarring, and often painful. Anna dying in Afrin had been a kick in the gut, and it felt like the momentum from that kick carried me to Rojava, where my body landed before my heart had a chance to catch up. But as my time in Rojava passed and I gained more understanding of the politics of the movement, it became clear that the last thing that revolutionaries from Rojava wanted was for internationalists to reject and cut ties with the countries where they came from.

Something that surprises a lot of internationalists who come to Rojava is that one of the central ethics of the Kurdistan Freedom Movement is love for your place, your country. We don't expect this from an anti-state, anti-nationalist and anti-fascist revolution, but time and again the importance of loving where you come from was emphasised. The Kurdish term for this ethic is *welatparezi*, which translates literally into 'to defend one's country'. The word *welat* — country – is a different word than what is used to mean nation, state, or even homeland. It's used to refer to the land, people and culture that you are from, and is seen as something sacred. *Parezi* means defence, or protection, so it's sometimes sloppily translated as 'patriotism', but *welatparezi* is never used as a reason to claim that other countries are inferior. It's just that the relationship you have to your country is special, and powerful, like the relationship you have to your family and friends. It's about the smell of the rain on the land, the way people prepare tea, the stories that people hold about who they are and where they come from.

When visiting Kurdish families, internationalists are often asked semi-seriously "where's nicer – Kurdistan or where you come from?" I felt like I was expected to say "Rojava is nicer", because in Rojava there is an anti-capitalist revolution, and my home is the heart of empire. But it felt dishonest – I was learning a lot from being in Rojava, but my heart longed for the people and places that I called home. I had come to rely on the strong, sugary çay tea that we drank constantly from small glasses, but I desperately wanted a mug of builders' tea and a long catch up with my loved ones. I eventually worked up the courage (and the language skills), to try answering in a different way. The next time I was asked whether I preferred Rojava or home, I honestly and warmly described the things about Rojava that made it a special and compelling place, but then I said "but England, that is my *welat*". Without exception, the response would be a smile, a knowing nod, and an acknowledgement that "your *welat*, that is something sweet indeed".

The ability to know, love, and defend the place you call home is non-negotiable if you want to build revolution. We can't fight nationalism and fascism by hating where we come from, we need to fight it through loving it enough to defend it from those ideologies. If we want to build up democracy without a state, it will come out of celebrating the richness of our diversity, and the strength of knowing what we are fighting for. Of course this becomes harder when the place you call home is also the home of Empire and capitalism. British internationalists (particularly those from England) often struggle with the concept of *welatparezi*, grappling with deeply ingrained reflexes to reject anything that has even a whiff of national pride about it. Internationalist volunteers from Catalonia and the Basque country would wax poetic about the liberation struggles of their people, and even the Swiss could get enthusiastic about mountains and fondue. Meanwhile, the English and Germans awkwardly pulled ourselves through emotional and intellectual gymnastics to try to move beyond the guilt and hatred we felt about our countries' brutal impact on the world.

Again and again, organisers from the movement would listen to our hand wringing about empire, and patiently tell us — "you can't defend something if you don't love it". They reminded us that our country, our *welat*, is not the same thing as the nation-state and government that's been imposed onto it. They didn't ask us to whitewash or forget the crimes committed by our governments and our ancestors, they asked us to also uncover the other half of the story, to connect with our collective histories of resistance. Of course this also means taking responsibility for the hard stuff, reckoning with how growing up as the beneficiaries of imperialism has affected our material and social realities. But they urged us to always look beyond what we are rejecting and towards what we are trying to build up. They reminded us that if you can't defend yourself, you can never be free. And that defending where you come from is defending the whole world, because struggles for freedom and justice around the world are all connected.

***

A few months after arriving, I was able to join a tour of North and East Syria with other international volunteers, visiting dozens of projects and institutions that made up the Revolution: schools, co-operatives, municipal courts, youth centres, media outlets, Neolithic sites and women's movement organisations. In most towns we would split into small groups and stay the night in family homes before reconvening in the morning for a ram-packed schedule of visits. The exception was in Raqqa: the local security forces had advised us against spending the night there. Since its liberation from the Islamic State, the security situation was slowly improving but fluctuating, and right then it was a bit too risky to scatter a bus load of foreigners across the city. Rather than getting off the bus, we drove slowly through the streets of Raqqa to be able to see the city that the Islamic State caliphate had declared as its capital.

We drove slowly into the city and the music that constantly blasted through the minibus sound-system somehow perfectly matched the feeling of that moment. It was an epic revolutionary Kurdish song with swelling instrumentals and a resounding chorus, the kind of music you can imagine as the soundtrack to the climactic battle scene of a movie. It had been over a year since Raqqa was the front line of the fight against ISIS, but the city still wore battle scars from the war. The buildings bore the marks of air strikes and bombings – many were only half-standing or completely levelled. Walls were ripped open to expose the remnants of kitchens and workplaces, and whole buildings were gutted, crumbling onto themselves. We drove past a row of busy kebab shops on the ground level of a multi-story building whose upper levels had collapsed. Mountains of rubble pressed down on the shops; business as usual at street level, complete destruction above. Every building that was not ripped open from airstrikes or artillery was riddled with holes from bullets and shrapnel.

I was so absorbed by the city scape that I hardly noticed the human life – whether there were any women on the street, whether people walked with ease or with worry, whether people wore different things than the cities further north. It had been a year and a half since the liberation of Raqqa, but the destruction still felt absolute. And the enemy is still inside. We drove past a partially collapsed building and caught a glimpse of people in a room where an Islamic State flag was prominently displayed, as if the 20,000 bombs dropped by International Coalition air planes never hit home, as if Raqqa was still a city where beheadings could happen in the main square.

Seeing the battered remains of cities like Raqqa and Kobane reminded me of the stories of World War II I had heard since I was a child. It made me think of what it must have felt like for my grandmother to return to Warsaw after the bombings to find her house completely levelled to the ground by Nazi warplanes. To not know where her brother was, waiting to hear the news that he had died in a concentration camp. To not know where her husband was, only knowing that wherever he was, he was risking his life. To look out over the city she had called home reduced to rubble. To take her young daughter's hand and face a future lined with loss. I don't think I had ever really confronted the reality of what happens between the destruction and the rebuilding, how long everyone in Warsaw must have lived surrounded by piles of concrete and stone, children playing among the remains of homes and bombs, above corpses buried in their houses waiting their turn to be dug up.

People in Kobane tell of how the city smelled for months after the final battle because there were so many bodies buried in the rubble, and as they rebuilt the city they would keep on uncovering bodies, so far deteriorated that they couldn't identify which side they fought on. How they wrestled with the need to lay the past to rest, with the need to remember. Which is why they didn't rebuild one ruined neighbourhood, leaving it to stand as a memorial, a reminder of what the city went through, of what price was paid for freedom. Between ripped up slabs of concrete, twisted metal armoured cars and heavy weapons stand rusting where they last launched attacks before being overcome. Within the shells of buildings sandbags encircle a small space from which the fighters defended the city, moving position every day to protect themselves from attack. Those sandbags are still there, left in position, so we can remember the path that we follow, what it means to defend something you love.

These are places that I carry with me into the struggle, threads of history that tie me to the places I have called home and the people who fought for, died for, rebuilt them. This is why we owe something to the struggle, and to every struggle. Because the mangled remains of someone's home are part of a chain bigger than any one person can remember, but it lives in our collective DNA, and weighs upon our conscience until we break the pattern.

***

Nine months after I arrived, Rojava still didn't quite feel like home but it was close enough for me to want to defend it as a new Turkish invasion threatened. Rojava wasn't where I was from, and it wasn't even somewhere I imagined spending much of my life, but I had grown to love it. It was an instinctive act of reciprocity with a place that had given me the strength and love to insist on hope. Because I loved it, I would defend it. And through defending it, I would know freedom — because protecting something you care about makes us free. After the heaviest part of the war passed, I realised that I felt more like I belonged there. Even though I knew I would be heading home soon, once travel became possible, I had drawn nourishment from the soil and the people there, and I would carry that with me forever. I don't know what came first, deciding to defend it, or it feeling a bit more like home.

For someone who has a mixed up heritage – Polish, American and English are all jumbled together in my identity – it was hard to put my finger on what *welatparezî* means to me. Maybe this is where internationalism comes in. To be internationalist isn't about where you come from, it's a political stance that emphasises the connections between the struggles we fight at home and those being fought around the world. It's not just recognising a common enemy, but seeing that what we are defending exists in humanity worldwide. So that the deeper we love and understand the land that we call home – the human and natural world that we inhabit – the closer we can feel to humanity anywhere in the world. This is what lies at the root of anti-colonialism, an insistence on the relationship between communities, land and self determination. For the Kurdish movement that meant standing up against colonial oppression on their land. But even if your background is bound up in the privilege inherited from that very oppression, *welatparezi* still means anti-colonialism. If we're willing to work our hardest to make reparations for the harm that's been done, we're not doing our own identity any disservice. It's exactly the other way around – we fight to get rid of the parts of those identities that are toxic and oppressive, and in doing so we have the possibility to bring to light the communities and cultures we really can love.

That relationship of land and identity is itself forged through love, which is a force that brings us closer together, rather than one that separates us. It's not limited to the borders of nation states or the technicalities of citizenship. It recognises that freedom, justice and dignity are connected to the land and the people who make us who we are. And so if we defend these things where we come from, we must fight for them wherever we find ourselves.

"We only had our history with which to defend ourselves, and we held it tightly so we would not die."
— *Zapatista communique*

BACK, WHERE I'M FROM

Jenni, August 2021

Our feet fall between the dashes of bright plastic, back to tarmac and headlights,

away from rust, crumbling cement, bold loving lines of graffiti painted slowly

metal tracks in the concrete that no longer have use or meaning but still trap the
earth

where starfish flourish in the depths if you know where to look,

where the mountains hold up a midnight blue sky, but not even our mountains are
as they should be, robbed of their trees and their wolves generations ago.

I've been feeling rootless, tainted, bought and sold, not sure what's me finding myself
and what's a desperate attempt to steal meaning.

The land around me is ripped up by arms depots, hotels and tourist spots, gaping
wounds that cars bleed through like an infection

and inside me, where there should be collective memory, there's spaces as blank as the
dark surface of the loch

there's cheapness, there's the lens of the rich and powerful over my eyes

there's every moment when I made things worse.

But the trees are reclaiming this spot, though it's not clear why they bother. Somehow
they grow in toxic earth

they clean it.

And we barely know who we are without the system but still we reclaim ourselves

with insecurity and kindness, and stumbling tries

we parody the steps they taught us and somehow something brighter shines through.

The mountains and the women of Kurdistan look on

the final chapter from a legend, immovable in beauty and strength.

But us, maybe we can ask this broken land to forgive us.

Maybe we can turn to each other

go back, and make something new.

The Martyrs' cemetery of Kobane

9. REMEMBERING

Grief, martyrs and struggle
Jenni

Death and grief knock us sideways out of time. All at once, the knowledge that we cannot go back in time becomes something too painful to hold. There is nothing more final than death. But in that moment of finality, time stops working in quite the same way. Five minutes lasts hours, a day lasts a year or gets lost while we turn our backs. Day to day time-keeping and schedules start to read like a foreign language. While the years, months, minutes and golden moments that we spent with the person we lost suddenly become their own special time. We reach for them like you reach for the face of a loved one on a video call – as clear as could be, but completely untouchable. Instead of staying in a neat chronological file in our histories, our lost loved ones break out and jog ahead to run beside us, waving... *remember this?* Remember does not just mean recall: it means carry, embrace, inhabit, re-live and re-breathe.

As I write this in 2021, almost three years have passed since our old and dear friend Anna Campbell was killed in an airstrike in the Turkish state's invasion of Afrin in 2018. Sometimes the realisation that she's gone hits me again like new. Other times I feel her by my side more than ever. There's no logic, of time or any other kind, to how this seems to pass over me.

A month after she was killed, we gathered together in a crowded community hall in Bristol, where she lived before leaving for Rojava, for her memorial service. We shared memories and raucously belted out songs from our shared squatting days, tears pouring down faces, fists raised to the sky instead of wiping them away. Her memorial was full of music, stories, whiskey, warm food, warmer embraces, and a lot of laughter. After we thought we couldn't talk or cry any longer we piled out of the hall and packed a pub with too many people and our own playlist, discovering that if nothing else, we could still dance. Some of us hadn't seen each other in years. But that time didn't matter either, it wasn't real, it was just an interval between our moments together.

In the same way, I sometimes feel as if I stepped straight out of the door of that memorial and found myself, not rowdy and howling on a rainy Bristol street, but sombre and sober in the martyrs' cemetery in the city of Derik, Rojava, one year later. Hundreds of people had gathered for the one year anniversary of Anna's death; the women fighters from the YPJ academy where she had been based, other internationalist volunteers from across Rojava, and local people from Derik. It was humbling to see so many people. I was acutely aware every person there had their own losses, in fact many more, or even more devastating, like the loss of a child.

The one year memorial service also marked another internationalist volunteer's death. Alina Sanchez was a doctor who had become part of the Kurdistan Freedom Movement and was a medical worker in Rojava when she was killed in a car crash just days after Anna's death.

With a backdrop of Anna and Alina's faces printed larger than life on a banner, speakers addressed the crowd through a sound system, their words echoing around the stone monuments and walls of the cemetery. Most people at the memorial had not known either of them personally and stood sedate — and respectful — throughout the service. Songs are considered inappropriate. Some of Anna's friends falteringly read a poem that we knew most people couldn't understand, trying not to cry because it's not the done thing in Rojava to show too much emotion when speaking at a memorial. Back in Bristol, we only kept each other afloat by holding on to each other like lifelines and screaming our feelings at each other until our throats were raw.

Superficially those days were like chalk and cheese. But in very different ways, they were doing the exact same thing. People need ceremony and ritual. Even though the Rojava version is more recognisably ceremonial, complete with flags and official minutes of silence and sometimes military uniforms and salutes, what passed in Bristol was also a ritual of sorts. Yep, even (perhaps especially) when we were rolling around on the floor to musical soundtracks and classic lesbian pop tunes. Without these rituals, we get stuck in time or dislodged from it, something just doesn't work properly. We need these ways to open channels so time can continue to flow.

Collective grief isn't just about healing and moving on though. It's also about power. There's a determination that pumps through the blood when we move — together — in the name of those we have lost that can be found in almost no other way. There were moments after we lost Anna when we felt like nothing in the world could stop us, both right after as we covered miles of a city in furious graffiti of her name and Kurdistan solidarity slogans, and the following year as we braced ourselves for the Turkish state's next invasion of Rojava. When grief divides us it weakens us and we fall deeper and deeper into the cracks it digs. But when it brings us together, however that may be, we get stronger, and much bigger than the sum of our individual pain.

The Kurdistan Freedom Movement has found a way to channel and organise that strength. The culture around *şehîds* (pronounced *sheh-heed*) is the practice of honouring those who have fallen in struggle and how that's made tradition and written into daily life. The term şehîd is usually translated as 'martyr'. For some, that word in English tends to set off alarm bells, invoking images of suffering saints or suicide bombers. But the word, and concept, of şehîd in the movement is both less fanatical and more generous. A şehîd is someone who has fallen in the fight for freedom. Someone whose life was devoted to building a better world, whose memory we honour. This means that you don't have to die in a war to be declared a şehîd. Like Alina Sanchez, a medical worker who died in a car accident, and other revolutionaries who died of cancer or other illnesses, şehîd is more about what you gave your life to than the way you died. It draws on cultural understandings of death and ancestors and on revolutionary love and respect.

In the very early days of the movement, comrades were murdered by the state and their friends vowed revenge. But this would not be a revenge that falls into a cycle of violence. Sometimes, it did mean to answer an attack in a powerful, immediate way. No death should go unanswered. But it's also part of the long struggle. Long term, they chose a slow, deep revenge made of creation. They would make what their comrades had fought for a reality, which is what their murderers were afraid of. This attitude has snowballed into a whole way of life. More and more people stood up for their land and for freedom and more and more people were targeted for it.

It's a grim reality, and not one limited to Kurdistan, that anyone on the wrong side of an oppressive system is always at risk of being taken from us early, ground up in the wheels of the machine that will do anything to protect itself. At the same time, if we can hold each other through it, this can fall on the fire of our rage like petrol, not water.

North and East Syria and the Kurdistan Freedom Movement know enough about grief and loss, and then a little bit more. From its birth in Turkey in the 1970s, the movement's first recorded martyr was killed in 1977, and since then the number has grown into the tens of thousands. There are only three ways you can handle that kind of pain: fall apart, cease to feel and care, or build something out of it. The option chosen, again and again, can be felt in the air you breathe at a memorial. The decision is to build, to create, to refuse to give up.

One of the women I worked with during the Serekaniye invasion shared with me one evening that everyone she had first become politically active with was dead. And her story was typical for anyone her age in the movement. Towards the end of the heavy phase of the invasion, we were all hit by a wave of exhaustion that seemed to bring a kind of nostalgia with it. Grief old and new became tangled up in memories in ways that didn't even seem to make sense. This was one of those nights, and it was a quiet one, over a glass of tea in the bedroom. She didn't give me any kind of fiery revolutionary speech about how we had to carry on their memories. She was obviously in a pain I could barely imagine. But it wasn't even in the realm of her imagination to give up what she was doing. That would be like stopping breathing, or stopping loving. I remembered the sense I'd had when Anna died—that giving up wasn't an option any more. Multiply that by so much more pain, so many more people, and no wonder you get a force to be reckoned with.

***

After Anna died, at first it was strange to know there were hundreds, perhaps thousands of people who'd never met her who were expressing genuine grief. Stranger still to hear her called a martyr. *"Şehîd namirin!"* — "Martyrs never die!" people shout at funerals, memorials or occasions to honour the fallen. At first you wonder if you're hearing a religious sentiment. But whilst many people in the movement do have a faith, the collective process around şehîds is one of an earthly, human spirituality.

To say they do not die doesn't mean they are sitting in some celestial kingdom, looking down at us from the afterlife (though many people might believe that and neither I nor the movement is here to argue about it. There's no contradiction in thinking that as well). It simply means that we will keep them alive. We do this by sharing stories, telling their jokes, doing what we think they would have done when we wish they were there, and by continuing their struggle. If we are patterns in time, then we continue to trace over the lines that our friends and comrades left.

We don't do this alone. We are joined in our remembering by countless others, and we ourselves add our grief to the collective. In Rojava, we attended countless memorials and funerals, for those recently fallen, and those whose deaths happened in the early days of the movement. At first I didn't understand what it meant to grieve for or honour those you never knew. I also didn't understand how people could stay so stiff and formal, or at least that was how it felt to me coming straight from the melting embraces and pouring of souls that was how my community back home had been grieving. As time went by I saw that those closest do actually show a lot of emotion, supported by those around them so they don't fall apart. But the overall formality is also a way to be generous in grief: it means everyone knows what to do, everyone is invited in and can share. It's only human to have some special connections, and that will include those we've lost, but when we have a format for ritual that is roughly the same, it means everyone gets the same treatment and respect.

It creates a pattern for drawing a collective grief out of individual loss, in a way that amplifies it and makes it stronger rather than watering it down. It's not a better or worse way to grieve — it is just as full of feeling, just of a different kind. Sometimes it feels like the mass expressions of collective grief mean that the pain and sense of loss gets distributed across thousands — even millions — of people, and so does the responsibility to continue the work that our loved ones have died for. A crucial result of this is that it builds social movements whose determination and power are strengthened through loss, rather than fragmented and weakened by it.

We make a promise with every death. Taking that promise seriously also teaches us about giving meaning to what we do. To see ourselves as part of their legacy means to be more respectful to ourselves, and to hold ourselves with dignity. An old friend of mine and Anna's once said that he appreciates hearing the funny and human stories of şehîds – times when they've messed up or really struggled with something. Personally he can't always connect with the formal, slightly heroic image. But not because he doesn't honour them, but because it reminds him what they were: just people, people who made choices. That's all a hero should be.

***

Rojava is covered in images of şehîds. Their faces smile down proudly from the spaces Western Europe reserves for advertising or government announcements. The majority of homes of families connected to the movement will have at least one photo on the wall of someone who has fallen, usually a formal portrait superimposed onto a blank background with the emblem of their organisation emblazoned in the corner and their name along the bottom. Sadly this image is often the child or parent of that house, though it can also be someone they had a connection with or someone well known who inspired them. Every public building, office, or collective space is covered with these images. We stand and take a minute of silence before important meetings. Series of seminars and eduction, institutions and new projects are almost always named after a şehîd.

Yet despite the fact that the faces and names of şehîds adorn public and private spaces, some even becoming household names, death isn't glorified by şehîd culture. The goal is and always must be life. Our fallen comrades bring us closer to life with everything they showed us, and we keep them alive in the spaces between us.

136

Formality in expressions of grief in no way means that the sense of loss is superficial. The sincerity in people's sadness for Anna also changed how I saw things. I was and remain sceptical of liberal media hand wringing in the West, over narratives claiming she went to save the poor people of the Middle East. But in Rojava there was a different quality. When people found out I knew her they expressed not just sympathy for me, but a real shared loss for a collective we are all a part of. To understand şehîd culture you have to see how it's connected to a broader movement. You know there's thousands of people you've never met who are on your side and pulling in the same direction as you. That connection is as real as laughter or pain. It brings you the strength to keep doing what you're doing and seeing the meaning in it. So when that collective loses someone you also feel that.

So I feel a part of the legacy of thousands who I never met. I feel a connection that motivates me to get up, link arms, and march forward. It reaches back to those executed by the British state, at home and abroad. It encompasses the likes of Rosa Luxembourg, who knew they would come for her and did the right thing all the same. And hundreds more we've lost, all the way to those from the Kurdistan Freedom Movement who I never met but I still know:

I remember Haukur Hilmarsson, a friend of many friends of mine, another internationalist who also died in the defence of Afrin, a few weeks before Anna.

I remember Farid Medjahed, an internationalist who spent time in the Hambach Forest occupation and a protest camp outside Newcastle where I too built pallet shelters, before travelling to Syria and the frontline against ISIS.

I remember Malda Kosa, the young woman who breathed life into young women's organising in Rojava, whose mother always invites us round and fusses over us with tea.

And I remember countless others. Mother Aqide, Amara Renas and Hevrin Xalaf, symbols of women's resistance who were killed in the Serekaniye war. Alina Sanchez who died within days of Anna and was a brightly lit bridge between the Middle East and South America. Serxwebun Ali, the young man run over by a Turkish armoured vehicle in his own village on my birthday in 2019. Andrea Wolf, tortured and summarily executed after her capture by Turkish soldiers in 1998, a long way from her native Germany but in the mountains of Kurdistan that had become her home. I spent months at the academy named after her in Rojava. For months I worked, laughed, cried, drank tea, wrote, and sang songs under pictures of her face and always in her memory.

While I was in Rojava a friend of mine back home took her own life. It made me think a lot about mental health and the quiet invisible war that is also waged on us by the systems we live under. As a trans woman with a long history of mental health problems, she took a sharper edge of patriarchal social relations than many people, but thousands of people every year end up in the same place as she did.

So I remember those who've been taken by the system in all those insidious, gagged ways. Those I met and those I didn't. Those whose struggle was fought just by existing against all odds for as long as they did. Killed by isolation, poverty, trauma, abuse, marginalisation or just the plain violence of the systems we live under. This is also a legacy of the fight.

The struggle is a long hard road and şehîd culture reminds us that we're a link in a long chain. Sometimes it's hard to see the legacy of anything, let alone the struggle for freedom, in our everyday moments. In the Kurdistan Freedom Movement we talk a lot about 'giving meaning' to things. This direct translation is a slightly odd but very beautiful concept in English. *Give,* not *find* meaning. We have to make an effort to see what we are a part of and in doing so become a part of it. We have to take ourselves seriously for the world to take us seriously.

When we perform our rituals and make our promises, we are giving meaning. But that doesn't mean we have to live solemnly. Our movements are nothing without joy and laughter. You need to live to the fullest to keep someone else alive. And here is something that's the same in Kurdistan and back home. Outside of the rituals, the ceremonial moments, long after the loss has passed through time but not fully through us, we sit and drink tea and tell a story that makes people smile. When we remember friends and comrades we've lost in all their imperfections and pratfalls, when we laugh until we cry and see someone else's face light up with joy even though they never met them, we are also giving meaning. They should still be here with us, taking pratfalls, making mistakes, and being our heroes. Sometimes the pain of that threatens to drown us in nihilism and meaninglessness. But we always have a choice, and we always have each other. Together we can decide what legacy they will leave.

"Let this radicalize you, rather than drive you to despair"
— *Mariame Kaba, Abolitionist organiser and educator*

An internationalist volunteer and one of the children of Jinwar women's village

10. STRUGGLING

Sometimes the revolution feels a lot like hard work
Natalia

"Fight my dear, fight strong! By fighting we exist. By fighting we become free
and beautiful and more. By fighting we love."

— *Şehîd Beritan, a Kurdish guerrilla in whose memory the first all-women's
guerrilla forces were created*

Life in Rojava was not what I expected. I was taking part in one of the most
effective revolutionary movements of our time, working towards a vision I deeply
believed in. I lived side by side with revolutionaries from around the world, and
was learning more than I had learned for many years. Yet a lot of the time I found
myself frustrated and unhappy, unable to find beauty or meaning in the work I
was doing.

One afternoon, I found myself hiding out in the stifling hot, wet air of the
greenhouse. I went through the motions of weeding, but what I was really doing
was surrounding myself by growing things and letting the familiarity of clay soil
on my hands soothe – or at least distract – me from my unhappiness. I had tried
to come to Rojava without too many expectations, but somewhere in the back of
my mind I expected time to move in epic sweeps, like a camera panning in slow
motion across a climactic scene. Instead, time felt broken and awkward, a video

skipping and distorted as I tried to bridge the gap between what I was seeing and what I was expecting to happen. Sometimes all I could do was step out of time and let a few deep breaths of morning dew on seedlings take me somewhere that I understood.

After Anna died, a lot of people reflected on the letters and phone calls they had had with her while she was with the YPJ. People often described her as so happy, more content than she had been for years. What was wrong with me, I wondered, that I felt so miserable? What did it say about my ideals, my commitment to revolution?

As time went on, I met more people who had spent time with Anna in Rojava, and a different perspective on her time here began to emerge. I heard stories about her frustration with being sent to a military base in the middle of nowhere, about times when she was feeling stuck, of feeling like all the action was happening somewhere else far away, of loneliness. Her story began to fall in line with my own experience and that of almost every internationalist volunteer. We arrive in Kurdistan lifted up by our daydreams and weighed down by baggage, and inevitably, the reality is both dreamy and heavy, and much more besides.

Sometimes it feels like we are walking a beautiful path that is changing the course of world history, other times we are confronted with the brutal everyday tedium of revolutionary life. Often it's both at the same time. It's not that Anna – or I – lied every time we wrote home saying how amazing it was to be part of the Rojava revolution. It's just that sometimes things can be amazing and difficult at the same time. Trying to find the right words to describe this feeling in emails I send back home, I found myself writing that 'It's hard, and I'm not always happy, but I feel like I'm in the right place."

While I clung to the sense that I was doing the right thing, I was finding myself worn down by difficult interpersonal dynamics with comrades, by the total lack of privacy, and by the inaccessibility of all the things that I was used to drawing comfort from. Things like going out with a hip flask of whiskey and dancing until the early hours, or ordering a small mountain of takeaway sushi and stuffing my face in bed. Or disappearing into my bedroom and watching period dramas all day, or even just having a bedroom to myself in the first place!

It had been a long time since I was somewhere where I didn't understand how anything worked, and I didn't like it. I was getting into fights with my supervisors, about everything from transparency in decision making to whether listening to Whitney Houston while cleaning the kitchen was 'counter-revolutionary'. One of the most memorable clashes was a very public argument about whether we should try to establish a grass lawn in the middle of our site, where my environmentalist approach to water conservation in a semi-arid region came head to head with the importance the movement places on aesthetics. It was after this dispute that I retreated to the greenhouse, stubbornly planting drought-resistant vegetable seeds into bags of earth, and waited for them to give a sign of life.

I had expected to pit myself against the fascism and violence of Islamic State and the global capitalist system while I was in Rojava. It felt less straightforward — and a lot less heroic — when the conflict I was grappling with was more internal, and didn't fall along fairly straightforward political lines. It was one thing to hear about the Kurdistan Freedom Movement's political culture of navigating conflict within a commitment to unity — sounds great! — and another thing entirely to actually have to live it. Humans are humans whether they are in a revolutionary movement or not, and that means personality clashes, different approaches and straight up political differences still exist.

So time and again I found myself at loggerheads with my supervisors, enmeshed in a battle of wills that was a constant background presence in my day to day. The tensions came to a head when the supervisors of the project staged a surprise training in how to respond to an emergency security situation. In retrospect, the whole situation was equal parts comedic and chaotic, with an elaborate staged breach of site security in which comrades from a neighbouring project snuck onto site at night and attempted to steal our shoes from outside the rooms we slept in. The exercise was a test of our diligence in carrying out round-the-clock security shifts, and our ability to follow the set process for when there was a security alert. It was a worthwhile lesson to teach us, and our failure to step up to the challenge showed that we had a lot of learning to do. But all the same, I felt that it was done badly and unkindly. It seemed that we had been set up to fail, that a significant amount of distress was caused by the absence of advance warning or preparation, and that we were being collectively punished for the inattention of a few individuals.

I found myself shaking with anger during the debrief of the training exercise, literally brought to tears by my rage. When our poor performance was evaluated by those running the session, they pulled no punches in telling us exactly what we did wrong, even laughing at us. I had already been angry at how the training was carried out, and now I was livid that our shortcomings were being held up in ridicule rather than in understanding. I couldn't remember the last time I had been so angry. Maybe years ago, plunging into shouting matches with swaggering men at house parties. Or a handful of times defending ourselves against the police at protests. But even in those times I had felt more in control, because I was able to see the person I was battling against as the enemy. I didn't have this sense of gut-wrenching betrayal, that a perceived wrongdoing was like a stab in the back, rather than an attack I could see coming and arm myself against.

In the course of the debrief and ensuing clashes, I felt really disrespected, and that my political perspective, identity and experience were marginalised and belittled. At the time, it felt like I was being punished for speaking out against the supervisors, and I was outraged that this would happen in a movement that placed such a high value on comradeship and solidarity. The response I was used to in this kind of a situation would have been complete outrage, calling people out and a subtle (or not so subtle) social blacklisting. Guest lists to events and gatherings would be quietly curated with the expectation that I wouldn't want to be in the same space as the people I was in a conflict with. Back home, I would have considered leaving the project in a fit of rage, and would have expected to be fully backed by my friends and political circle in doing so. But here, that was neither logistically possible nor culturally acceptable. It was weird to not have this immediate vindication of being able to say "you are wrong and I am right" and have my whole world back me up.

Of course there was backup from the people around me – some sneaking off on the motorbike to bring back ice cream, others taking the time to chat and expressing support, experienced comrades from other parts of the movement giving hours of their time to talk and explore options, give wider context and suggest possible directions and actions. But throughout all this, there wasn't a public spectacle, there wasn't a big drama, a big split. There was certainly no airing of dirty laundry on social media, and that was only partly due to very limited access to the internet.

I think I was expecting some kind of showdown, my political muscle memory waiting for the moment where some people were declared right, and the rest, wrong. But mostly, we just got on with it. And throughout this time, I never doubted that I would continue to have a place to sleep. To continue to have food three times a day and a virtually endless supply of strong sugary tea. That I would continue to have work to do and a place within the project, responsibilities to fulfil and the same rights as everyone else.

Through long conversations with people who had spent years organising within the movement, I was encouraged to not see myself as a victim. Instead, I was lovingly but firmly pushed to learn how to struggle within my collective to make it better. At the same time, I was encouraged to take time to reflect on the dynamics I brought to the situation and what I could learn from it. I unpacked how behaviours I internalised from my school days — competitiveness, a phobia of 'poor performance' and the idea that we succeed and fail as individuals rather than as collectives — were playing out in my reactions to the situation. I noticed how I defaulted into an 'us vs them' dynamic and wanted to blame those in positions of official leadership for my sense of disempowerment in a way that reproduced the dynamic of 'state' and 'subject', rather than exploring how I can see myself as a leader even when I'm not in charge.

I found it strangely reassuring how many weathered organisers and veterans in Rojava, when talking about the revolution, would say: 'It's hard. It's long, and it's hard". It meant that the fact that I was finding a lot of things hard didn't mean I was somehow doing it wrong. In fact, it maybe even meant that I was doing it right.

Another thing they would say is that "after the revolution... there is more revolution". Revolution isn't an event or an endpoint, it's a life's work, an approach to how we live our lives and how we struggle. We can't live our lives waiting for it to be over, we need to embrace it and see the beauty in it. This might sound tokenistic or naive, like a cliche trotted out by those who understand revolution only from Hollywood movies and rose-tinted history books. But in the Kurdistan Freedom Movement, it is a truth lived by people whose lives are a testament to struggle, who wear years of struggle in the lines of their faces and the shrapnel buried under their skin.

The insistence on not only the necessity of struggle, but the beauty of it, is central to the movement's approach to revolution. Struggle is seen as resistance to wherever and however oppression and injustice show up. Struggle is not the same thing as suffering, but it does mean not always taking the easy path. It means doing the hard work of revolutionary change; whether that work is on the front lines, in community organising, in working through conflict or unpacking the oppressive behaviours we've all internalised. Struggle means aligning your thoughts, your feelings, and your actions so you're able to bring your whole self to the work, celebration and connections that make up a revolution.

In the political organising I was involved in in years past, struggle all too often felt like bashing my head against a brick wall again and again. I think I saw activism as something that — if we were lucky — might bring us closer to a moment of revolution which may or may not happen in the distant future. Now I try to think of revolution as something that grows out of – among other things – people choosing to take a revolutionary approach to how we struggle. If we take the path of resistance, of beauty in struggle, then we will experience liberation through walking it. That's where the joy comes from — not because it's easy or pleasurable, but because through it we can feel ourselves becoming more free.

When I first arrived in Rojava, this was not something I was willing to do. I loved a lot of things about political organising — the community, the feeling of collective power, the sense of living my values — but I wasn't emotionally ready to commit to struggling for the rest of my life. All the stuff about struggle being beautiful is easy enough to believe in theory, but harder to put into practice. If we haven't genuinely embraced struggle, then we will always be looking for an easier way out. This can mean going down the path of flashy and photogenic mobilisations and the low hanging fruit of winnable reforms rather than deep political organising and revolutionary system change. It can mean engaging in political change only to the extent that it is comfortable and doesn't challenge our individual footholds in the system. It can also mean falling into cynicism and not really believing things can change, or limiting ourselves to political spaces where we already agree with each other.

The year I spent in Rojava, I was constantly challenged to dig deep into myself and discover what it meant to struggle in a revolutionary way. It meant always being open to reflecting on my behaviours, my thoughts and my desires, and being honest when they did not match up with my values and my stated commitment to change the world for the better. It meant not keeping my vulnerabilities and difficulties to myself, instead learning to trust my comrades and work through things together. It meant not seeing people as disposable if they pissed me off or weren't 'woke' enough, and committing to building trust and relationships with them anyway, because we were all part of the revolution.

I wasn't used to living like this, so that year was one of the most challenging years of my life. Some days I was better at embracing this struggle within myself than others. On days that I was particularly exhausted or unmotivated, I would imagine being home and getting wasted and dancing with my friends, or just tapping out and ignoring the rest of the world. When struggling to stay focused – or awake – during long seminars, I listed the restaurants I wanted to go to and holidays I wanted to escape on in the margins of my notebook. Sometimes I even daydreamed about the security blanket of dabbling in politics in a way that made me feel good but was confined to a manageable section of my life, testing out whether it was something I could go back to. Time and again, I came to the conclusion that no, it was not a life I could return to. The feeling of rightness that came from knowing that I was fully immersed in struggle alongside many thousands of people was something I couldn't turn my back on. And for the rest of my life — whether I was in Rojava, England, or anywhere else — this meant not shying away from struggle.

What does it look like in practice? In my diary entries from Rojava, I complain that most of my energy was going towards unpicking difficult interpersonal dynamics and endless confrontations with the supervisors of the project where I was working, rather than figuratively waving flags on the front line of the revolution. It felt like a distraction, a waste of time and energy from the real work. But even after just a few weeks within the movement, I could hear the voices of wise revolutionaries in my head: "where do you think the front line of the revolution is, if not inside yourself?"

It was hard not to feel impatient, not to feel like revolutionary life was meant to be more glamorous. I had friends on the front lines, watching the territory of the once-vast ISIS caliphate shrink to a tiny patch in the Deir ez Zor region. I had friends working with the women's movement, spending time with amazing women revolutionaries from across Kurdistan as well as from across Europe. Meanwhile, I was trying to keep our greenhouse from blowing away, clashing with the toxic masculinity of young male internationalist volunteers, and having fights about grass.

Although I can look back on those months with a certain level of relief that they are over, there's no denying that I went through a huge amount of growth and learning during that time. Before arriving in Rojava, I would have described myself as being pretty self aware, but while I was there I got to know myself on a whole different level. Sometimes international volunteers joke that being in Rojava is like an extended therapy session. But crucially, it's conducted collectively with your comrades and through the practice of revolution – of struggle. So within that framework I was pulled up on more than I would have liked to admit: from my reliance on irony and cynicism to keep hope at arm's length, to how I am resistant to opening up and sharing what I find challenging, to my lack of trust in my comrades and seeing my personal needs as separate from collective needs.

It was in a conversation with one of my supervisors who I was engaged in perpetual wrangling with, sitting on the floor cushions in the small project office drinking tiny cups of instant coffee, that I began to understand and embrace this approach to struggle. In imperfect English, she tried to explain to me: 'the highest points...you have to struggle... the times that it's the highest, you know... progress". She smiled at me, half serious and half cheeky, as if she was acknowledging that she was one of the things I was struggling with the most, and that was okay because through that conflict I would grow. It's true – I learned so much about struggle, about persistence, about solidarity and about hope, that I wouldn't have learned if I was only learning things from people I got on with, or somewhere where I wasn't committed (or compelled) to push through, past my comfort zone. I wasn't given the space to run away from myself, so I had to face myself and — with the support of comrades — grow into a stronger and more aligned version of myself.

Anyone who's been on a sports team knows that you have to train as hard as you want to be able to play on game day – your strength and skills and reserves need to be built up through practice. Although political struggle is not as cut and dry as a sports competition, revolutionary struggles throughout history and around the world tend to come down to the wire. At that point, victory and failure comes down to being able to stick to your guns no matter what. When it's the crunch point, there's no space for having doubts about whether the struggle is 'worth it' — you need to be committed and in love with it.

This level of self knowledge and commitment on an individual level can only strengthen our social movements on a collective level. Reading about historical failures and setbacks of the left over the past century, I've been struck by a few writers noticing the same thing. That however important external factors were in determining the failures and setbacks of key struggles – the rising force of neoliberal capitalism, criminalisation from the state and changing social contexts — the crises of confidence and compromised political principles within the social movements themselves were just as critical. Whether it was out of self preservation, hopelessness, or lack of political commitment, those who organised within these movements – and particularly those who held leadership positions — looked for an easy way out and struck a fatal blow to the movements that they should have been accountable to. From the cooperative movement, to anti-colonial independence struggles, to union battles, those in leadership positions didn't hold the line and settled for too little. It wasn't enough for them to be convinced of the worthiness of their struggle in their brains. We need to be convinced of not just the logic of struggle, but of its beauty: it needs to be in our hearts, our guts and our bones. I look back on my years of political organising and I can spot the times when I was convinced on an analytical level, but not on an embodied and emotional one. Unsurprisingly, those were the times I gave up.

People in Rojava often describe the revolutionaries who have fully devoted their lives to the movement as the most 'clean' people you can meet; that inside they are clean. This isn't a word that I originally felt at ease with – it implied some kind of weird dogmatic purity or quasi-religious absolution of sins. But it's something different – to be clean as a revolutionary means to move through the world with a resolve and a peace that comes from knowing what you believe in, and knowing that you are living it. So that whether you yourself are in a position of leadership and responsibility, or you are someone holding those in positions of leadership to account, you have the clarity and strength to know what you're accountable to.

For all of us who want to shape the future, it's a heavy responsibility — to become as clean as we can inside, to work on our mentalities until we take out the bits of capitalism, patriarchy and domination that have infected us and that stop us from truly imagining and working towards a better world. It's exhausting — picking yourself apart over and over, and knowing that the work never stops, that we're going to have to keep on doing this again and again. But crucially, we do it together, learning that while struggling on our own can be oppressive, to struggle together is revolutionary.

So there is a lot of internal work we need to do as part of building a revolutionary approach to social change. We need to develop the strength and clarity to struggle against the systems we are trying to change, and also to struggle within our movements and ourselves to make them stronger. I'd love to see our social movements develop the ability to hold conflict and differences of approach or analysis within them. This will only help our movements grow in size and scope, while still sticking to core values and a shared vision. It gives us the resilience to overcome failure and resist dogmatism, and the adaptability to take on board learnings.

Sectarianism in the left is a tired and tedious reality that many of us have accepted as an inevitability, rather than seeing it as a product of a political culture that we can — and must — change. There are of course real differences of ideology and direction. I'm not saying if we all just chilled out and listened to each other better we'd discover that we agree on everything. There are red lines we have to stand firm on, there are hard conversations to hash out. But by not being able to sit round the table and have these conversations, or work with each other strategically, we are stunting our possibilities.

I think one of the most valuable lessons I learned in Rojava was developing my ability to struggle *within* a group or *alongside* an individual, rather than *against* them. It meant learning how to work with people who had different organising cultures and approaches to me, and who I often came head to head with. This meant taking the time to talk to people to establish common ground, and developing a strong culture of education and transformation, so those who are involved in conflict are supported in their growth and learning. It means learning the art of balancing the insistence on constructive criticism with the understanding that change can be slow.

Patience, faith, and the resilience that comes from knowing what you're fighting for and knowing that it is worth it, all open the door to building mass movements that are capable of shattering the stronghold that capitalism and the state have on our lives. Of course there are still groups or individuals who we consider ourselves to be struggling *against* — but those who we work with and with whom we engage in struggle *within* or *alongside* will be a much larger group.

No matter how many times you ask revolutionaries from the movement "what are the red lines?" — hoping to receive a nugget of wisdom or a handy formula for figuring out how much divergence is *too much* divergence, the answer always comes back the same: 'It depends on your particular context, you need to find the red lines for yourself". But it goes without saying that the 'us' is going to be much, much bigger than the 'them'.

This emphasis on unity is one of the biggest differences in the political culture of the Kurdistan Freedom Movement and my experiences of the left at home. The commitment to working together stands even when things don't go your way, and it extends to spaces in which you are uncomfortable. It means that you don't have to agree with everything that is happening in order to be part of it. Instead, you build up your understanding of what you're fighting for so that you can work with people you disagree with in a way that strengthens your position, rather than watering it down. A commitment to unity is made possible through our commitment to working for change, rather than being in opposition to it. In the words of Mariame Kaba, an abolitionist organiser and education from the USA, "my political commitments are to developing stronger relationships with people and to transforming harm", because transformation is not possible if we are not in relationship to each other.

I was reminded of this approach again when the Zapatista delegation to Europe in 2021 prefaced their visit with the declaration that what social movements need most is unity – not a lack of disagreements or divergence — but an insistence on unity despite and beyond them. The Zapatistas reminded us that social movements are like families — and families are never free from disagreements. But, if we want to be a strong family, we learn how to work through and beyond disagreements.

The ability to do this is based on a few things: the existence of a set of shared values, a culture which insists that people can change, and processes which are strong enough to hold those disagreements. So when I was seething with rage at my supervisors for the training that I felt they had really messed up, I was given a space in which to unpack that. I was able to share my critiques and analysis of how the behaviour of my comrades (because just because they're my supervisors doesn't mean they're not comrades) was oppressive and disrespectful. In turn, they were able to offer reflections on my defensiveness, on my lack of humility and how my resistance to letting collective learning take precedence over personal comfort was getting in the way of all of us learning together. Together, we could pool our perspectives and analysis and then take action as we felt necessary. This was abolitionism in practice – an attempt to move away from a punitive culture by setting up systems and culture that offer an alternative.

The process wasn't perfect – it was bumpy, and squeezed around and under a too-busy schedule and personality clashes that weren't going to suddenly disappear. But the combination of having collectively held values and even just the bare bones of a process through which to struggle *within* a group or movement **rather** than *against* each other created a fundamental shift in how I could engage in that conflict. When my time in the project came to an end, I was able to say goodbye to my supervisors and the male comrades who I had constantly clashed against with genuine comradeship and warmth. Had we resolved all of our differences? Not even close. But through our arguments and criticisms and tensions we had affirmed our common dedication to our struggle. We took our commitment to freedom and justice as a starting point, and dug down into what it looks like to embody those values in who we are and how we treat each other.

This was an important lesson for me to learn, to not just organise in places that feel comfortable and in line with my political beliefs, but to forge a unified resistance through disagreement and difference. This is something that a lot of people involved in front line struggles already know – whether the front line is a fight to save local welfare services, grass-roots housing unions or migrant solidarity. We see it too across history, like the women in Black liberation struggles in America who fought on two front lines: that of white supremacy across society and that of patriarchy within their movements.

There were times throughout my year in Rojava that I felt intensely uncomfortable. There were even times that I felt belittled and disrespected, exhausted and overstretched. Sometimes it meant that I wasn't as happy, or comfortable, or well-rested as I could have been. At the same time, it meant that I wasn't complacent, and that I didn't fall into a sense of helplessness and hopelessness. It meant that I didn't automatically prioritise my own wants over everyone else's, and that others in the group did the same.

Somehow the ability to feel ownership and trust in the collective was able to sit alongside conflict, frustration and even alienation. This was at least partly because both materially and socially I was still seen as part of the group, even when I was fighting with the supervisors or railing against the entrenched patriarchal attitudes of the men who made up the majority at the internationalist project where I was based. The same emphasis on the collective that I had at first found stifling and restrictive, I now recognised as a form of security, an expression of unconditional belonging. Held in this way, I learned and grew so much through these experiences, more than I had in a long time.

On my return from Rojava, I expected to be overwhelmed and alienated by the relentlessness of consumerism and the politically reactionary mainstream. It's true that I had to close my eyes and gather my strength as my Megabus rolled down London's Oxford Street; consumerism on a scale I had grown unused to. But far more jarring was the negative language that fellow leftists used when talking about each other. It was a punch in the gut each time I heard either subtle put downs or unrestrained trash talk of different groups and individuals — and it seemed to happen constantly. I was surprised to realise how much my standards had shifted in relation to how we talk about others within the wider movement, even (especially) those we disagree with. It wasn't just about language — my intuitive understanding of who the 'us' is when we talk about 'our struggle' had grown much bigger than it had been before.

It's not that in Rojava there are no tensions or conflicts between different groups and individuals operating within the movement. But the understanding that we're all in this together sits a lot closer to the skin. The culture of constructive criticism fosters a commitment to mutual learning and transformation, and strong organisational structures between different areas of work and levels of activity translate into a sense of accountability to each other.

Driven by that culture of accountability and everyone's inalienable right to offer constructive criticism, those in leadership positions try to lead by example. In fact, it's often those in leadership positions who model what it looks like to give insightful analysis of their own journey in trying to liberate their mentality from internalised oppression. Nobody and nothing claims to be perfect, but everyone has the responsibility to learn and progress. It's an incredibly hopeful approach, because at its root is the belief that everyone can change. It requires long, hard struggle within ourselves and our movements so that we can live up to the task before us. This kind of work can feel thankless and endless, but as the saying goes, 'If it was easy, they wouldn't call it struggle".

I would like to say that after my time in Rojava, I am able to joyfully engage in 'struggle within' or 'alongside' rather than 'against' comrades I find myself in conflict with, and that I don't fall into pits of frustration and fits of anger. This wouldn't be true – I am still human and although I hope to learn to be more patient and understanding, I also know that anger is an expression of believing – fiercely- that things could be different. But I have learned how to sit with discomfort a bit better, and to take responsibility for the dynamics that I bring to a difficult situation. Sometimes that approach has put me at odds with some fellow organisers back home. I'm more willing to work alongside groups and individuals whose politics I disagree with, and often push back against approaches to organising (including some versions of 'safe spaces') which seek to eliminate difference rather than finding ways to hold it in a principled and transformative way. There's never just one right answer for how we navigate divergence and conflict in our movements, but it's a question I want to keep on asking.

I'm sure that part of the transformation I've experienced comes from a previously unparalleled experience in my life: I knew that any one of us could have died in carrying out our work in the resistance to the Turkish invasion, and that was something that we were willing to give to each other. But it also comes from something deeper: I have seen people change. I have seen people dig deep inside themselves and recognise how patriarchy, individualism, and capitalism have taken root inside their minds and then embark on the messy, imperfect and endless work of rooting it out. I have learned how to collectivise struggle and to seek ways to bring people together to confront a problem intentionally, rather than flailing at it like a moth throwing herself into a flame. Insisting on learning how to work together is not just a strategic necessity so we can achieve the critical mass we need for power. Instead, it is deeply visionary and hopeful, reminding us that the world we are trying to build is only possible if we believe in each person's capacity for change

As time passed, I began to feel more at home in Rojava. I started to find my place, which meant not only learning how to navigate the processes and ways of working in the movement, but learning to rely on them and instinctively reach for them when the going got tough. After a while, I even found that I wasn't reaching for the individual coping mechanisms that had occupied my daydreams so intensely in the months after I arrived.

Life began to feel normal and filled with an everyday happiness that isn't particularly unique to any specific place, like dancing to music (sometimes Britney Spears, sometimes revolutionary Kurdish tunes) while cleaning the kitchen floor after dinner or singing songs in crowded vans driving down dusty roads. Other days I got that slow motion epic feeling I had been missing when I first arrived. Times that felt momentous and left me searching for a record button in my brain, knowing that these were memories I wanted to hold on to. Some days were still hard, and there were times that I sought escapism whenever I had a chance. But I always came back — I was done with running away from struggle.

"Freedom only exists if you fight for it every day – and you're in a car that's picking up speed"
— *Pussy Riot, Russian feminist protest art collective*

DIFFERENCES

Jenni, summer 2021

I sit in the muted chatter of a 'beer garden' (well, a couple of picnic benches backing onto a side road). The pub door swings occasionally behind us. The city centre rumbles away to our left and the east end starts to sprawl not far to the right. There are more people in this city, where I moved a decade ago, than in any city in Rojava. The rumble of life is both energising and humbling.

I'm awkwardly perched, not sure what position to sit in, how much skin to show, what to drink. Luckily everyone else is covid-awkward: full of anxiety and confusion and need and loneliness. I'm not the only alien here.

Next to me is one of my old friends. We've been partners in crime in the same small crew for a long time and have the stories and scars in common to show for it. We took direct action on shoestring budgets, cared for and supported those around us, weathered arrests, tried to make sense of the world. We had hyper-radical stances, no compromises, very little strategy, almost no coherence.

Across the table are two other women. The same age as us, from the same part of the world. A lot in common. While we were running around chasing the heat, or maybe our own tails, they've been directing their love and rage into unions, political parties, mass mobilisations, conference rooms, lobbying, structured organisation...

We're all of us hungry for something different. We've been talking for ages and we can joke, and we can dig deep into what we care about: revolution and care, feminism and class, community and organising. Why have we never all four sat and talked like this before? How have we been so close for years and missed each other?

It could be the disconnection in our movements. But I don't believe it's just that our circles were somehow too far apart and we never bumped into each other. Let's be honest. I don't think we would have been comrades if we'd found each other. Instead of complementing, sharing, finding common ground, we might have judged and dismissed each other, competed. Seen difference as division instead of possibility.

I can't speak for anyone else, for what they might have done or the journeys they might have been on. But it seems I had to go halfway across the world just to learn to sit well with people from my home and from my city. It's a bit embarrassing. And honestly, it's still not always easy. But there's a big difference.

Traditional Kurdish dancing at a celebration at Jinwar women's village

11. SURVIVING

Conflict, collective care, critique
Natalia

When it comes down to it, all revolutionary struggles are about survival. About overthrowing the systems which seek to wipe us out and holding each other through the worst bits in the hope that we come out the other end. Trying to stay whole and human as we fight, and ultimately building something beautiful that will survive us after we're gone. The Kurdistan Freedom Movement is no exception.

I wasn't prepared for just how much I would learn about survival during my year in Rojava. How much I would learn about strength, about the line between vulnerability and weakness, about what it means to fight. About how easy it is to lose the things that are so precious to us — care, nurture, survival – to the individualism that our society is steeped in. Much of what I learned came to me through the women of the movement; the seasoned fighters who had been links in the DNA of the movement for decades, the mothers and grandmothers who dreamed of their children's futures while offering shelter to Kurdish guerrillas heading for the mountains, the young women who came of age at a time of revolution and carried freedom comfortably on their shoulders.

Women's organisation within the Kurdistan Freedom Movement is the midwife of the movement's vision. The Kurdistan Workers' Party (PKK) was first founded in the 1970s, and from the beginning small numbers of women made their mark on its development. In the 1990s, the trickle of women joining the movement swelled to a flood and autonomous women's organisational structures were developed. Now, through the Rojava revolution, the principles of the women's movement continue to be implemented on a mass scale. Like many women's movements around the world, the Kurdistan Women's Movement has found itself pulled between the possibility of gaining power within the existing framework, or trying to change how power works in the first place.

One of the many amazing things about spending time in Rojava is being able to meet some of the women who are part of this history. At a political education session for internationalist volunteers, an older woman who had been in the movement for decades came to tell us stories of the early years of the women's movement. She held our attention easily, her hair pulled back in a long braid and shoulders straight in a no frills button up shirt. A traditional Kurdish scarf wrapped around her shoulders was the only splash of colour or ornament she wore, but the laugh lines etched around her eyes and her quick smile stopped her looking severe. She looked like she would be equally at home chairing a meeting as firing a Kalashnikov — and she probably was.

She told us about the push and pull that women who joined the movement experienced. The pull of emulating patriarchal forms of power, which meant that a lot of women in the movement adopted traditionally masculine behaviours and attitudes in an attempt to be empowered. But at the same time, the push to understand a different kind of power, a kind of power that grows through cooperation and lifts other people up rather than using them as steps on the climb to the top. The women in the movement knew that it would be easier to take up patriarchal weapons to play a man's game, but they chose to change the rules of the game instead. So they took up the weapons of radical honesty, commitment and building trust. They honed their patience and built up their perseverance and strength. They laid out the new rules of the game: we believe that people can change; we believe that women have a responsibility to show the alternative to patriarchy; and we know that we will only be successful in this if we work collectively.

***

As I was learning hard lessons through conflicts with my supervisors, I had to ask myself how we can nurture and care for ourselves and each other when the movement asks so much of us. As I learned to offer constructive criticism and not escape into individual coping mechanisms, I was faced with another challenge which made me question truths about how change happens that I had taken for granted.

A few weeks after arriving in Rojava, I got the opportunity to take part in an education 'term' for several weeks at the project where I was based. During the education, we attended hours of seminars and workshops each day, but the real education was everything that happened around them. We were encouraged to push ourselves as much as possible, in every arena. It meant a gruelling schedule and not enough sleep. It meant never having time or space to ourselves and facing constant pressure to strengthen our relationships with each other, way past the point of comfort or personal boundaries. Stripping down personal possessions to the bare minimum. Sitting in plastic chairs while listening to lectures for hours upon hours. Being pushed to analyse and challenge ourselves through the lens of revolutionary values, and always being called upon to serve the needs of the collective, always everyone else before you.

It felt like we were being pushed to our limits – physically, socially, intellectually, emotionally. Yet all the time we knew that this was nothing compared to what revolutionaries in the movement had lived through. Many of the Kurdish organisers' experiences of political education had taken place in prisons as part of the mass prison resistances that span the movement's history. This has led many people to refer to prison as 'Kurdish university' – partly tongue in cheek, and partly recognising how crucial it is to drill deep down into what we believe in, even in the most brutal of circumstances. As internationalists experiencing the discipline and focus required by the movement's approach to political education for the first time, we mulled over theories about why we were encouraged to embrace discomfort, rather than minimising it.

We stashed sweets in cupboards and shared them out during breaks, savouring the moment of rest as much as the sugar rush, and threw around theories about what we were meant to be learning. Whether it was immersion therapy to break us out of deeply entrenched habits of individualism, liberalism and capitalism. Whether by wearing us out we'd lose the ability to hide behind the facades we were used to, and the stuff that we try to hide – our deepest insecurities, patriar-chal attitudes, capitalist thought processes — would come spilling out for every-one to see so that we could collectively understand and unlearn it. Whether it came from a macho attitude towards stoicism, a belief that suffering builds char-acter. Or maybe it was giving us an opportunity to learn and grow strong so that when we needed to draw on emotional and physical reserves in order to survive, we would know how.

In the days before the start of the education term, internationalist volunteers from all over the world who were going to participate assembled at our project. Although we were predominantly white Europeans in their 20s, there were also folks from Latin America, North America and the Middle East. Some interna-tionalists came to Rojava in their late teens, others in their 30s (like myself) or even their 40s and 50s. Our stories of how we got here varied as well – some of us seasoned political organisers, some having no background in activism at all but feeling compelled to go after hearing about Rojava on the news, or YouTube. We were all shaped by the positions of privilege and marginalisation we held, through gender, class, race, sexual orientation, neurodivergence, and the countless other ways we experience life. We came from anarchist, communist, feminist and eco-logical struggles, and sometimes felt like the differences in our political perspec-tives and life experiences outweighed what we had in common. But what we did have in common was that we were all asking questions, and the search for the answers had taken us to Rojava.

I was getting to know people and starting to form friendships, but I soon found myself butting heads again and again with another internationalist volun-teer, a young guy from Germany. My feminist hackles immediately went up. It wasn't just me – all the women in the group found him patronising, disrespect-ful and macho. In such an intense setting, the friction between myself and the male comrade who I found so problematic was impossible to avoid. There was no escaping the reality that we had weeks ahead of us of brutally early mornings, shared meals, hours of seminars and evening workshops together. Whenever I saw him walking towards me – while I was weeding the garden, washing up after dinner, or making cups of tea during breaks in the seminars – half of me would tense up and get ready to verbally spar, and half of me would roll my eyes, exasper-ated because I had to deal with him.

This is how it would have continued – some of us waging battle when we could be bothered, some of us avoiding him, and all of us complaining about him when it got too much – if it weren't for the input and intervention of the supervisors and some of the more experienced women taking part in the education. We were told, sternly but patiently, "don't just complain – organise". We were reminded that patriarchy is not just a question of individual men but a whole system, and as individual women we would never be able to dismantle it. But if we worked together, if we were organised, we held the power to not only take down patriarchy, but build something else in its place. As people who have moved through the world as women, we have knowledge of not just the violences of patriarchy, but of ways of being that run counter to it. We build on the legacy of the generations of women and oppressed genders who have come before us, and find ways of making decisions, holding power and building connections which value life and freedom.

So when an issue of patriarchy arises within a collective or organisation, the women within it have both the right, and the responsibility, to take action to confront it. But what does that look like? I experienced it for the first time early on during my year in Rojava. It meant first of all meeting autonomously as women to develop a collective analysis of how the behaviours of the male comrade showed up in patriarchal and dominating ways. This way, we had a shared understanding of the situation, rooted in our values. If there was a major disagreement within the group of women, we would discuss it until we developed a shared perspective that we were happy to support. Then, two delegates – one of the project supervisors and me – met with him and shared our feedback. He was then given time to reflect on it, and an opportunity to change his behaviour. For some people, this would have been enough to trigger at least an attempted shift in behaviour. Unfortunately, this wasn't the case for our comrade.

We touched base as women again to plan the next step – asking him to prepare and present a session on how we internalise oppressive systems into our mentalities, on how our upbringing and identity shape our behaviours and world views, and how we can transform ourselves in order to fulfil our revolutionary potential as individuals. This was an opportunity for him to support our learning as much as we were trying to support his, so we could reflect on how we all carried aspects of patriarchal mentality within ourselves.

Throughout this process we had to be aware of when our own frustration came out in unhelpful ways. Instead of sarcasm, arguments or cold shouldering, we were encouraged to use the formal process of *tekmil* (critic and self critic) to work through difficult interpersonal dynamics. We were challenged to do so in the spirit of collective reflection and learning, not just using it as a space to vent.

When I felt really frustrated by the comrade we were trying to work with, it was tempting to be vindictive and shaming in my criticisms of him. I had to recognise that using criticism to tear someone down rather than building them up was in itself a form of internalised patriarchy, and find a way to communicate my feedback in kindness rather than in anger, or hold off on sharing it until I could. We were also reminded by the more experienced women in our group that change wouldn't happen overnight, and that we were looking for small changes in behaviour, or increased self awareness and insight, not a radical wholesale transformation. We had to learn to hold patience and understanding in one hand, but insistence on change in the other.

It's important to emphasise that the male comrade in question was never threatening or violent. This is a red line that would have triggered a different course of events. But neither was the problem minimised just because there wasn't an immediate and severe threat to someone's physical or emotional well-being. We were pushed to work through our annoyance and exhaustion, and to resist the temptation to just give him up as a lost cause. It was seen as crucial to support him to unlearn patriarchy, because the revolution needs to take place in our minds as well as in systems of government and economy.

The revolution doesn't expect us to arrive perfect, but it needs us to work on ourselves from when we first arrive until... well, for the rest of our lives. Sound grim? It's not. Because you're not doing it alone, and you're not being punished for getting things wrong. You're expected to fail, and to try, and fail again. Failure isn't seen as a bad thing unless you don't learn from it. And the collective processes for giving feedback and evaluation means that we don't have to wait until we mess up to learn something, we learn from each other and embrace every mistake as an opportunity for everyone to grow. As I slowly took steps to unlearn defensiveness and insecurity, I felt a huge relief that I was constantly being supported to learn, and that my mistakes were seen as opportunities for transformation, rather than judgements on my worthiness as a human.

Although the process of confronting the behaviour of the male comrade pivoted around his behaviour as an individual, the lens was always brought back to the systems that we were trying to dismantle. Fundamentally, through this process we were trying to safeguard the strength and health of our collective. In the complex interplay between the individual and the group, we learned to see each individual as a vital part of the collective, and the collective itself as a vital part of each of us. At first I was really resistant — I was in my 30s and I had grown used to having the first and final word on how I go about my life. I took it for granted that I could separate out my needs and make sure they were met before seeing if I had capacity to meet the needs of others — but in the movement, this isn't only criticised, but deemed impossible.

Years of having unquestioned language around self care and boundaries to fall back on came head to head with how I was being asked to live. At first I was grumpy and even scornful, but as time passed I began to question my assumptions about what makes revolutionary political organising sustainable. I saw how the unconditional care and trust that the movement insists on builds strong collectives which are greater than the sum of their parts. Rather than a transactional and patriarchal way of approaching care in which individual needs are separated, and the needs of some are prioritised over others, we followed a model that was more maternal and nurtured a sense of kinship with each other.

I realised that part of the reason why I was so reluctant to stop seeing my needs as somehow distinct from those of the collective was because fundamentally I didn't trust the collective to meet my needs. This is what Thatcher and generations of those on the side of capitalism and the nation state want us to feel, because if we don't trust the people around us, then we will always fall back on the powers of the state to safeguard our needs. But humans are social creatures: we can't separate the needs of the collective from our needs as individuals, or our needs as individuals from the needs of the collective. This doesn't mean that all individuality is lost and we become anonymous members of the group. Instead, a strong collective produces strong individuals, and our diversity makes a strong and resilient collective. And I saw this taking place in collectives across Rojava. Despite lots of challenges, and by no means perfectly, community groups, workers' cooperatives, educational institutions and military units found ways of working that made it possible for all members, across age, gender, disability, personality and culture to be nurtured by the collective and to nurture the collective in return.

Based on the belief that collective organising makes hard revolutionary work sustainable and effective, women support each other to step up and tackle issues of patriarchy head on, rather than fighting on our own. It takes a lot of effort to hold men accountable, and many of us have had exhausting and unsatisfying experiences of trying to do that on our own, feeling like we were pouring our energy into a black hole that threatened to swallow us whole. I've done it myself when I was younger: at house parties where I debated for hours with rape apologists before retreating to smash glass bottles on the pavement in rage. I did it in a romantic relationship, feeling myself grow smaller and smaller as I took responsibility for changing the man I was dating. So for years I avoided doing it at all, drawing hard boundaries and saying that it wasn't my job to change the men around me. But there's a world of difference between trying to ride into battle against patriarchy on your own and being part of a united, militant women's movement which insists that men pull their socks up. This is why one of the golden rules of the Kurdistan Women's Movement is that a woman is never sent to do anti-patriarchal work on her own. But nor are men allowed to do it on their own.

As part of the ongoing process with the male comrade whose behaviour was so problematic, we identified a general culture of toxic masculinity, and an absence of men who proactively challenged the behaviours of their male comrades. So the women of the project made a proposal that all the men take part in a workshop in which they unpack how their behaviour reflected a patriarchal world view. Because women play such a key role in the revolution, this was the kind of proposal that you couldn't really say no to. So two of us — myself and another woman at the project — facilitated a session for the men in which we shared the perspectives developed in the discussions that we had been having as women. Afterwards we debriefed with the rest of the women, shared what was hard and what felt positive. I went to sleep that night feeling stronger than I had before.

After I arrived back home, I found it hard to translate the beauty and strength that I experienced from this approach to collective organising without sounding like I'd lost touch with tenderness and compassion for people going through a tough time. After all, we are all just trying to cope with the shit that capitalism, the state, white supremacy, patriarchy and other systems of domination are throwing at us. It's scary to have to let go of our coping mechanisms in order to build a totally different way of doing something. But we know it's possible because against all odds, our comrades in revolutionary movements have done it. The women in the Kurdistan Freedom Movement are one example. They've done it while facing every form of violence possible – genocide, torture, rape – and still they insist on the beauty of the struggle. Because the way we struggle, the relationships we build and the care we give to each other, bring to life the world we are trying to build. Through the struggle we taste freedom.

***

Through all of these experiences, I grew to understand the role that women's autonomous organising plays in the Kurdistan Freedom Movement's ideology and mode of organising. It's not to give women a 'safe space' away from patriarchy. It is a tool, a weapon, that we need in order to dismantle patriarchy. In autonomous women's structures women are able to nurture and establish non-patriarchal ways of organising, and use them as a launching pad from which to fight against patriarchy in mixed gender spaces. They are also spaces in which women challenge each other on internalised patriarchy and push each other to grow and learn.

Within the Kurdistan Freedom Movement, the right to autonomous women's spaces – and their recognition as an organisational and ideological authority within the movement – means that the analysis and decisions of women are centred rather than sidelined by the wider movement. This achievement was born out of decades of hard struggle by Kurdish women revolutionaries who organised as women to confront patriarchy within the movement at the same time as they fought as part of the wider movement to resist state fascism and the genocide of their people. Unsurprisingly, they don't mince their words in reminding us that if we want freedom, we need to be prepared to fight for it.

It's absolutely crucial that our political movements actively and explicitly align themselves with, and organise within, communities who experience the sharp end of capitalism, patriarchy, transphobia, white supremacy and state violence. But in order to dismantle those systems of oppression, our political arena cannot be limited to spaces in which everyone is on the same page. We will all need to fight for change on the streets and in toxic board meetings, in our neighbourhoods and in our workplaces. This is why expressing alignment isn't enough on its own, we need active collaboration and significant transfers of power and resources towards those who struggle to survive and resist state capitalism.

Women in the Kurdistan Freedom Movement have the organisational and ideological power — matched with material resources — to self organise in order to challenge patriarchy. We need to also find ways to leverage whatever power and resources we have to create spaces from which marginalised communities can move from a place of strength. This means creating autonomous groups or caucuses for women, queer and trans folks, black and brown people, disabled people, youth, migrants and any other marginalised identity – not just as safe spaces for discussion and mutual support, but as places from which political analysis and action is born and spreads outwards. These places will never be given to us, we have to fight for them the way that women in the Kurdistan Freedom Movement fought for autonomous women's structures and equal leadership. Now, if you ask anybody, they will say that the women's movement is the backbone of the revolution.

Before my time in Rojava, I would have thought that demanding so much of people would create exhausted, bitter individuals. That the only way to survive through struggle was to have limits on how much you were willing to give, and if all else fails, an exit plan. So what made it possible for us, and countless other revolutionaries, to step into a movement that asks so much of you, and be strengthened by it? Once again, the crucial detail is that you're not expected to do any of this alone. The whole collective has to take responsibility for resolving tensions and conflicts within the group, whether the issues are taking place between one individual and the rest of the group, between two individuals, or across everyone. All of these dynamics affect the whole group, so we are all responsible for building the strongest collectives that we can. This doesn't just mean the group of people we work or live with on a day to day basis, although that's often where it makes sense to start. It's also a responsibility that extends outwards; we are held by, and hold, the whole movement, and the society that we are a part of.

A few months after arriving in Rojava, I wrote this in my notebook:

I'm better at sharing, I'm better at being uncomfortable, I'm better at taking a moment to do something for someone else. And I feel held by a net of these practical solidarities – I know that if I am hungry I will be fed, if I am lost someone will get me to where I need to be, if I am cold someone will give me a jacket or share a blanket. I know that people do hundreds of things each day that make my life more comfortable, and I do those things for them in return. From filling the water tanks at dawn to making food, to security shifts at night to making cups of tea to pass around every time there is a break, to the whole movement funding our existence here, to the people who have died to make this area safe from ISIS, to build defences against Turkish invasion. And they did it for their families, their neighbours, and for people they have never met. They did it for us. People we meet make sure we are safe, even if they have no idea what we are doing here.

Looking back, I see this as a bit of a turning point for me in moving towards a culture of collective care. I was realising that the alternative to interpretations of self care which prioritise the individual is not a macho approach that rejects care, but an approach in which we all nurture each other. That when all of us put each other before ourselves, we are all taken care of, we hold each other up. Many movements outside of Kurdistan, from disability justice to abolitionist to feminist movements, also refuse to draw a line between care and struggle, the individual and the collective. This is what our social movements need to be seeking to build – not more opportunities and permission for opting out, but more commitment to seeing each other through thick and thin, and more trust in each other.

Describing this to lots of people back home after returning from Rojava, I was regularly met with mutterings of 'sounds like a recipe for burnout". But the proof is in the pudding. Burnout isn't endemic in the Kurdistan Freedom Movement the way people seem to assume it must be. In our movements at home, it sometimes feels like burnout is seen as an inevitability. In the Kurdistan Freedom Movement, people do get exhausted, people do wear themselves out, but the strength of the collective catches them and holds on.

Too often, we focus too much on what is taking our energy away from us, rather than what gives us energy — whether that's education, dancing, meeting new people — and finding a way to weave that into the struggle. What would our movements look like if we didn't draw hard boundaries between our political work and the spaces where we regenerate, celebrate and connect? Resting and partying are part of our political work, because without joy, healing, and reflection, revolution isn't possible. When we look at it that way, we realise that sometimes rather than giving less, we need to give more. That although it feels like inevitably the more you give the less you have, when there is a collective commitment to each other and the world you are fighting for, you find yourself holding more than you ever could have held onto on your own.

Youth and children organise as part of the revolutionary process

12. RESHAPING

Unlearning the system, learning to be us
Jenni

I never would have said I was an individualist. Of course I thought about my own survival, getting my life the way I wanted it, the friends I wanted around me, and how I took care of or expressed myself. Who doesn't? But I wasn't *selfish*. I shared what I had, I took care of other people, I was capable of putting aside my own needs for another person's.

In North and East Syria I found out that individualism doesn't just mean selfishness. It's considered anti-social to make a cup of tea just for yourself instead of a pot for everyone, but not only because other people might want tea. Rather, because we should see ourselves as a group, think in collective terms, and realise that coming together is just as important as meeting our personal needs. It's not that we can't think about ourselves, but we shouldn't be able to disconnect *me* from *us*.

In some ways this was an affirmation to me, soothing a part of my soul that had been aching for a long time and not known why. But in others, it was one of the hardest things. I'm still not there. Because a really deep individualism has been with me my whole life: from my upbringing in a nuclear family cut from community, to the way I went out into the world, earning money to get by and enjoy life, all the way to deciding I wanted to go to Rojava and be a part of the revolution.

The ability to know yourself, take personal responsibility and a step forward, is essential to being a whole human, let alone a revolutionary. But the priorities we base action on, who we think we are, and where we are when push comes to shove, reveal a lot about how we see ourselves. There is something that lies at the base of that lack of trust in people, of putting our trust first and foremost in the state. It wasn't always common sense.

When international volunteers come into contact with the Kurdistan Freedom Movement we are suddenly confronted with criticisms, jokes, debates, and analysis that all revolve around 'liberalism', and within that 'individualism'. We realise that both are pretty much dirty words – and also that in Kurdistan they don't mean what we thought they did. It becomes a running joke long before we really understand it, as we provoke repeated exasperated tuts, patient explanations and affectionate head shaking.

Organisers with the Kurdistan Freedom Movement are determined to dig deep into what liberalism really means, and share those discussions with us. They are so determined that despite being at war on multiple fronts, they give a huge amount of energy to push our boundaries and challenge our assumptions. In rows of school desks, sweating in broken air conditioning, on too little sleep and tightly rationed coffee, we pinched our legs to stay awake through the second hour in an afternoon of lectures on 19th century philosophers. We tried hard to be respectful and to engage in the discussions but at first, we were all thinking, *'what does this have to do with us, though?'* Well, unfortunately, quite a lot. Liberal philosophers, most of whom were doing pretty well out of the emerging new capitalist world order, promoted a lot of the things that we grew up thinking weren't just true, but *obvious*. Common sense.

A lot of 'common sense' is actually an ideology. Liberalism doesn't mean a position of rational neutrality, as it has tried to portray itself (and what I'm talking about here also doesn't have anything to do with left-of-centre voting, reading the Guardian, recycling, or being pro gay marriage). When we look for liberal ideology, it is everywhere, wedged deeply into our most personal relationships, what we think freedom is, or how we understand intelligence and rationality.

The ideal liberal character is a rational individual. It comes naturally to them to take care of themselves first of all. They have the right to act and speak freely. They stand apart from the world, and can assess it objectively. Of course, this cuts off connection with the rest of the world, and often from half of ourselves. Liberalism is capitalism's secret, silent weapon. It goes deep, deep inside; especially for some of us.

For years I worked with animals and the whole time I could see that often the drive to make a profit meant they weren't cared for like they should be. Not only was I capable of going through with my work anyway, of putting my heart on ice until I got home, the world encouraged me to do so. Work is work. Compartmentalise. Separate. Just do your job. Yes, I needed the money to live. But how far does that take you? There's no end to the horrors that this attitude can make normal people a part of, from prisons to battery farms to government administration. I'm not blaming individual people, I'm saying that without the double think liberalism allows for, the system couldn't function. That we have to be conscious of the system inside, and how it connects with the one on the outside.

It wasn't like work was exactly fair on the humans either. I was often working for less than minimum wage, or 'self employed' in a way that basically meant I got no paid holidays and my bosses had less responsibility. Not only did I not find ways to organise against this, I often welcomed things that seemed to give me more freedom or flexibility, or work out for me personally if I put in the extra time. I didn't always think about what that did for people like me as a class or a collective. This chipping away at class or collective power in the name of individual freedoms happens across the board, on any line of oppression you can draw. Liberalism provides the chisel.

When I went home, kicked off my boots and showered, I was a different person. This was the part where I could be who I was, talk about what I believed in. My partner and I lived together just the two of us, and no one else really had the right to comment on what went on behind that door. That's just common sense. As it happened we were happy. We were very lucky to live near a lot of friends: a crew of working- and middle class young folk, dotted about in romantic or flatmate couples. We were mostly just concerned with getting by and being ok. We started calling our block of council flats 'the warren' because someone joked there were so many little burrows that connected together. It didn't really matter whose living room we were sitting in smoking weed at the end of a day.

But there were many lines we didn't cross. We always shared beer, but our survival methods and life paths (be that study, work, or benefits) connected us to the state or capitalism, not each other. Even unofficial or criminalised forms of work were a separate, private matter. We didn't really comment on someone else's business even when the shouting came down through the floor. Not even when someone moved in with a partner smiling and full of life, and left grey and drawn headed for the local mental hospital. Not when a friend withdrew and self destructed, or someone started to show signs of losing their grip on reality. We cared. Deeply. We talked in hushed, select moments. We wanted to reach out. But none of us really knew how, and if someone tried, often they were pushed away. Private life was private. Personal choice was personal choice- even if it was tearing your friend apart in front of your eyes. Politics, if we thought about it, was something separate. So separate that I felt like I had to leave 'the warren' and seek it on the horizon. I couldn't see that the battlefield with capitalism, liberalism and the state was there within our lives: in everything from the freezing mornings squeezing my cold hands together in my gloves at the start of the work day, to the battered old sofas where the evenings passed us by.

For better or worse, like it or not, if you spend time in the movement as an internationalist volunteer in North and East Syria you are pretty much never alone. You eat, sleep, work, learn, grow, rest, exercise, train, get sick, succeed and fail in a group, connected to those around you. It can be really hard to find out that not only is there almost no privacy or private space, but it's even frowned upon to want it. I found it hardest when I realised I couldn't hide my faults. There was no space to take myself away when I wasn't my best self, or to choose what sides of me people saw. But as unsettling and humbling as the process is, I found out that it's only when people see all of you that you can get perspectives to help you really change things. By living so close to everyone and taking on the group's needs and problems I was also forced to dig deep into my strengths and discover I could do and be more than I realised.

Of course almost no one can live up to these principles all the time, but even just trying really teaches you things about yourself. One thing we learnt is how strongly attached we are to a liberal model of each of us as an island, a unit, and how hard it can be to break that. We get angry about our own 'rights': to independence, to withdraw commitment at any time, to always understand everything that's going on and be in control. Any infringement on these feels like authoritarianism. I'd experienced a lot of attempts at collective living before I left for Kurdistan. I often felt blocks and obstacles that I couldn't quite explain. With some distance, I started to feel like we couldn't begin to live communally until we understood what that meant. We had been confusing collective care for getting all our individual needs constantly met; collective life for lots of individual people in one place.

Rojava and the Kurdistan Freedom Movement are full of diverse, colourful, complex, weird and wonderful individuals. But people are not understood as a separate bubble of personhood that stands in proximity to others, like balls in a ball-pit. While I was in North and East Syria I realised I used to see a group or collective as a coming together of individuals. Now I think that a healthy group *produces* individuals. That's where we grow. It's not about sameness, or enforcing strict codes. Differing, thinking, arguing, diverse individuals are the sign of a healthy community. But the collective they come from needs to be bound together by something. Maybe something stronger than 'you do you, and I'll do me' because then we can never truly rely on each other. If we start with isolated individuals that might be all we can get to.

I was always proud of being independent and self reliant. I 'stood on my own two feet'. But what does that actually mean in the world we live in? It means I gave all my effort to work that ultimately was built on exploitation. It meant I'd sooner ask the state for support for education or housing than a community. This independent figure I was so proud of being was no such thing. She was a poster child for liberalism, so it's no coincidence that she needed the state.

From the Middle East to islands washed by the North Sea, wherever you are, when you prioritise *we* over *me*, you might lose having every individual need met all the time. But you gain real collective care. You might lose total independence but you gain trust and commitment. You might lose some days to things you'd rather not. But you gain the long term future and a widespread network. You might lose a private life delineated by boundaries, but you will also lose loneliness, and gain strength you never knew you had. You gain a *we,* and all of the things that are only possible if we do them together. Like resistance.

Of course, many communities exist everywhere that don't accept these liberal standards and don't operate on them. I know of plenty where I'm from and I've been part of a few. Life has insistently burst individual bubbles and resisted liberal values. Those values have taken hold most among the middle class, who are also the most invested in the state and capital. Groups and communities the system stamps on every day have little choice but to resist just by existing, and existing in ways that defy liberalism's attacks. But middle class values have power, and it can be hard to imagine a different way of being when the liberalism shapes not just our day to day lives, but our imagination.

Some of us have been trying to make ourselves and others feel good, somehow *be ok,* in a world that has isolated us and stripped us of our values and connections. It simply isn't working. We are learning this the hardest way, by watching increasing numbers of friends decide they don't want to live at all if this is the only way to live.

The pandemic and the response to it has exposed the ugliness of this way of living to the cold light of day. Some people started to ask themselves if this was really where and how they wanted to live once they were forced to stay at home. Started to question their priorities. The pandemic has also exposed the nonsense of the idea that what we do *doesn't affect each other.* Whether you are scared of contracting or spreading the virus, or scared of the accompanying authoritarian crackdown, you are locked in a web with the people around you. Government responses, far from recognising this, have capitalised on the moment to drive even bigger wedges among and between communities, opening the door to division and repression. It's suited the state, grabbing this opportunity to refine systems of control, just fine that we've turned on each other and see each other as a danger or threat. But the seeds for all that were sown long ago.

During lockdown, people with gardens shamed those who crowded into parks to soak up the summer sun, and in response to this local councils locked the gates to public green spaces. Neighbours called the police on each other, and within some mutual aid groups judgements were passed about whether or not someone was deserving of help.

Sometimes we even take on the role of the state and police each other from a place of mistrust. The state wanted us to do this in the pandemic – to blame young people, migrants, or 'feckless party-goers' for the devastation of the pandemic, rather than a society plagued by inequality and a healthcare system that has been starved of funds for over a decade.

In the moments where we feel scared or out of control we aren't always our best selves, but these reflexes expose what happens to a society where liberalism has run its course. When our basic sense of self is as an individual, and the one thing we can always rely on being there (whether it's actually helping or not) is the state, we'll continue to turn to it in a crunch point.

Because we've internalised the idea that not 'standing on our own two feet' is shameful, ways of living which don't rely on state power – and the individualism that it is premised on – are marginalised. We undermine them economically and materially, and look down on them socially. We mock children who stay with or near their parents as adults as codependent or underdeveloped. There's no recognition of structures outside the nuclear family. This means that the close extended family, communalism or the local networks of many poor, working class or migrant communities are invisibilised and get no support. We don't listen to these communities about their needs, and we see many of their strengths as problems to be fixed.

Individuals are often able to access at least some support in our system, as liberal democracies so proudly point out. But this support is dependant on the individual accepting the liberal values of the dominant class, complying with the state and continuing to think along individualistic lines — thinking first and foremost of themselves, chipping away at communities.

It's difficult to know how to respond to the ways that the state weakens our ability to live without it. It's self-defeating to the point of comical to blame individual people for how we move within this maze of individualism. I'm not proposing trying to check out of the system. In fact, presenting that as a solution is one of liberalism's greatest tricks. There is no checking out. There's only collective resistance. If we seriously want to be a part of that, we have to look at what's going on inside, question some of our assumptions, and really dig deep into the network of human relationships that the system dictates. We cannot dismiss these questions as small, nor can we solve them just by saying that we don't want to live like that.

The Kurdistan Freedom Movement teaches us to always put ourselves in service of something bigger, not to seek affirmation and applause for ourselves. Revolutionary work is taken deadly seriously, but that isn't the same as personal arrogance. Back home, in the circles I was in anyway, we often didn't see activism we were doing as important, didn't take it fully seriously. But we still somehow managed to carry weighty individual egos, take ourselves as individuals far *too* seriously. We can (and many people do), flip this around: take ourselves just a bit less seriously, but give what we are a part of the respect and dignity it deserves.

There's plenty of space for playfulness, for different personalities, for personal faults and failings, and for room to grow. There's no demand in the movement that you prove your worth by being super skilled at everything. Instead, there's almost no higher value than *hevaltî*, meaning 'comradeship' but also carrying the weight of 'friendship' in the deepest sense, and understood as a model of how love and connection can look beyond patriarchy and capitalism.

Back in 'the warren' we wanted to be around people because we liked each other better than we liked others. We wandered around assessing people as consumable goods, until we found the ones that suited our tastes the most and unsettled or challenged us the least. Then we collected our favourites like Pokemon and affirmed each other. It's not that we didn't love each other deeply. But that's how we showed love, and we thought love meant choosing the right people and then things would be easy. When things got hard, or we fell out, sometimes people just left. Sometimes we didn't even know where they'd gone.

In Kurdistan, when we were asked to live and embody the values of *hevaltî* – *revolutionary friendship* — we were expected to love, respect, and try to understand whoever was around us. When people behave in ways we think are wrong, we face that and challenge it.

In this model of relationships, no one should be excluded. Everyone should be listened to. We are trying to create a group, not a series of one on one relationships that just happen to align with each other. It means we take values like mutual aid, support, and communal life seriously. Only offering these things to certain people takes all the meaning out of them. And only feeling like we deserve them if we can be liked by the right people isn't a nice feeling.

It was only when I was pushed to try and live more like this that I realised how much I had always seen people as consumer choices, options I could take or leave. On some level, even if I didn't articulate it, I'd felt that if I didn't like or get along with someone, in some way they were less deserving of respect or inclusion. I realised how many spaces I've seen fall apart due to us not being able to get along with each other- houses, community spaces, political organising. I now understand why the movement puts such an emphasis on this. When we are together and strong we can achieve anything. When we tear ourselves apart, it doesn't matter what material or technical advantages we have. The system doesn't even have to bother to attack us.

Comrades from the movement tell us that when we struggle to get along with someone, that's exactly the relationship we should be putting energy into. I could parrot this back to them after just a few months, congratulating myself on having totally got the idea. But when a new friend arrived in our academy and her approach grated on me like nails down a blackboard, a voice in my head insisted "yeah, but not *that person*, right..?"

I found her rude and abrasive and I felt like she didn't take politics and the movement seriously. Part of me just wanted her to leave. It would just be better if she left. She didn't seem interested in any of the work we were doing or willing to contribute anyway. I caught myself starting to slip snide comments or frustrated glances in when she came up in conversation. Whether consciously or not, I was looking for people to join me in agreeing that she wasn't really one of *us*, that we didn't want her around.

In the culture I grew up in I found plenty of that. Often social circles define themselves by who they dislike or exclude. I wouldn't even have been conscious of it happening. Instead I only realised I wanted that option of exclusion because it hit a brick wall, and was echoed back at me. What was echoed wasn't pretty.

So I took a deep breath and challenged myself to really move towards the friend. Not performatively, but sincerely. I took more time to spend with her, I asked her more about herself. I bothered to speak up and critique her in tekmil, honestly but not unkindly. I listened when she did the same for me. I learnt about myself, and we started to find our common ground.

Of course we will clash and struggle with some people. Comradeship has to go hand in hand with critique and a healthy way to treat conflict. You won't be best pals with everyone. But we come out of it, if not all sunshine and rainbows, then stronger and safer as a crew. The other option is ripping ourselves apart.

In the case of this friend, we didn't just learn to get along with trust and respect, as is often the case, and the expected baseline. We actually stumbled into an unexpectedly close friendship, a loving and special dynamic, at times a double act. Which threw it all into question in another light: the movement also warns us to be careful of relationships that are too 'exclusive'. That prioritise one comrade above the others. Back home, that was what I looked for in friendship: since the anxiety of teenage girlhood and the eternal question of who was your 'best friend', the terror of not having one, or enough friends in general has lingered in my subconscious. The need for affirmation by being liked, but not just liked: liked *more than others*.

I'm not saying we won't or even shouldn't have special, extra close relationships. During my time in Rojava, I came to see that everyone in the movement has friends who they feel particularly connected to. But rather than only put energy into those connections and let the rest go, we could celebrate them as beautiful things, but acknowledge they will take care of themselves naturally and that more conscious effort might need to go elsewhere. If we have a base level of respect, trust, openness and honesty that goes across the board, then extra emotional intimacy isn't excluding or damaging. It's not wrong to have special relationships – but what do those relationships do to a group? Can we use them to lift other people up, and bring them in? Or are they shutting people out, or dividing a group?

As part of the women's movement, we are encouraged to work especially on this solidarity between us. Patriarchy is based on conflict between women and other oppressed genders just as much as it is on male dominance. Liberalism is capitalism's modern way of maintaining that conflict. It's what makes us jealous, competitive, insecure, mistrusting. It's what makes it possible for us to mainly see difference between us and leave each other to the clutches of bosses or institutions instead of building solidarity.

In Rojava, we were pushed to work through deep wells of these emotions and pain that we'd all brought with us from our whole lives. It wasn't easy, and it's a constant process. But we won't get anywhere if we don't work on it.

This is a fight that happens in the smallest of moments, in the biggest of ways. We can't quantify or prove how we fight it, it has to be felt. It's about treating love and comradeship as things that multiply when they are spread, not a scarce resource we have to fight over. It's about not holding back our material resources either, not always having the escape pods ready, but entering into a sharing that redistributes and brings us more eye to eye. Then we start to see the image that's so big we don't notice it.

THE NIGHT THE CALIPHATE FELL

Natalia — March 2019

The night the Islamic State caliphate fell, the clouds broke open and pounded endless rain onto the streets and houses of Derik.

The world went opaque, a solid sheet of rain filling the spaces between buildings and cars, the river breaking its banks and pouring onto the roads. Like a biblical flood, washing the world clean of the horrors humanity had created.

The morning dawned bleary eyed and tired, a hazy sun rising over tens of thousands emerging weary and hungry from tunnels beneath the roads where the caliphate made its last stand. One battle won, but the sun sets on camps straining from the thousands who have traded one hell for another.

As the shadows shift, the battle-worn people of Kurdistan scrape together food to feed enemy fighters, their wives and their children. They bring medicine, and know it is not enough to heal the hurt.

The struggle shifts from front line to breadline, keeping those who started the war alive, the latest in a long line of enemies who set their sights on genocide.

The sun spears the clouds as we meet to dance, music pounding from the sound system, fighters joining hands with youth, with traffic conductors, with women in high heels and high fashion.

There's a muted tone to the celebration, something that holds struggle, pain and celebration tight in its arms at the same time. Their colours run together and paint the scene in new subtle tones.

I swallow my awkwardness and join the dance, letting myself be carried by the moment. When I look back at this day, I want to remember that I was dancing, that I was witnessing history being made, that I was part of it and I knew that the future is ours for the making.

The rain returned with the dusk and turned dust to mud, found its way into houses through cracks in the walls, ripped laundry from the lines and drummed relentlessly on windows roofs.

Pulling our jackets tight around us we rounded our shoulders, pushed homewards through the storm.

Do not forget that the way is long and hard, the rain said.

Do not forget that you have each other -

Do not forget where you are going -

Do not forget that there are seeds underground, and when the sky clears they will open, and reach towards the sun.

Residents of Jinwar Women's Village process the harvest together

13. SEEDS

Getting our hands dirty
Natalia

The summer I was in Rojava was the year the whole world caught on fire. The Amazon rainforest burned, bushfires blazed across Australia, flames devoured California once again, and even parts of the Arctic Circle dried out and joined the conflagrations. In North and East Syria, countless fields of wheat smouldered, thick snakes of fire glowing orange against the smoke-laced darkness. Others burned more extravagantly, lashing out, plumes of smoke forming a grey wall reaching for the sky as the flames advanced like a battlefront towards us. The growling racket of harvest machinery rumbled around the clock, fluorescent lights tracking back and forth across the fields in the dead of night in a desperate bid to get the wheat harvest in before it burned.

The pillars of the Rojava revolution, as we so often hear, are grass-roots democracy, women's freedom... and ecology. I was drawn to the women's revolution as much as Jenni was, but I also had a background in environmental activism and food growing and I wanted to get my hands in the soil and see the green side of the revolution. I'm not sure what I thought it would look like, but it was definitely not what I expected. I think back to the wet February I arrived in Rojava, trying to get a soggy pile of cardboard, plastic and tin cans to burn with the help of generous splashes of low-quality diesel. I had just arrived and was still getting used to how everything worked, including how we processed the rubbish.

Face to face with the thick smoke and chemical flames of the smouldering trash pile, I had to reckon with my convictions about how we get the world out of the ecological disaster it's in. Before arriving, I hadn't really thought about what kind of waste disposal systems there would be in Rojava, but I can't say that diesel and a lighter was what I expected to see in a revolution that saw ecology as one of its three core pillars. But it was this moment, watching black bin bags full of plastic bottles, tin cans and polystyrene send clouds of greasy smoke and toxic fumes into the air, that opened a new understanding for me about what it means to change everything.

As a long time activist and political organiser, I had come to Rojava hoping to learn from the political culture, ideology and structures of the ongoing revolution. As someone who had worked in gardening and food growing for the past seven years, I was specifically joining in the ecological work of the movement and hoped to make myself useful in some way. As with most things in Rojava, it wasn't quite what I expected. Although we were planting trees, planning a sustainable water recycling system, and building compost bins, we were also burning through countless litres of low quality diesel for heating, driving, and — of course — trash burning. On every road, ancient trucks spouted clouds of exhaust from their engines, and mountains of litter accumulated along roads as the rubbish collection system struggled to keep up. What's the difference between an ambitious ecological programme wrestling with and overcoming challenges, and simply one that's falling short in the face of too many obstacles?

Looking back, I can see that I arrived with a set of assumptions about what ecological action should look like that were the result of the capitalist and individualistic society we have in Western Europe. The reality in Rojava is shaped not only by being in the Middle East, but by coming out of an ideology that puts ecology at the centre of its world-view alongside radical democracy and women's liberation. While back home I'd got used to seeing the environment as an issue that we take action on, in the Kurdistan Freedom Movement it's seen as the starting point which we move from, the very framework which shapes our actions.

Democratic confederalism is the movement's political model, replacing the state and embracing devolved power, assemblies and cooperative, worker-controlled economies. This is what's built on the foundations of women's liberation, democracy and ecology. When the whole system – political, economic, cultural — is geared towards developing an ecological society, then you don't fixate on whether each bit of work ticks all the boxes in terms of sustainability. Instead, its relationship to the other aspects of the movement — building an economy that meet the needs of communities and the planet, nurturing and defending life, equipping towns, villages and cities with the democratic autonomy to build a different kind of world — are just as important as what the work itself accomplishes. It leaves a lot more space for getting things wrong and learning how to do it better, for experimentation and exploration, and always the emphasis is on the collective progress towards an ecological society, rather than individual progress. A solution that only a privileged few can manage to live up to is no solution at all, and the movement in North and East Syria doesn't even bother discussing them, whereas in some parts of the world we've become fixated on them.

This approach is crucial in the context of North and East Syria, where there are countless obstacles in the way of developing ecological sustainability. We are faced with the reality of a region where fossil fuels are locally abundant and cheap, an economic embargo is strangling the economy of the region, and scarce resources are directed to support the fight against ISIS and defend against the attacks and occupation by the Turkish state. This situation didn't come about by accident: for decades the authoritarian Assad regime treated the fertile and oil rich region of North and East Syria as a source of raw materials. Cash-crop monoculture was enforced, so rather than meeting its own needs, the people of Rojava had to grow wheat, cotton and barley through intensive agricultural practices that depleted the soil and locked them into dependency on imports. The flow of crucial waterways for irrigation is being pinched off by the Turkish government's dam-building projects across the border, and vital infrastructure has been bombed throughout years of conflict. The ecological struggle is bound up in the political power struggles that criss-cross the geography and history of the region, weaving a net that constricts the possibilities and pathways of change.

It can be tempting to feel hopeless in the face of all of this. And yet, all over Rojava, people are planting trees. Each municipality, district and region has an Ecological Committee that aims to set up ecological projects, and dozens of environmental cooperatives (food production, tree nurseries, greenhouses) have been supported by the department of the self-governance system that oversees economy.

As I continued to mull over the ecological possibilities that emerge through burning plastic, a group of us visited a tree nursery located on the outskirts of Derik city. The tree nursery – which was run as a cooperative made up of a couple of Kurdish workers and an Arabic family – was located on land that had belonged to the brutal Assad regime before the revolution expelled the regime from most of Rojava. As always, the question of land and who owns it is a thread woven through liberation and environmental struggles around the world and throughout history.

At the tree nursery, just like everywhere else, we first sat down to drink tea. The strong brew was made directly in the electric kettle and brought to us by one of the kids of the family who works there. As we sat in battered plastic chairs, one of the founders of the cooperative chatted to us about their work and their lives, occasionally getting up to greet and help folk who who came to pick up saplings potted in emptied vegetable oil canisters, or ask for planting advice.

He openly shared some of the challenges they faced in their work, like the prejudice some Kurds hold against Arabic people, meaning that they can be reluctant to approach the Arabic workers of the cooperative for help. He acknowledged that this prejudice came in part from decades of anti-Kurdish policies and violence enacted by the Arab-nationalist regime based in Damascus, but he emphasised the need for education in order to build understanding and cooperation. It was clear to see that the existence of the tree nursery in itself was working towards this aim through building up a collective economy run by Kurdish and Arabic communities together.

After tea and conversation, we got down to business. The workers in the cooperative had generously invited us to take cuttings from their olive tree orchard so we could plant them in our tree nursery. We wandered through the muddy orchard with our clippers, taking armloads of cuttings from trees that had themselves been rooted from cuttings of trees from Afrin before the region was invaded and occupied by Turkish forces in 2018.

When our bags were crammed to capacity with tree cuttings, we exchanged goodbyes and walked back to the road to hitch-hike home, easily picking up a lift in the back of a truck heading in the right direction. As the driver dropped us off, he asked us what we were up to – a handful of foreigners with bags full of olive branches. We explained to him that we had come from different countries to join the work of the revolution in nurturing seedlings and planting trees, restoring the land and rebuilding our stewardship of the natural world. We told him that the branches we held were from trees that had grown from cuttings of Afrin olive groves, and how we planned to root them in our soil, every tree a promise to one day liberate Afrin.

He smiled, and told us that he understood – he himself was from Afrin and had fled the region when it was attacked. His brother, who had chosen to stay, had been killed by one of the Turkish backed militias now controlling the territory, punishment for being unable to pay a demanded bribe. Since the invasion his community had scattered and life had become much harder. Before we said goodbye we took photos together on the side of the road, arms full of olive cuttings that told a story of a revolution that has the patience to plant trees.

***

The tree nursery we visited is only one of many examples of ecological projects working to rebuild North and East Syria on a foundation of revolutionary values. The poor condition of the rubbish collection system has been noticed and worked on: a comprehensive, state of the art rubbish collection and recycling system has been planned and costed, but has stalled due to shortages in funds and materials. In the meantime, more and more places are being linked up to a garbage collection system to reduce littering and the need for each household to burn its trash. A cheap, accessible public bus system was launched in Qamişlo city, and solar panels are starting to adorn the rooftops of traditional clay buildings in villages. On their own any of these initiatives would be an insignificant droplet, but linked together they can change the tide.

These projects, spread across an area the size of the south of England, are connected and coordinated by a well organised social movement, which provides financial support and oversight. The democratic structures that have been set up by the revolution incorporate cooperatives and ecological projects in the committees and councils that govern the territory.

But they are also linked by something less tangible: a set of collectively held visions and values that provide an unshakeable set of roots so that the work can continue despite the immense challenges it faces. I was used to environmental campaigns which tend to wobble and collapse in the face of far smaller challenges. In my years organising within ecological movements in England, I noticed a tendency to either fall into dogmatic purism or neoliberal reformism. I imagined what would happen if someone had started burning the trash with diesel at an environmental protest camp: we would have ripped each other to shreds within an hour!

From what I saw in Rojava, it seemed that a big part of what gives the revolution the strength to overcome obstacles and face its shortcomings, while maintaining integrity and hope, was a huge amount of clarity about what it stands for. This clarity goes far deeper than superficial goals like 'renewable energy' or even 'a system of governance in which minorities are represented'. It's nothing more or less than a total paradigm shift. The only effective way to dismantle the capitalist system, which is based on the domination of human over human, and the domination of human over the natural world, is to nurture an alternative paradigm – one based on an ecological economy, gender liberation, self-determination and freedom. Which means that there's no way to 'get it right' within a particular project or area of work, they all depend on each other and we need to learn to work through the imperfections as we move towards deep systemic change.

***

As revolutionaries from the movement explain, our response to state capitalism needs to be rooted in something outside of state capitalism, otherwise we will never be able to develop the tools we need to overturn the paradigm (as Audre Lorde *put it, 'the master's tools will never dismantle the master's house'*). This is why the Kurdistan Freedom Movement looks as far back as the Neolithic Revolution thousands of years ago for the solutions to the political, economic and ecological crises we are faced with, because anything more recent can't help but take capitalism, class society and the state as the foundation. This doesn't mean that the movement is primitivist: technology is seen as a powerful tool and

192

plays a crucial role in the building of a new world. It's not pre-capitalist lifestyles that the movement is trying to return to, it's pre-capitalist values.

I slowly digest all of these ideas as I tend vegetable gardens, water the tree nursery and burn the trash. My brain isn't used to thinking in such long time spans, but the land here remembers the time before. I imagine that with each seed we sow and each tree we plant, the earth is welcoming us home. And in this fundamental shift in how we relate to nature – seeing ourselves as part of it, rather than something that we either exploit for profit, or have to protect from ourselves – we will unlock our ability to change the system, and not just how it's dressed up. This means seeing ecology as not just an issue on which we take action, but as our political philosophy. Capitalism breaks up our communities and disconnects us from our homes and our history. Fighting back against this means seeing humans not as a collection of independent individuals, but as an interdependent web, an ecology of our families, our communities, our landscape and our ancestors.

In the Kurdistan Freedom Movement, an ecological approach means that organising on the collective, rather than individual, level is non-negotiable. Ecological thinking means that individual freedom cannot exist without collective liberation, that all of our struggles are linked. This is why the Kurdistan Freedom Movement has been actively internationalist for decades. The constant presence of internationalists has created a fertile space as ideas and experiences cross pollinate. But it's always clear that those of us from the West — particularly Northern Europe and America — are here to unlearn the individualism that forms the bedrock of capitalist world-view.

Like lots of internationalists who joined the revolution, I was confronted with how deeply individualism is rooted in our mindsets. How uncomfortable I was with focusing on what the movement and my collective needed over what I personally wanted to do. I struggled to see how the needs of the collective were actually my needs, as if I could opt out and default to being an individual separate from the collective. I was confronted with how much I equated personal choice with freedom, and personal status with respect and worth. I was able to see how perceiving ourselves as separate from each other is part of seeing ourselves as separate from nature.

Coming to terms – in a lived, emotional way – with the reality that we are nothing without each other, and without the earth we live on, was a homecoming of sorts for me. It was as if the thousands of connections that make me who I am had suddenly lit up, and I could see and feel how I was part of something so much bigger than myself.

By no means is this holistic approach unique to Rojava. Those who work the land all around the world live the reality of interdependence from the moment our sweat mingles with the soil. The immense power of the global peasants' movement is channelled through La Via Campesina, whose 200 million members urge us to look at the connections between land, gender, freedom, health and justice. Indigenous communities around the world have lived this knowledge for generations, and are often at the forefront of defending the land and more-than-human world from extraction and mega-projects. Tucked away in the nooks and crannies of deeply capitalist societies we see projects like Phat Beets in Oakland and Granville Community Kitchen in London who weave the threads between community, food, culture and power.

Only through basing our struggle on this philosophy of interconnectedness — with nature, with each other, with a wider movement for social change — can we build up our own paradigm and bring to life our response to the interconnected systems of capitalism-patriarchy-white supremacy-imperialism. This is the first step to getting serious, to having a roadmap that guides our strategy, and a vision that feeds our hearts. Rather than falling into a reactionary politics of panic and protest, we can set the terms of the struggle ourselves. A paradigm shift means that we are no longer just fighting against fossil fuel extraction and airport runways and carbon trading, we are fighting for and building up an alternative system.

Of course it's crucial to continue mobilising against the destructive actions of government and corporations, and to see these actions as a form of collective self defence. It can also be important to engage in electoral and legislative campaigns to challenge injustice. But we need to integrate these actions into the web of resistances and alternatives that we are part of. This is not the same as simply acknowledging that of course all issues are connected, as so many of our movements already do. It's about building analysis, alliances and organisation that mount a coordinated resistance. It's about doing the long, hard work of political education and coalition building so that we can develop a shared idea of what we're fighting for together, rather than just uniting briefly over an action or flashpoint, and then dispersing after the fight whether we win or lose.

There's no use pretending that it's not a huge and daunting task, but speaking for myself, I have found a lot more hope in taking incremental steps towards changing everything than huge leaps towards changing nothing. What steps can we take in developing this paradigm shift? We can change the way we talk about nature – emphasising our connection with it, and our reliance on it for energy, food, medicine, beauty, spirituality. We can lift up city gardens and farms, because they rebuild our connection with nature and community in our highly urbanised and individualised world. Most importantly, we must develop collective strategies of struggle and forge a common path together, not letting ourselves get sidetracked and stalled by the clever marketing ploys and co-optation of capitalism.

***

In 2018, under the hot Syrian sun, dozens of women put their hands and feet into the red clay soil and made bricks to build houses. Using natural building techniques older than living memory, they sweated and smiled and laid the first bricks of the autonomous women's village and called it *Jinwar — the place of the women*. As the houses were built, women and their children moved in and set themselves to the work of making the village home. Both economy and ecology have the same root word – from the Greek *oikos*, meaning house or home. So from this understanding that the natural world is our home, and that economy should mean tending to, rather than extracting from it, they built up a collective, ecological, feminist village economy.

The houses in the village are arranged around a garden, a communal kitchen and a covered area where the women of the village share bigger meals, welcome guests and hold celebrations. Each household also has its own small garden, and a kitchen big enough to meet the needs of the family who lives there.

The life of the village takes a similar shape – each household has its own patterns and particularities, but they face towards the collective centre. Women take it in turn to herd the goats and sheep, tend the garden, work the fields and make bread in the bakery. The village comes together for bigger tasks – harvests and dances, planting the fields and celebrating the children's educational achievements, putting up a new building and observing holy days. At the same time, the women of the village explore what it looks like to build community without patriarchy, finding new-old ways to make decisions, navigate power and sustain life.

The community hall hosts educational sessions from women from around Rojava and the local area, and a natural health centre has been established to research and share medical practice which is based on the unity of body, mind and spirit. The knowledge of healing, just like the growing and agriculture skills, are not newly made up and flown in from above. They look back at traditional, pre-capitalist ways of interacting with the land and our bodies, trust that we came from the earth and nature and that we can learn again how to understand ourselves as a part of it. This is what environmental action looks like when we use ecology as a frame, and a whole paradigm, rather than seeing it as an issue.

Without such a well-articulated and deeply held alternative paradigm in the West, our attempts at resistance are often absorbed by the dominant capitalist paradigm. Working on sustainable technologies becomes a business opportunity for corporations, and attempts to live our values in how we live and what we consume become individualistic statements about our 'footprint'. Because capitalism disconnects humans from nature, we don't realise that it's our relationship to it that's broken – not nature itself. This means we can fall into the trap of thinking that we could fix things if only we had the right technologies or the right laws. So called 'green' capitalism produces endless false solutions — like GMO crops, renewable energy that exploits workers, carbon offsetting – that are still based on extraction, individualism and the profit motive. Doubtless some of these technologies could be useful, but they won't be until their use is guided by a bigger shift in values. State-based political systems make token accommodations such as superficial climate change regulations, and politicians pay lip service to sustainability. Unsurprisingly, these so-called solutions are never effective in the long term, because they don't address and challenge the fundamental relationship of domination between humans and nature.

If people want to wage an effective resistance to environmental destruction, we have to make this paradigm shift in the way we think and talk about climate action. When we see ourselves as part of nature, taking action against ecological destruction becomes self defence. It means that radical climate action neither begins nor ends with how you get rid of your rubbish, that's just one of the stops along the way.

"Even a wounded world is feeding us. Even a wounded world holds us, giving us moments of wonder and joy."
— *Robin Wall Kimmerer, Potawatomi writer, botanist and educator*

Internationalist volunteers participate in political education at the Andrea Wolf Institute in Rojava

14. KNOWING

How we think makes us who we are
Jenni

I've been home for Christmas more often than not since I first moved out at 16. My folks still live where I grew up, and the patterns of farmland and the bends in the road welcome me back as much or more than the people. After moving out, my brother, sister and I often congregated at our parents' and dutifully observed traditions. We opened presents, ate chocolate in our pyjamas for breakfast, and my mum spent hours working in a kitchen she could barely turn round in, pulling together an amazing meal in a half broken oven with whatever Christmassy fare Tesco's had that didn't break the bank. Once we'd eaten, still at the table, my dad and I usually launch into another seasonal ritual: having some kind of 'debate'. It could be about a range of things: democracy, power, history, news. But only within a given framework of what is 'political', what is up for serious debate, what can be abstractly reasoned.

As a young girl with a strong streak of logical, analytical intelligence, and a bolshy, assertive arguing style, I fought tooth and nail to prove to him and to the world around me that I wasn't stupid. I managed it. Despite retreating to the kitchen to avoid our head-butting, my mum always winked at me and would later remind me that I'm pretty much the only one who's a match for him and actually makes him stop and think, and that it's good for him to be challenged.

Our sessions left me energised as well, a world apart from the real arguments we used to have. But still, there was always a knot of discomfort in my stomach. I know I am not completely myself in those moments, that I'm speaking a language that is not mine, that limits me. But that language has a lot of power in our world.

My dad taught me a lot about the world: about history and politics, as well as how to express myself a certain way. He gave me his battered old textbooks about sociological theory; Marxist critiques of 'great' English literature; working class socialist polemics. Without him, I would have taken a lot longer to find any kind of political way of expressing myself, any explanation for what I could see in the world.

At the same time, I learnt that there was a correct way to see things, and that it came with sounding a certain way. I built up an armoury of weapons to prove my point or take someone else's to pieces, to hold my own in any debate. It also meant building a thick shield around certain parts of myself, not giving space to emotion or intuition when I was in political discussion mode, or at least not unless I could justify those emotions on certain terms. It meant insisting on tearing everything — ideas, experiences, reality — apart into little pieces that could be defined.

With the training I got at home, by the time I was arguing with not-very-interesting-men-in-pubs it was a doddle. I became 'the clever one'. I was rewarded by some men with their grudging respect, while being fancied by others because I was (implication: unusually) 'smart'. Other women often agreed that I was (implication: they weren't), and cheered me on, as a kind of tactical weapon to be deployed. I didn't notice that I was reinforcing this. I felt like I was achieving something, proving something. I'd learnt to play the game extremely well.

The game is not just in the social circles I was around when I was young. It's much bigger than that. There's a particular way of thinking and being, that has been around for a long time, but it really came into its own in the Enlightenment of the 18th century — that period of time Europe and the West are so proud of. The time when we apparently emerged from backwards, childish, superstitious ways of thinking into the glorious light of reason. That's when the philosophy of 'positivism' really found its feet.

Positivism – roughly speaking – is a way of thinking that puts emphasis on the scientific and rational over the emotional and immaterial. Rather than looking at the relationships that connect humans, ecosystems and the world in general, positivism breaks everything down into disconnected units: human as separate from nature, outcome as separate from process. It imposes binaries and borders, rather than being open to the richness, complexity and fluidity of the world we live in. It says that the only real kind of knowledge is what can be proved (or shouted) in these black and white terms.

When international volunteers come to North and East Syria, we are confronted with a lot of talk about positivism and why it's steering us all wrong. Most of us had never heard of it before.

In our society, you don't have to be explicitly taught what positivism is to learn that it's a good thing. In fact, it works better for the system if it is unnamed, showing up only when disguised as 'truth' or 'science'. Our whole education system is based on it, on cold dead facts and information, and learning that only certain ways of explaining truth are justifiable. It's no coincidence that that same education system grew from the top down, from the boys groomed to become men who run empires, down to the poor and working classes kept in line; we are educated to all know our neatly classified place in the world.

***

I grew up hearing Tony Blair and his cronies push "education, education, education", and this is what they really meant. Very unusually for my generation, I didn't actually go through the schooling system they were so keen on. My parents, once teachers themselves in England, had run a mile (several hundred, actually, to a muddy Scottish hillside and a long way from a teacher's pay cheque) from a system they didn't think had anything to do with real education. My siblings and I were raised instead on a mish mash of the outdoors, age-inappropriate reading at the library, playing with matches, old radio shows, and the conversation of our parents and their friends.

My mum was the full-time carer while my dad worked seven days a week to try and keep us above water now that he was starting a small business from scratch. Day to day life with my mum fed the other part of my soul, the one that I had to shut down when I wanted to win at masculine debate, in ways I never even realised until later. She never preached politics explicitly but she never let me forget that "things don't have to be the way they are".

She didn't make us sit down in lessons, or divide the world into subjects neatly closed off from each other. She read to us and told us stories, so much I'm surprised she didn't lose her voice. Stories don't divide, they connect. The capacity to connect and empathise that stories teach us makes it much harder to ignore the state of the real world. To learn only abstract facts and figures makes it easy to grow up and keep seeing things that way. When we think only in terms of 'practical' solutions, we are stuck in a mindset the Kurdish movement often calls too 'technical': bogged down in material and practical things, looking only at the immediate moment and not the root causes. Above all, we see everything as distanced and disconnected from ourselves.

My dad was just as committed as my mum to not sending us to school. If they hadn't been so committed, they could have both worked, and he might not have spent my childhood driving himself into mental and physical ill health and a fair amount of debt in order to get by. I understood that the decisions they took meant that we were raised, though by no means poor, generally struggling for cash, and without the luxuries other middle class families seemed to take for granted. Instead, I grew up understanding that values and principles are important, or more important than scrabbling to maximise your status, and that's something worth teaching a kid.

We can see how the mainstream education system has left its mark on generation after generation, who are primed to memorise dates and pass exams at the expense of cultivating curiosity, nurturing collaborative relationships and asking the question of how we want to bring kindness, fairness and beauty into the world. It's not like me and my siblings escaped it: despite not going to school, we were still a part of the same culture, the same society, and absorbed it at college, work, or socially. Whether your class or other privileges set you up to succeed or fail at this game, you learn to play it and to measure yourself by it.

The outcome of this way of thinking, writ large, perpetuates imperialism and capitalism. It also plays a role in the failure of projects that sought to be the solution, including attempts at communism and socialism.

The Kurdistan Freedom Movement looked closely at the fall of the Soviet Union, questioning not only why it ultimately fell, but why it — and many other national liberation struggles that drew inspiration from it — defaulted to

authoritarianism and brutality. There's hundreds of factors that led to the death of those 20th century revolutions, to torture chambers and concentration camps, struggles for dominance and control. Among them are the reliance on the state as a road to freedom, the betrayals of a popular movement, and the failure to centre the question of gender liberation. But crucially in there as well, the Kurdish movement concluded, was that although socialist revolutions changed who had power and how the system ran, they did not effect a revolution in the *mindset* of those leading the revolution, or the people living it. So the toxic mentalities such as those of domination, capitalism and positivism remained, and poisoned it until it betrayed everything it stood for.

To overcome this challenge will take more than a change of material systems, no matter how radical. How do you create deep, internal change? In part this means learning how to add a question mark to how we move through the world. In the Kurdistan Freedom Movement, this process also includes getting philosophical. Asking questions like 'what is truth?" is seen as a pressing task for revolutionaries, because in order to build a new world we have to understand what reality is and how we shape it. This too is revolution.

And so, far away in the Middle East, the same region where Tony Blair himself created so much upheaval and bloodshed, a very different band of people started to insist on a very different kind of 'education, education, education". I had no idea that my life would lead me there, among them, still debating and discussing the important questions of life but this time with my whole self.

***

Education might be the single most important principle of the Kurdistan Freedom Movement. Everyone is seen as deserving of education, and on the flip side, no one is ever seen as having had 'enough' education. Across society, people from all walks of life are encouraged and supported to take part in education – to get to know their history and culture, talk about patriarchy, power and the system, and develop themselves. This can take the form of long, closed sessions, and I joined one in Kurdish, spending several weeks with women from society across Rojava who were given time out of their normal jobs to attend the education. When that's not feasible it can be weekend seminars, evenings, or a day a week at your work. It goes without saying that all of these educations are free of charge, including accommodation and food.

Sometimes people come to these educations just barely able to read and write, or still learning. Other times they have been through high levels of mainstream education. Still, there's no tiers, everyone goes into education together regardless and has just as much to learn from each other and to bring. Although understanding things intellectually is seen as an important part of learning, the ultimate aim is to bring knowledge into your day to day life, to understand it on an emotional level and embody it through practice.

Seasoned full-time organisers sometimes spend weeks or months attending seminars, having discussions, reading texts, and practising collective self reflection to analyse and develop themselves according to revolutionary values. They are supposed to represent those values but the truth is they don't always manage to. They let themselves and others down all the time. We all have the system inside us. To be a revolutionary is to promise to never stop learning, never stop looking at yourself. Education is the safety net, the engine and the grease that makes this possible.

Towards the end of my time in Rojava I was offered the chance to attend another round of education. I wavered. I had a lot of work to do. Would I be able to wrap things up in time? Would someone else be able to take things on? My supervisor at this time sat me down and gently but firmly told me that none of that mattered. They saw it as extremely important that I went, and if I wanted to go, then that was the end of it. Work would be figured out collectively, but this was a priority. What's the point in working and being productive if you don't understand what you're working for, if you haven't reflected on how you should do it?

So we gathered together in a big, slightly dilapidated building that had belonged to the Assad regime before the revolution. We handed over our phones to minimise distraction, made cooking and cleaning rotas based on the rooms we slept in, and started getting to know each other. This was fitted into the gaps in a gruelling schedule of seminars and lectures that started early, finished late, and were delivered by women from across the Middle East with decades of experience in changing their world. We talked about everything from capitalism, the state, history, gender, and self defence, to love, perception and time. A generous supply of notebooks decorated with love hearts or cartoon characters were provided for us to scribble notes in, and strong tea and coffee to keep us fuelled. Our group contained a lot of international volunteers, and we wanted to wring out all the knowledge we could from this experience. We asked almost all of our teachers what they thought was the biggest challenge the revolution faced and what the most important work was. Without exception, they all said *education*.

In the left in Europe we can shy away from the idea that education is important, worried that means either becoming academic, or saying that we – or the folks we organise with — are stupid. But we don't live in a vacuum, and the system is extremely good at pumping misinformation into us. Schools and universities are part of the system. There's an unimaginably vast media industry spreading the same ideas, or providing distractions so we don't question it. Whether you think it's a conscious plan to keep us docile, or a blind, self-perpetuating system that has just emerged alongside global capitalism, it has a big impact on our lives.

Despite having more information at our disposal than at any other point in history, we seem to have a lot of memory loss in our culture. We (should) know that the British Empire and the wealth of Britain today was built on the stolen land, blood, sweat and labour of hundreds of thousands of enslaved peoples and people of colour across the world, including in Britain itself. But British schools don't teach this to kids, although they find time to relentlessly browbeat about Nazi Germany. This helped allow the Brexit campaign that ran in the years before I left for Kurdistan to be based on a vision of an independently successful, white, unified Britain protecting itself from impoverished hordes.

The witch hunts of mediaeval and renaissance Europe were a massacre that changed our communities and histories forever. They left gaping wounds in the individual and collective psyches of thousands of women, across Europe. But all to often if we look back on the trials at all it's to claim they were a moment of backwards irrationality, rather than part of the war waged on women and communities by the powers of church, state and capital.

None of this memory loss is entirely an accident.

We need to fight back, understand this stuff as an attack, see the need for self defence. This has to include taking education — real education — into our own hands.

That doesn't mean we act like the state and start to fill people with information and insist they follow our line. I was in a few different periods of education while I was in Rojava. Sometimes, as we sat in rows of chairs like the school I never even went to, struggling to concentrate through the third hour of a lecture, I did feel that we were falling into the same patterns. But that was at least discussed, an open point for critique and reflection. As our comrades there pointed out, there's also nothing wrong with pushing ourselves, developing our focus and discipline, as long as it's driven by our own commitment, not punishment from above.

There are no tests in political education in the movement. We were never posed a question where the goal was to see if we passed or failed. The goal is to really connect with content, for everyone to take away what they need. You don't come out with a qualification that's meant to prove something. You just come out different. The process is the goal. It's untestable. That also removes a whole stack of pressure that other education I experienced had always had. It meant that even when methods were quite traditional, different learning styles and different brains weren't forced to bend themselves quite as rigidly to fit – you engaged how you could and took and gave what you could in that moment.

At other times, women organisers in particular broke from traditional styles, and guided us with participatory methods, songs, images and stories. There were sessions that worked in movement. No matter what the style, we were always encouraged — in fact pushed quite hard — to speak up, debate, share our personal stories, and give our opinions.

As internationals in particular we were told we should never hold back: criticise, question, say what you really think, not what you think you should say. Then, real conversations emerge. Perhaps most significantly, it was one of the reasons that it was possible for us to become a part of the movement in a meaningful way. Often when Europeans and those from countries enriched by colonialism travel to other places we come in from the top down, obliviously swinging our entitlement and privilege around, neo-colonialism disguised as solidarity or aid. There's considerably less space for this in the Kurdish Movement, not because anyone is turned away, or because we don't come in with colonial baggage, or act in appropriative or prejudiced ways. But because the system of education, and embedded processes of learning and development, guide us to reflect and grow.

***

The Kurdistan Freedom Movement is never content with just criticising. We have to come up with alternative proposals. The question of knowing and knowledge is no exception. Over the last fifteen years, the women's movement has been working hard at a bold, all encompassing proposal that refuses to stop digging until it finds the roots of what it means to know something.

Jineolojî, the 'science of women', is a radical intervention into science, social science and knowledge. It's the Kurdistan Women's Movement's proposal for a holistic, deep transformation in how we see the world. Science should be in service of society, not the other way round, it says. We need to put social sciences at the centre of all knowledge, and social sciences themselves need an overhaul. We have to start asking *why* and *who for* when it comes to science. The only way to ensure it works for the good of everyone is to put women at the centre. Not only to ask *'how does this affect women's collective position?'* or *'what does this mean for social well being?'* in any change or development, but also to study women and women's history and knowledge, gender itself and gender oppression and to uncover history and knowledge that has been suppressed by patriarchy.

Ten years before I came to Rojava, Abdullah Öcalan had proposed the idea of jineolojî in the writings he produced from the prison island where he was — and continues to be — held by the Turkish state. The Kurdistan Women's Movement picked this idea up and ran with it. As well as including jineolojî in all educations, they've created the Jineolojî Academy, an autonomous women's institution composed of research centres, institutes and committees. Regional academies and centres can be found across all four parts of Kurdistan, North and East Syria, and in Europe as well.

The Andrea Wolf Academy is one of the jineolojî academies in Rojava, and exists in part to support internationalists arriving to join the work of the revolution. Both Natalia and I participated in a term of education there, and found it to be a whole lot more than just seminars and lectures. It was a way of living together, developing ourselves and each other, and reimagining what it meant to know, or understand the world. *"What is truth?"* we were asked, and we asked ourselves and each other, gathered in groups under fruit trees or in shipping-containers-cum-classrooms, sweating from the heat, exhausted, and in love with each other and the fight ahead. *"What is a free life? What is love?"* These questions flowed between us until the light faded, our stomachs growled and our heads nodded... and inevitably some*one burst into a rendition of "What is love? Baby don't hurt me, no more!"* and we collapsed in a round of delirious giggles.

One important point about jineolojî is that it's not tied to one context and can be practised by anyone anywhere. In fact, it must be. The different realities, perspectives, meanings and histories of women and anti-patriarchal struggles have different colours and textures, and these are what give it depth and strength. Just like knowledge itself, jineolojî is not set in stone, despite not accepting a soulless 'no such thing as truth' relativism. It is a field for debate and discussion, that can unite women and other genders across the world, just as it's already the meeting point for so many with the Kurdistan Women's Movement, like our group gathered under those trees.

Jineolojî also means looking deeply at our histories, recovering untold stories, making visible that which the system needs to make invisible; whether that's knowledge, memory, labour, resistance, or even our bodies themselves and how they are suppressed and co-opted by oppression and capital. It means listening to people we don't listen to enough, such as mothers and grandmothers, for a start.

We used our minds, of course, like sharp, precise cutting tools. We analysed, we debated. We were presented with facts and we made logical assessments. But that wasn't all we did. We talked about our life stories and how we had become the people we are, and reflected on how living in a patriarchal, capitalist society had impacted our families, our relationships and our sense of hope that a different world was possible. We dove into uncertainties and contradictions without the need to surface with a clear cut 'answer' in our grasp. The way we lived together wasn't separate from what we were learning, and the kind of world we were trying to build. We wove our analytical intelligence with intuition and emotional intelligence, allowing them to work together and support each other. When you tear one away the other staggers, wobbles, will blunder and go wrong. For far too long patriarchal thinking and positivism have pedestalled analytical intelligence and in doing so made it something dangerous, unprincipled, volatile. A tool is a tool, it shouldn't steer the ship.

Positivism is rife across our society and leftists, radical communities, and political organisers are no exception. We seek technical, material solutions, needing a certain kind of proof or results to believe something is working. We remove questions of ethics or values from our understanding of truth, and think we can stand and objectively view the world instead of being part of its flow.

***

I know that what we experienced in North and East Syria was real education because I always came out of it with more questions than answers. But they were new questions, they were shifts, they were tools, and maps, and I was changed. Far from sending me home convinced I have the answers, I arrived back humbled and shamed by how little of the history of my own home I know, or the context of the struggle I want to be a part of, or the story of where we came from and who we are. I see everyone around me as a source of amazing knowledge and wisdom. I keep insisting on our household giving each other little talks or holding discussions, especially when a difficult topic comes up.

Before I left I'd have been a mix of baffled and resentful at the idea of taking weeks to reflect and discuss. The first time the movement proposed that I attend an education, I thought it was self-indulgent nonsense and that I was 'far too busy' (which I think was actually much more egotistical than the self reflection I was rejecting). Now I completely understand my Kurdish comrades who jump up at the thought of education like it's a birthday present. Half-slept nights full of security shifts; a repetitive diet; no personal space or even elbow room for weeks; relentless classes until your head bursts and interesting thoughts bubble out of your ears; seminars that spill over into the evenings just when you thought you were done; being challenged, made angry, pushed to the limits, forced to hang every detail of your personality out on all the theory and take a long hard look at it... Great! When do we start? You always come out of it full of love, and twice as ready for the fight as you were before, even if you also seriously need to catch up on sleep.

This motivation, connection and love isn't separate to facts, history, philosophy and ideology. They can't be. They need each other. We'll never get anywhere in the big or the small if we can't unite our heads and our hearts.

WHAT WE LEARNED

Natalia

Night falls on our last day together, and I hear voices raised in song across the garden.
Unfurling from solitude, I sing harmony with paper and pen.
I write our stories — how we all ended up in an old house with paint peeling off the
*   walls, surrounded by evergreen trees.*
The smell of roses soaks the night air, white mulberries fall from branches into our
*   outstretched hands.*

Something ancient bears witnesses to our promises – a scorpion, a snake, a shooting
*   star.*
We're still young enough to be afraid of poison, but when we're old and wise we'll
*   come to fight with venom on sharpened teeth and snakes twined in our*
*   hair.*
We'll raise our arms to the clouds as the heavens rain down vengeance for the wounds
*   our mothers carry on their backs.*

We'll walk like giants among the rubble of the old world, scattering seeds to the
*   wind.*
Calendula for healing, chamomile for forgiveness.
Sunflowers for strength and sage for those who have fallen.
A lemon tree for Anna, apricot for Malda.

We've spun something beautiful here – we've given each other our pain and trusted
*   each other to hold it steady while we wove: anger for warp, hope for weft.*
In and out, each day setting down layer after layer, until the tapestry of swifts duck-
*   ing through the sunset sketches our histories onto the sky.*
And when the time comes we will rise together, backs straight and hands clasped,
*   and meet the battle with our songs.*

The road leading to Kobane

15. FREE

The road to liberation

Jenni

"Jin! Jiyan! Azadı!" "Women! Life! Freedom!" I knew this chant in Kurdish long before I could form a sentence. This is the chant that resounds across the Kurdistan Freedom Movement, from the cities of Northern Kurdistan, to the mountains of the South and East, and over the dusty wheat fields of Rojava and Syria. In October 2022, it spread even further as it was cried out at the forefront of the uprisings across Iran. In Rojava, you hear it daily. We chanted it whenever a group of people left our place, surrounding minivans and clapping as the glimpses of waving hands and laughing mouths inside pulled away. Huge crowds of people shouted it in defiance of warplanes and chemical weapons. It gets recited by pairs or individuals into video messages, refusing to feel silly chanting it alone because really, you are joining a chorus.

Years before, I came across the memoirs of Black revolutionary and writer Mumia Abu Jamal. He was a long time member of the Black Panther Party, fighting imperialism, white supremacy, and capitalism right in one of their strongholds, the USA. He wrote from prison, but he wasn't just talking about prison when he entitled his book *We Want Freedom*. I was (and remain) awed by his life, but also by his way with words and ability condense something so clearly and neatly it feels like you can fit it right in your pocket, but so powerfully it keeps your heart beating the whole time it's there.

We are fighting for our freedom. It's as simple, and as complicated, as that. It's so cliched it's almost lost all meaning, right up until it hasn't. Right up until it's suddenly everything. People die for freedom every day. Why? What is this thing that seems to trump survival as a human need?

I knew I wasn't free from a young age. I believe we all hold this sense somewhere deep in our guts, no matter how differently the world has hit us. I didn't know what I was railing *against*, but I was railing. My greatest fear was to end up *stuck*, trapped. Tied down.

Growing up relatively isolated in the country, I was desperate to learn to drive. I wanted to be free to come and go as I wanted. I wanted to be able to hit the road. I was fiercely proud of my independence, of working and paying my way from a young age. I told myself I was making myself free to live how I wanted. I accepted the story I'd been told, that as long as I didn't get in the way of anyone else's freedom, I could and should be free this way. I hit the road in a battered old car made mostly of fibreglass that cost me £200, and felt like I was getting somewhere.

The road stretching out before me still makes my heart lift like almost nothing else. I get high on it: on the physical reality of a flickering white line and the hum of an engine, and on the freedom it stands for. I don't think I'll ever lose it, one of the first and deepest loves of my life. But now I look back occasionally and wonder where that road was headed. Why it took me quite so long to ask some deeper questions about freedom.

Because there's a trick played on us. People know we are not free, we know there's a problem. We can sense it clear as day, and so we strike out blindly to try and grab it, not sure what we're chasing or how to get it but sure that it matters, that there's a part of us missing. Rather than clunkily try and crush this, as some socialist states have a history of, capitalist culture sells us a forgery. It dangles a fake for us to chase, to fool ourselves into thinking we're becoming free. A pre-mapped road to get those feelings out of our system. What we're doing is nailing our own coffin.

So there I was, just like millions of young people in wealthy parts of the world: free to buy whatever I wanted (if I could afford it), say whatever I wanted (as long as I didn't act on it), wear whatever I wanted (up to the point it was 'asking for it'). We are free to go wherever we want (if we have the right papers, be that a passport or a vaccine certificate). We're free to sell ourselves and others over and over again, and free to spend what we get on something to numb the pain. We're even free to rebel, as long as that involves buying something, Che Guevara's face on a t-shirt perhaps, or individual self expression that ends up little more than fashion.

In Kurmanji Kurdish there's two words that you translate into English as free or freedom. They're not interchangeable, and are used in totally different contexts. If someone is going to tell you to do whatever you want, or that it doesn't matter what someone does, they'll say *serbest*. There's no real value judgement on whether this word is a good or a bad thing. It could be either depending on context. It could be, 'let the kids be free to play wherever they like just now, it's fine". Or it could be, 'that person acts like they are free to just walk into our space and take whatever they want". It just means there are no restrictions.

I was pretty sure that's what freedom was, for a long time. I found people who agreed with me. We stuffed our pockets with tinnies, pills and directionless rage, and painted the town all colours of red. It's not that it was always a bad thing. Yes, sometimes we hurt each other. Violence and oppression hid behind the lights, hard to challenge because everyone was there to be free to do whatever they want. But other times, a lot of the time, it was fun. It was fine. We were certainly *serbest*. But freedom is a bit more than *fine*.

It just never fully satisfies, this unrestricted, blind, immediate individual freedom. It turns out what we are getting, or even fighting for, is our identity as individuals broken from any kind of community. Take any of us out of modern society and we wouldn't last long. Neither would most people I know. We're not even meant to; macho individualist survivalism isn't actually how we got by before the modern world either. We got by, thrived, learned to value things like freedom, by working *together*. Even in the world we live in now the image of self-sufficiency is a thin facade. It drops away when I'm sick and you bring me food, when we put our heads together to solve a problem, when when hold each other while we shake and weep. It drops away when I feel my friends step up behind me, warm, and solid, when someone threatens me. It drops away when we lift, bathe, comfort, and feed the elderly, just like they did for us when we were small.

If we slip away from each other, if we don't want to be 'stuck' or 'trapped' by all this, then we are on our own. On our own, we need the state. The state grew and became strong as the idea of 'man as an island' was born. All those times when we're unwell, threatened, old or young, we turn to the state if we are not part of a community. The state is about control, and it always will be. We can't be free when we need the state. In the meantime, when we are apparently fine, we turn to capitalism for our food, housing, clothes, and the very freedom that we are so fond of. The freedom of the market.

Are we just doomed to need other people, but forever trapped by this need and desperately trying to carve out our own space? Liberalism certainly wants us to think so, wants us to think freedom is a tug of war with humanity, that communities are a stern overbearing father endangering our freedom. The freedom of an individual to do whatever we want (be serbest) at any particular time.

If you are going to talk in *Kurmanji* Kurdish about political freedom, the freedom of a people or many peoples, the kind of freedom that is the opposite of domination and oppression, you say *azadî.* Azadî is what you chant at the darkening sky under fluttering flags. Azadî is what millions of people across Kurdistan will tell you they are ready to die for. In English we might better express the idea by talking about *liberation. But I've noticed we are often shy to use that word, and even when we do it too can sometimes start to sound more like the absence of restrictions.*

Azadî isn't the absence of anything. It's the presence of empowerment. Of being able to be our full selves. It's collective. It's *we* who want freedom.

After I left home, I was still a long way from finding this word, or any others, for what I felt was missing. But I could feel it. I was convinced real freedom was out there, and that I just had to push harder, look farther afield. Hit the road again. This time that looked like standing by the side of it, thumb stretched out in hope and humble request. Together with a friend, I travelled thousands of miles of other countries' roads, in other people's cars, pick ups, and lorries. I fell in love with the white line over and over again. It seemed like it never let me down. We met people and saw places we'd never dreamed existed. Despite every difference, we made real connections. We found that book, with Mumia Abu Jamal's words in it, somewhere along the road. We raced along like we were looking for something. I guess we were.

216

Every time we crossed a border we could just pull out our passports. It might get complicated, or expensive, but because of where we were from we could basically go wherever we wanted. Our money, even earned shovelling manure and stacking shelves, went a long way. No matter how far you go, how long your road is, the systems that both shape and control us are always with you. Freedom is not just the absence of restrictions, and it's certainly not just the absence of restrictions *for some*.

Years later, I was on the road again. This time headed for North and East Syria. I numbed my brain with movies on the plane that took me to the Middle East. I get dislocated and anxious in airports and on planes. My soul travels best somewhere between 50 and 90mph, depending on the bends in the road and the state of the engine. On the ground again, I was excitedly eyeing up all the vehicles; endless parades of pick up trucks, rusty old fake Toyotas mixed in randomly with shiny real ones; minibuses bursting at the seams; three wheel motorbikes; DIY armoured cars; 4x4s with blacked out windows. I was itching to try my hand at the roads, dodging donkeys, potholes and drivers with a death wish, for a taste of that freedom I always felt behind the wheel. I was ready to be patient though, and it didn't even have to be the drivers' seat. I just wanted to get going.

It turned out not to be that simple. Suddenly we had to ask to go anywhere or do almost anything. Often the answer was no, or even more often *wait*, without much of an explanation. It wasn't just about getting places. Most internationalists who show up to be part of the movement struggle with a sudden loss of loads of freedoms.

Hitting the road in Rojava seemed to mean waiting all day for a lift, with no idea if it will be five minutes or five hours, no control and no information (but woe betide the comrade who's not ready to jump when it *does* arrive). Depending on the situation, you often can't even just nip to the shops. Let alone jump in a car and visit someone in another city. Meanwhile there are some things we *have* to do, even if we don't particularly feel like it.

Sometimes it takes a while to shift this view of freedom, like one of those magic eye optical illusions. When you first look at it, you see what you expect – a jumbled mess of colours and lines. No freedom here. But then when you learn the trick of looking at it a certain way, of squinting your eyes and looking from a different angle, a whole new shape pops out. This freedom is bigger than us. Choosing as organisers to give up some freedoms, to not always be *serbest*, allows us to create the kind of collective that can fight for real freedom, for azadî. Freedom is a collective process. Only together are we strong enough to resist.

In Rojava, we are free to imagine the world a whole different way, to grasp the idea of revolution with both hands and make it come alive. The decades of collective struggle have created a society and political culture that has thrown the horizon wide open for dreaming, imagining and hoping. We hold the tools to freedom in our hands – they were forged and tested by others, so that we may use them. As women, we have the freedom to fight for our liberation. We do this through discussion, through education, through evaluation and criticism. It's hard work, but at no point do men get to opt out and say 'I don't want to do this, you're restricting my personal freedom". Rather than seeing a free society as one in which each individual moves through the world in their own bubble of freedom, bumping up against other people's bubbles, we see a free society as a web, where freedom is made up of the strands that connect us and strengthen us. It's a freedom that doesn't pretend that it's disconnected from the kind of world we want to live in.

Because we *are* connected. It's one of the few things we can be sure of. We come into this world quite literally part of someone else. As soon as that physical reality shifts, we become part of an incredibly complex social web that gives our selves and our worlds meaning. We remain physically helpless for a length of time unheard of anywhere else in the animal world, relying completely on that web for our bodies and souls to survive and thrive. This web of relations is how we first stood up and looked around, starting talking, started thinking. Our freedom must lie here too.

The state and capitalism have used liberalism to convince us we are individuals, made us fear committing to communities of shared values, in order to make us weak. Collectives can reproduce, defend, develop, nourish and fulfil themselves. We have to stay a *we*. Collectives need collective values, and these have to be held in some way. Different collectives and communities have organised differently for their freedom over time. Forms of leadership or negotiation look different. But however they look, we need to actively build freedom up from blocks of unity, empowerment, mutual aid, discussion and debate, and commitment. We won't find it in the falling sensation of cutting ties with those around us.

This is why the Kurdistan Freedom Movement says that a free society is a society that has collectively held ethics, or morals. Without them, we need to rely on the state for laws and bureaucracy to shape how we live. Unless we learn to find and hold our shared values – across all of society – we won't be able to free ourselves from state domination.

The same friend I spent all those months on the road with years ago found his own way to the revolution in Rojava as well. In all those months that we hitched around the world together, whenever we mentioned that we were from Scotland it was only a matter of time before someone brought up the movie *Braveheart*. It turned out North and East Syria was no different. The first time we saw each other after he arrived (and it was quite a while after, because even though we hadn't been that far apart, we had to wait until work and life gave us the chance to meet), he told me about working in a medical point near the front lines during the invasion of Serekaniye. A Kurdish man who had been recently wounded and was still in a critical condition called him over, and my friend was expecting to be confronted with a sudden loss of blood or other medical emergency. Instead he was presented with a phone screen showing Mel Gibson cantering up and down on a horse and asked if what he was shouting truly was "azadî"?

Despite most Scottish leftists' cynicism about a historically inaccurate Hollywood action movie, he did what any of us would have done. He gritted his teeth and agreed that yes, that movie is about *azadî*. Partly because when someone still has shrapnel from Turkish-backed jihadist shells in their leg and your shared language is faltering, it's not the time to get picky. But partly because even when Hollywood has hollowed something out and sold it back to us, we know what it was playing on, or perhaps even genuinely trying to say. The fight against imperialism is never a fight to just be serbest. It is a struggle for *azadî*.

Because of course freedom isn't only in autonomous territories like Rojava. Hundreds of movements are building freedom on the same principles. We are free to protest, to strike, to care for each other, and not because any government recognises these freedoms (they often don't), but because those who came before us and struggle alongside us have carved out that space. We have fought for every bit of freedom we have. But we have to be careful that liberal models of freedom don't sneak in and take what we've achieved, repackage it, and sell it back to us all hollowed out.

The momentum behind liberal understandings of freedom sometimes sweeps us along with it and it pulls against us when we're trying to build communities of resistance. We try to juggle and balance different ideas of freedom, but the pull of this dominant view is strong: the more free I am, the more likely I am to take away someone else's freedom. We are so paralysed by our fear of restricting an individual's actions in the moment that we cannot always fight for real freedom. Sometimes, when we say "we want freedom" I can't help but hear 'serbest' not 'azadî', and 'I' not 'we'.

One sure-fire sign that collective freedom is truly a threat to the system is how hard the state and capital crack down on it. The fake freedom they try to sell us is *part of* that crackdown. We need to learn to recognise it as a fake when it's waved under our nose. One way to tell is to ask, does the system give me this freedom? For example, the freedom to indulge; to treat interactions with other people like a fairground ride I can buy a ticket to or not; to spend my money however I choose; even love who I choose as long as I love the *way* I've been told. If so, it's probably not worth fighting for. What the system fights so hard to destroy is much more likely to be what really undermines it. What it tries to destroy is strength in unity, a coming together of the ancient and the new.

I still love to hit the road. Back home, no longer completely surrounded by the organising structures of a movement, I can once again take a spontaneous decision. I can choose to get up early to squeeze in a mission of hundreds of miles, or to drive home late, alone with the radio and the white line. It's one of the things that grounds me, feeds me, keeps me steady. If there's any reason to be on the road, my heart still lifts.

But I try to think hard about the map I'm using to guide me. To ask who's on the journey with me, and where we're going. The fight and the work we have to do will doubtless take me still more places I've never dreamed of. But I'll let that happen as it happens and I won't pretend I can just drive out of the system. Or turn to the white line just because things get hard.

Freedom is a struggle. It's a struggle because we are a long way from it, and as soon as we open our eyes and refuse to close them we see we have a long fight ahead. And it's a struggle because we make it *in* struggle. When we fight we are free, no matter how many doors are slammed around us.

"Freedom is a process by which you develop the habit of being inaccessible to slavery."
— *Alla Gutnikova, Russian student activist in exile since 2022*

Rooftop breakfast in Iraq after leaving Rojava

16. RETURNING

Coming Home
Natalia

Rojava.

Nearly a year after I arrived in Kurdistan, I start to feel that it's time to go home. As I begin to make plans to leave Rojava, I feel closer to it than I ever had before. Over the previous months, I had felt the distance growing between me and my home in England, the war like a wedge driven between realities, pushing us apart. By choosing to defend the people, the land, the very idea of Rojava, my relationship to it shifted. Maybe it was just feeling like I belonged there more, that it had become a home of sorts. Or that I had passed the point of being able to explain everything I had been through, the promises I broke by staying there and how much I had changed. I didn't know when it happened, but a bit of my soul had taken root there: it had snuck up on me, the way that falling in love usually does.

I know that I'm headed home, headed to where I want to be in the long term. But I also know that I will leave a piece of myself in Rojava when I leave. In the weeks before I go, I move through moments saturated with nostalgia even before I have time to conjugate them into past tense. I begin to miss things before I have to leave them behind, trying to press them into my memory and my DNA to make them a permanent part of myself. On the day I leave Rojava, I sit in the back seat of the car with my face pressed against the window as we drive to the border.

I drink in the brilliant new green of the shoots in the fields stretching from the road towards the hazy mountains on the horizon, thirsty for a future in which I would see the fields grow high with grain, where the mountains were always just out of reach at the bottom of the sky.

Iraq.

Sulaymaniyah in the Kurdish region of Iraq is the first stepping stone on the way back home. I stay there for a bit over a week with a couple of other internationalist volunteers who are heading home at the same time as me. We spend our days exploring the city and eating shared meals on the floor of our hostel room. There is a sweetness about this in-between time, like the moments suspended between sleep and wakefulness where we move differently through time. We make friends and go on picnics in the countryside, drink from a freshwater spring steeped in local legend and buy scalding hot coffee from the stands lining the bustling streets of the city.

One afternoon we go with a local friend to visit his sister in one of the luxury high rises on the outskirts of the city. The day is grey and wet, and as the car drives up the hills and into the gated complex we can see the city spread below us, colours muted under the filtered light, sounds smothered by the low-hanging sky. We step into the lift, wet from the rain, and are faced with the bleak uniformity of modern living. What used to be so familiar — an apartment block offering housing, but no community — now feels foreign and uncomfortable. In the lift we read the printed list of rules for the building. How to use your kitchen, where to put your shoes, how to clean your balcony. It feels almost comical, like we've stepped into another world, so far from the gleaming porches of concrete houses across Rojava, meticulously swept and washed clean from the endless dust, even though there isn't a noticeboard telling anyone to do it. But in the margins of the rules notice someone had scribbled the letters – '*YPJ! YPG!*' – with a ballpoint pen, a small rebellion, or perhaps just a reminder that this, too, is Kurdistan. Inconsequential though it was, it's a scrap of familiarity in the oppressive anonymity of this building, and it soothes something inside me.

We knock on the door of the flat and awkwardly shuffle inside. I'm struck by the wrongness of it, this open-plan, cream coloured, carpeted apartment that tells the story of a Kurdistan that I don't know, foreign precisely because it feels so familiar from a different context. I know it's only a matter of time before I'm submerged in European fashions and aesthetics, but something inside me rebels: I'm not ready yet. Our friend's sister greets us, friendly but reserved, fashionable in leggings and lip gloss. I find myself ungenerous, comparing her with the women I had met in Rojava and finding her wanting. We stumble awkwardly through small talk about her life here, the time she had spent in Europe. I think of the seasoned YPJ fighters who can shake foundations with just one sentence, and the grandmothers who lead the demonstrations and defend their neighbourhoods, every word they say an act of resistance. But she, too, is a woman of Kurdistan, part of the tapestry of survival woven out of history, land, people.

We drink water poured from a cut crystal bottle. Everything is sterile — clean in a way which comes from catalogues and money, not from scrubbing and bleach-chapped hands. Gucci and Chanel design books perch artistically next to the television, carefully curated to invoke wanting. I sneer internally at the stylish apartment and matching glasses, thirsting for something else. At the same time, I know that my harsh judgement of our host and her home comes from my own inner battles, a small voice inside me telling me that I'm not ready to return, so I lash out at this simulacrum of Europe here in Kurdistan.

As if to throw the European aesthetics of the apartment into stark relief, our host's mother sits in an armchair, dignified and silent, timeless in the midst of this cream coloured modernity. She is jarringly out of place, shrouded in black robes, traditional face tattoos blue against her wrinkled brown skin. She does not smile. I wonder what it's like for the mothers, seeing their children leave home in search of something better – safety, opportunity, success – and come back having learned how to invite people to stay for dinner without really meaning it, having learned how to bring their loneliness inside themselves so that they are alone even in a room full of people. I feel that I'm about to make the same journey in reverse, but feel just as lonely at the other end. I am uncertain about what space I will occupy in the country I call home. Will I live up to the responsibility that my comrades have tasked me with: to bring the revolution home with me? Or will I stand stiff and out-of-place, unable to translate my experiences into relevance? I look out of the window which stretches across one wall offering a panoramic view of the city. We watch grey clouds clamber over the mountains and move towards us across the rooftops, swallowing the city like some nebulous beast, turning the world grey.

Europe.

I step out of the airport into a grey winter day. I go first to my father's house, pausing here for a little while before continuing on my journey back to England. Here the nights are longer and darker, in the morning the grass crunches under my shoes, hard with frost. I think back to mornings in Qamişlo, where the church bells in the Christian neighbourhood reminded me of home. Then, at some point home shifted to Qamişlo without me noticing and now the village bells I hear from my father's house remind me of there. I remember winter mornings when we would wake early to stretch before a day sat at our computers, huddling close to the heat of the diesel burner for warmth. In the quiet we could wake up our bodies as the slowly rising sun lifted the darkness, the deep-breathing bodies of our still dreaming friends arranged around the edges of the room. Back in Europe, I wake up alone in the house, in a village full of people I don't know. I make a pot of tea and breakfast for myself. There is a certain comfort, a quietness that suits me. All day long my body is charged with electricity – sparks flash every time I touch metal and the smell of smoke from the wood burner lingers on my hands and settles around my shoulders. I sit at my father's desk wrapped in his woollen sweater, and try to remember all of the things I feel sure need to be written down before they slip away.

The night before, I lay on the floor, Kurdish music playing tinnily from my phone, feeling out of place. My father spent the night in the city to start work early in the morning, so I had the house to myself. This was the first time I had spent the night alone in a room – let alone a whole house – in over a year, a year that felt much longer. A year can be a lifetime, as we are reminded each time we look back on one. My feelings are complicated and all tangled up in my chest – the immense and minuscule all crowded together.

I feel scared that the Turkish state will launch another invasion and chip away – or completely destroy – the revolution as it has unfolded so far. At the same time, I feel overwhelmed at having a fridge full of food to choose from. Touched that my father thought to buy soy milk for my arrival, a small tenderness that throws our distant and awkward relationship into relief. I realise I am lonely. I had become used to being with someone else almost all the time, whether in silence, conversation, or working side by side. I feel like I am constantly waiting for someone to come into the room, although my father won't be coming home until the next day. Then, longing. Longing for the dynamic, determined energy of the organisers from the movement, kind eyes looking out from faces young and old alike. A worn out wanting for being surrounded by complete dedication and steadfastness of vision, fierce intellect, serious mouths pursed in thought but always ready to break out into laughter, a playfulness and wildness beneath steady sensibility. A blurring of memory and dream, future and past, the space between fable and history.

England.

I arrive in England in time for the crocuses. Bold and bright, pushing up through muddy grass in gardens and verges, ringed around trees next to playgrounds and sports courts. They seem more real than the rest of the world, more immediate than either where I'd come from or where I had arrived. Most days I walk for hours across the city, wearing blisters into my toes, trekking mile after mile of pavement. One foot in front of the other, feeling like as long as I keep on moving I'll know where I am going. I take deep breaths of city air – wet park grass blended with car exhaust, the deliciously greasy scent of chicken shops, underground trains teeming with humanity and the thick water of the Thames – and try to root myself to this place, this time. But mostly I still feel like I'm in the wrong place, like when you get on the wrong train but only realise it after the doors shut. And suddenly things are moving too fast around me and I find out that I'm much farther away (from what?) than I thought.

I'm happiest when I can talk about politics, about what Rojava is like and how we can apply lessons to our context. Like talking about a crush, always ready for a giddy release, grabbing at any opportunity to unpack and analyse, describe and desire. Sometimes I launch into an explanation of how things work in Rojava, and after a minute realise that the faces of the people I'm talking to are shocked, maybe even a bit uncomfortable. I don't know whether it's what I'm saying, or that I've been talking too long, too desperately. So many things that I consider to be normal now, or even beautiful, jar against this reality I've landed in. I forget to buckle my seatbelt every time I get into a car. I catch the eye of an attractive stranger and half-remember what it feels like to flirt. I walk into a room and resist the impulse to shake everyone's hand. Tidal waves of emotional muscle memory crash into each other, my grasp on this reality precarious because I had lived another one so intensely. I can feel a hunger inside me, more anger than longing, wanting to fall in love the same way I want to start a revolution. I want to feel everything, sound system basslines pounding deep in my bones, the push of bodies against police lines, sweat and glitter, broken glass and barricades.

I have never felt so foreign in a place I consider my home. When I first arrived in England — 18 years old and out of place — it was a bit like moving through a darkened room, an awkward shuffling across unknown territory, groping in the dark to find my way. But coming back from Rojava is like entering a familiar room and reaching for the light switch only to find out that it has inexplicably moved across the room; rolling out of bed in the morning and bumping into a wall where I thought there would be a door.

The longer I am back in England the slippier the sense of political clarity and purpose that felt so easy to access in Rojava becomes. It's dizzying, constantly juggling the culture, norms, ways of communicating and lived experiences of Kurdistan and Northern Europe. One hand grasps the profound relationships I forged over the past year in Rojava through day to day interdependence and a total dedication to a shared vision, and the other hand holds onto the relationships surrounding me in England, stretching back over years of political organising, living together, supporting each other. The more people I'm in a room with, the more lonely I feel, so I seek the company of trees, fields and hills. I'm saturated by wanting, for something more, but I can't put my finger on exactly what.

I struggle to imagine what I want my life to look like, whether to start making decisions while I still have the clarity and strength of purpose from having just arrived, or whether I need some time to readjust to being back home so I can make wiser decisions. Suddenly wise seems like something that isn't so clear any more. Wise used to mean nuanced, balanced, considered. Wise meant not going too far or too fast, meant having a safety net of some kind. Now wise feels more wild. It feels like throwing yourself into the struggle and rejecting compromise. It means knowing that the resistance we are waging now is more important than our ability to grow old in good health. It means believing in something hard enough so that it drives you through the hardest times. It means trusting that we are on the right path, even if there is no rational way of measuring whether this is true or not.

I find myself constantly trying to hold back an irrepressible flow of analysis, critique and proposals for how we bring a revolutionary approach to our political organising. My earnestness jars against the deep cynicism of most of the people I speak to. I keep on telling people that I feel optimistic about our struggles. I present my case: the political and economic situation here has created the conditions for revolutionary political change, we just need to hold up our end and build the energy, the hope, the vision. People don't seem to expect this optimism, and I'm often met with a sort of half-baffled, half-pleased politeness: "well it's nice to hear you say that." Not many people ask "okay, where do we start?" I feel out of place with my excitement, and feel the need to rein it in so people don't write me off as either deluded or evangelistic. It only takes a few days before I feel myself hesitate before I use the word 'revolution'. I feel a quiet uncertainty about how to live here, how to interact and speak. I can feel that the social rules have shifted slightly, and I'm out of my comfort zone.

In the world of sustainable gardening, there's a saying: 'cultivate the edges and value the margins'. It refers to the idea that the most diverse, dynamic and fruitful part of an ecosystem is along its edges, where it encounters another ecosystem. Like tidal pools teeming with life where the edge of the ocean meets the shore. Or the edge of a forest where different species of plant and animal can benefit from both the trees and the open space beyond them. I would say that in our human communities and social movements this holds true as well. Perhaps this edge space – one foot in Rojava, one foot in England — is the most dynamic and rich with possibility. When we see that multiple worlds exist we understand clearly how we can shape them ourselves. But how do we live in the edge space without losing our balance, without suffering from isolation and alienation?

I walk down city streets disorientated by the reflections, finding it hard to adjust to how shiny everything is, how everything feels like it's for sale — not because you need it for living, but for image, status, or just for the sake of having stuff. There is so much 'identity' to be acquired everywhere – people expressing who they are through how they dress and what they consume and how they move. In many ways identity was reflected through image in Rojava as well – you could often interpret political, ethnic and religious leanings by how someone would dress. But wherever we came from, we were invited to ask ourselves — what does the way I present myself say about my values and how I move through this world?

I think about the straight-backed volunteers in the local security forces, raising a hand in welcome as they walk over to greet you. The plump mothers in long skirts and lined faces and tea-stained teeth, smiling as they invite you into their homes and also as they relentlessly criticise the way you do the washing up. YPJ fighters in uniform with long hair styled in complex braids, entering a room with a quiet confidence that comes from knowing how to defend yourself, who play silly pranks on each other and grow vegetables in plots at their bases. The young teachers on the street at a protest, some bare headed and some wearing hijab, but all of them crisp and professional, hands lifted to the air in victory signs and voices raised in chanting.

Identity is crucial in the Kurdistan Freedom Movement: only by knowing where you come from, and knowing who you are, can you begin to know where you are going. There is a lot of value placed on being rooted in your culture and your collective history, and seeing the work you do as part of a legacy of struggle. Because of this, organisers in the Kurdistan Freedom Movement often look critically at the counter-cultures that we create — punk, anarchist, queer, eco-activist, hippie – seeing them as rebellious but not revolutionary. It's hard to argue against this perspective when it feels like these identities are based on a bitter rejection of wider society and amount to a substitution of broader collective struggle for the comfort of an 'in group'. It's true we need to haul ourselves out of our niches. At the same time, it's often through these subcultures that we are able to scrape together a sense of community and collective care that runs counter to mainstream individualism. It's through these communities that we build a common language to dismantle oppressive realities, and find allies in our insistence on self-defence.

For me, being a queer woman and a part of the queer community was deeply embedded in my political bedrock, and I couldn't imagine being part of a social movement which didn't centre queer liberation. Of course that changed when I became part of the Rojava revolution. Just like in the England, views on queer politics and the gender binary vary radically across the Kurdistan Freedom Movement, from celebration and acceptance, to tolerance, to outright hostility and denial. In my time in Rojava I came across people who had read and appreciated Judith Butler, others who claimed that there were no gay people in Kurdistan, and those who were queer themselves, navigating their own reality just as I navigate mine.

Of course, in any group of people spanning millions there is unlikely to be a uniform perspective on queer politics. But this was a political movement that I had chosen to align myself with, so I couldn't just put it in the same category as smiling and shrugging when my Polish Catholic grandmother asked me if I had a boyfriend yet. It's not that back home I had never experienced homophobia – it's just that the scale of political organising I was involved in meant that I never had to choose whether I align myself with people who I might experience it from. So it felt hard to accept that queer liberation wasn't a core tenet of the revolution, and that for most of my time in Rojava I would be closeted to varying degrees. I experienced and witnessed some homophobia from people within the movement – often from those who had actually grown up in Europe – and was involved in pushing back against it when it felt possible. I drew a lot of strength from the memory of Anna, knowing that she also held this tension and still insisted on going to the front lines to defend the revolution. But it wasn't always easy, and there were times where I felt anger, grief and bitterness.

At its root, my struggle with being a closeted queer was about being part of a huge collective when it didn't always meet my expectations as an individual to be seen and heard, or to have my political beliefs and identity acknowledged and affirmed. So I struggled not just about my queer identity – I struggled when I didn't agree with or understand decisions that I had to abide by, when I wanted personal space but there was none, and when I wasn't consulted on issues that I had a strong opinion on.

Through my time as a semi-closeted queer in the revolution, I met so many other queer, lesbian, gay, trans and non-binary people, Kurdish and internationalist, who had come to the same conclusion as I had: that it was worth it to be part of something so huge, powerful, inspirational and unstoppable – in short, a revolution. In fact, our collective survival hinged on it. Together we can create something bigger than the sum of its parts, which means that it's bigger than any of us. Unless we think that everyone should – and can — be just like us, it means that it won't look exactly like any one of us either. Part of our political work will be to change the movements we organise within to make them the best version of themselves possible. And even though the path is hard and bumpy as hell, we know in our hearts that we're headed to a better place. And it needs all of us to get there.

I had expected that the parts of me that had felt marginalised and out of place in Rojava, like being an out and proud queer, would breathe a sigh of relief and leap into action once I came home. Instead, in coming back the main thing I was struck by was an overwhelming feeling of isolation from a broader struggle, and how painfully I missed the sense of hope and strength that it brings. I can't help but feel these two experiences: the frustration of not feeling represented as an individual in Rojava, and the deep fragmentation and loneliness of Western life and political organising – are somehow related. That what we get in the West is the ability to put our individual identity front and centre, but at the expense of becoming profoundly part of something bigger than us. That only by unlearning some of our desire to centre our individual identities can we access the strength – as individuals and as a collective – of being part of a mass resistance. Back in England, I realised how hard it was to begin to describe what it feels like to know you are part of an intricately woven tapestry – the words I feel I should use are strength, power, strategy, but I find myself reaching for words like love, beauty, joy, and hope, words that don't feel at home in our political vocabulary. I reflected on the humour of the situation – I had shifted from being a closeted queer to being a closeted revolutionary.

When catching up with a friend who had returned from Rojava some months before I had, we talked about how the way we organise and the way we live out our values in Europe has to be different from when we were in Rojava. "We can't fight as hard here", she said — "we don't have as much to put into it, when we have to make money to survive, when we are so much more isolated from each other". It's true that a lot of material conditions make it harder to fully devote ourselves to struggle – but it doesn't just come down to a cut and dry equation of rent, precarious work and the cost of bus tickets. It has to do with the strength that we draw from each other, the care that flows unconditionally across our networks, and the hope that gives us the energy to keep on fighting.

The more that we come together and celebrate, the more picket lines we bring biscuits and coffee to, the more we challenge each other to grow and learn – the more we will be able to face this huge task we have in front of us and feel like we're up to it. The extent to which we're able to do this grows exponentially in relation to how many of us there are, and how organised we are. We can fight harder as part of a bigger whole. And this means that sometimes, a revolutionary political process won't fit like a glove. It will challenge us to work with those we disagree with, disappoint us when it doesn't live up to our expectations, and hurt us the way only the ones we care about the most can. And yet if we don't square our shoulders and consider ourselves up to the challenge, we'll stay painfully inadequate to the work we have ahead of us.

The future.

So what does it mean to come out of the closet as a revolutionary, to live life according to my values? Cynicism is a comfortable rut to be in, which is why so many of us choose it. How do I face up to the fear of full commitment, of getting hurt by putting my heart into a struggle again and risk getting it broken? It's hard to be really honest with myself about how much of my resources – emotional, social, financial, professional – are channelled to create enough of a safety net for myself so that I have something to fall back on. What does it look like to invest those resources into collective safety nets? In some ways it's hard to even begin to answer the question "what does it look like to give everything?" let alone actually do it. But something that a lot of us are guilty of is trying to answer all the questions before we step out onto the path. Drawing on the old Zapatista saying, "walking, we ask questions", we need to be ready to hold uncertainty and discomfort, to get dirty and to make mistakes – revolution is a messy process.

Some days I still feel sick with how much I miss it – not necessarily physically being in Rojava, but of being so firmly part of a movement that I could live and die for. When I feel close to it I feel euphoric, I walk home grinning and giddy, asking myself if I'm in love. And on the days that for one reason or another I feel far away from it, I'm heartsick and hollow with the loss of it. Most days I grapple with how I translate the words, the feelings, the ideas of the movement into our context here, knowing that sloppiness is an inevitable part of the process.

Sometimes I long for things I've never held, a sense of home that has yet to become familiar. I long for the mountains. I dream in Kurdish, fumbling with words and sentences that are just as out of reach in my sleep as they are when I'm awake. When I feel bereft, all it takes is a reminder of how I am still part of it to launch me again onto a wave of euphoria. I am not alone. None of us are – we must remember that we are not alone. I think of revolutionaries in Rojava – those who I've met and those who I haven't — and remember how connected we are, how the bonds of shared experiences and struggle continue to link us now as they will for the rest of our lives. I think of the organisers we have in this country who have been building a movement their whole lives and I feel honoured to walk alongside them in our struggle. I feel butterflies in my stomach and head over heels, reckless in love, a promise on the tip of my tongue before I've found the words for it.

Anna Campbell sees how many revolutionary puppies she can hold

17. TOMORROW

Hope

Jenni and Natalia

"Tomorrow doesn't grow in the spotlight. It is nurtured, cared for, and born in the unobserved shadows during the early morning, when the night just begins to cede ground."

Zapatista communique

Natalia

Although my father's family are farmers in Poland, I grew up among the trimmed, manicured lawns of midwestern American suburbs. I was raised to expect and embrace a future behind a desk, with nature as something that was appreciated on holidays and weekends. Each year, as the bitter Ohio winter thawed and the snow melted, there would come a day – sometimes in March, sometimes as late as May — that brought the smell of spring on the air. And without fail I would rush home from school, dump my backpack and jacket on the driveway, and crouch in the garden to clear the brush from around the crocuses pushing up from the soil. Each year I met the flash of colour from the blossoms with wonder and joy, a promise kept and a promise made at the same time.

A couple decades later, I am sitting at my desk and writing on a cold February afternoon. The nights have been long and dark for months now, and it's hard to remember that spring will come. This is especially hard in a world where coronavirus is still spreading, and we've been isolated and claustrophobic for most of the past year. But this year, like every other year, people are breathing in the smell of rich soil, the cold air turning each exhale into a cloud soft with possibility, and sowing seeds. Even after years of gardening, there is still something improbable about a tiny seed becoming a leaf, a flower, a fruit. Seeds don't need us to believe in them in order to sprout, but if we're trying to grow a garden, they do need our love and attention to thrive.

Anyone who has tended a garden can tell you that to garden fundamentally shifts our relationship to the earth, to seasonal cycles and to time. As I harvest the fruit of the seeds sown months before, I plant new ones to nurture over the coming months. I notice when it rains and when the frost comes. I move through the seasons with the soil and seedlings, and see how every year follows patterns, but still has its own character. So when I squint doubtfully at the tiny seeds I hold in my palm as winter sits defiant on the land, I rely on hope to believe that they will take root and grow towards the sun.

It can be hard to cultivate hope sometimes, and often we forget that it's not something that just comes and goes without our say so. It's something that we need to work on, a fire to feed in ourselves and in others. This is something that a lot of internationalist volunteers with the Kurdistan Freedom Movement discover. Many of us arrive in Rojava expecting to receive a top up of our hope balance, putting ourselves in the position of consumer rather than a creator. But hope which is entirely dependent on an external source would only yield poor fruit, it can never thrive in the harsh conditions of the struggle we are in. So we need to insist on hope, not just wait for it to arrive. The hope inside of us lives in a reciprocal relationship with the world around us. Much like the interdependence with nature that we belong in, the wider struggle feeds us and fuels our hope, but in turn we must build our ability to hope and use it to steward resistance.

It's not surprising that the most precious thing we brought back from Rojava was a sense of hope. This time it wasn't the effervescent hope of youth and novelty, but something more solid, deeply rooted and hewn out of hard struggle. In some ways this whole book is about hope, and why it's one of the most important things we need to nurture if we want to win.

When we dare to let hope out, let it grow stronger in the light and air, when we work for it, we discover it makes us stronger than we ever knew in return. Suddenly, we can give everything, with love and joy, and then there's no limit to what we can do. We can face moments of pressure and crisis and years of long, dark, boring haul.

Jenni

In Kurdistan, you dance a lot. You join hands and make a chain, and that chain carries us through lines of hundreds of strangers under a beating sun, round and round your living room at midnight learning new steps, following in the shadow of those with real flair as they stomp and twirl and grin back at us as they bring us along.

Behind me I can feel the firm grip on my elbow of a folk dance in a Scottish community centre, as we pass ourselves from person to person, everyone dancing with everyone regardless of age or gender. I can feel myself pressed up against other sweaty, grinning revellers in a club or a sprawling tent, or someone's crowded, smokey living room, as we talk without words and become much more than the sum of our parts.

The line stretches out in front of me to my return from Kurdistan. Suddenly we didn't gather in large groups any more, but despite that, it only takes the handful of us who live together to turn the living room into a high spirited karaoke night. My sister and I will start the day with music, just the two of us and some fairy lights under a low, grey sky. I dance alone, more often than I should probably admit: hotel rooftops in Iraq on my way home from Rojava; nearly missing the turn on snow-covered country roads under the stars back in Scotland because I'm enjoying a song too much. I never feel alone in those moments. We're part of that chain. When we dance we can feel that there's more to us, and more to life, than dull mechanics. When we dance we reconnect our souls and our physical selves. We remake that promise of hope.

There are a lot of reasons to lose hope with the world the way it is. But there are many more reasons to keep it. High among them is the fact that our enemies want us to lose hope. If we lose hope, we will not fight, and they will have already won. So we should be suspicious of any philosophy that tries to say things are hopeless. And we should take responsibility to create our own hope. It's part of the fight, a part of our struggle. And if that means we need to dance, then we'll damn well dance.

While we were in Kurdistan, the rage and beauty of resistance poured out across the world. Fibre optic cables fired images of struggle to and fro. In particular it seemed like women's resistance, gender struggle and the fight against patriarchy were taking front and centre. Of all the riots, communiques, actions, marches and call-outs, what really bridged the gap was a dance. Those fibre optic cables, wonderful though they are, tend to strip the human soul out of things. A dance put it right back. Chilean feminist art collective Las Tesis wrote a simple song and dance that everyone could follow, and they did, thousands upon thousands of feet stomping out the dance across the world. It was about who our enemy is, and it was angry. It was also about who we are. It was uplifting.

They say we might have sung before we talked. It seems obvious that we danced. Every child does. Our bodies rock and our feet lift and drop, lift and drop, simultaneously responding to and creating the beat. Our bodies, moving, in the moment but always anticipating the next step, are the common denominator that runs across the world.

Dance is one of the most present and immediate things we ever do, and yet, it is filled with a promise of the future. A promise of hope.

Natalia

Ten years ago, and it's a cold and grey October. I drag myself onto the train and into work, still reeling from the brutal eviction of the Dale Farm

Traveller site a couple days before. I stand between the ramshackle vegetable beds of the community garden where I work and wonder what I'm doing there. As the families from the tight-knit Dale Farm community scatter to sites and lay-bys across the country, and as solidarity activists from the eviction resistance are released from police cells and hunker down in cold squats for the winter, I grow vegetables, make compost and prune fruit trees. I learn to call plants by their names – salvia officinalis, solanum tuberosum, daucus carota. I spend so many hours picking bindweed out of the soil that I see its white tangled roots in my mind as I drift off to sleep. I don't realise it at the time, but the earth is healing me. Even while I wrangle with the hurdles that humans impose onto something as simple as land — funding, trustees, policies, ownership – I find peace and meaning in coaxing life out of the earth. Something as simple as gathering a harvest from a patch of earth that I had tended through the seasons is deeply restorative. It reminds me that despite the cruelty that exists in the world, the earth still cares for us, and the life-giving cycle of soil to seedling to fruit to soil continues. There is death, and suffering, and conflict in nature – but nature heals and turns towards survival.

Healing is part of hope, the ability to keep fighting and keep believing that change is possible. If we pay attention to the good earth that is our home, we come to know that change is inevitable and the world is bountiful. The smallest patch of earth contains an infinite amount of cooperation and interdependence, from the tiny microbes in the soil to the towering heights of sequoia pines. Hope and healing are also a collective project, something we cannot achieve on our own.

You know the spirit of the Kurdistan Freedom Movement has sunk in when failure or imperfections, rather than making you lose hope, serve to strengthen it. Being faced with the shortcomings of the revolutionary process in North and East Syria demonstrated that something as beautiful and powerful as the Rojava revolution was built out of humans as imperfect as any of us. Its achievements aren't premised on some mythical humans arriving perfect to the struggle, but rather on the ability of humans to learn from their mistakes, to find new ways of being in the world, and to help each other grow. If we're doing it right, hope can be strengthened through imperfection and failings, rather than weakened by it. It means that we don't give up on each other, and we don't let each other lose hope. We are able to bring action, healing and hope into a dynamic relationship with each other, in which each one fuels and feeds the others.

How do revolutionaries in prison keep hope alive? The ongoing stories of prison resistance in the Kurdistan Freedom Movement are echoed across the world and history: from Ireland, to Algeria, to Indonesia, and to all those imprisoned for whatever reason. Kept behind bars for years with no rights, under attack every single day, and cut off from their communities, they fight back. They fight for life, for the future, and for what they still believe is possible. If people can maintain hope under these conditions, we too must work to find the hope in our lives and struggles. Not that we 'have it easy' as such. We are also under attack, just in different and more subtle ways. But one of the most important ways we can defend ourselves is to refuse to accept hopelessness and nihilism.

At Anna's funeral, one friend of hers recounted a story of when they first met, when they were preparing for an action. Anna was laughing, joking, almost making light of what was going on. At first, her soon-to-be-friend thought her attitude was childish, or that she saw organising as a game. But soon she realised, as she put it 'that it was just that everything she did, she did with joy." When this story was told, two hundred people gave a collective sigh of recognition. That was Anna, alright. And that joy gave hope and that hope bred more joy.

Jenni

Late at night, a handful of internationalist volunteers hunch over computers next to coffee cups long since emptied and turned into ash trays, occasionally making a futile effort to roll cricks out of our necks. We're translating interviews with YPG fighters and local politicians, sending emails about human rights violations to institutions who are programmed not to care, trying to learn how to use video editing software from YouTube tutorials. There's a critical mass of English and Scottish volunteers in the room, and that means (along with a bit more swearing and occasionally upsetting Kurdish comrades by putting milk in the tea), we are basically talking as though everything we're doing is pointless. We fuel ourselves with sarcasm and self deprecation, expecting bad news before we even hear it. Yet, we all keep on working, as hard as anyone. When someone starts to flag, more tea, coffee, cigarettes and a shoulder rub go without saying. If someone expresses that they really can't go on any more, that they've lost all faith, we pull them back. Probably not by mentioning the big picture (the one that actually makes all our efforts make sense) but more likely with a joke. Maybe the black humour and cynicism we've cultivated are a sort of Trojan Horse for hope. We make light of things so that we can keep going, so that we can appear cynical but somehow still be there from dawn until the depths of night. Maybe it's what we've needed to shelter the little flame of hope long enough to get us through hard years, get us where we are right now, thousands of miles from home, in the middle of a revolution.

But I'm starting to think it's only going to get us so far. We have to use that flame, we have to relight the fire. And now that we're here in North and East Syria our cynicism suddenly looks different. Earlier that day I was out of the office, in a family's home. It's much harder to be jaded when you're looking the kids from the region in the eye, effectively acting like they have no future. And when certain other comrades join us at the desks, and the language switches to Kurdish, we drop a lot of the attitude along with the English language. These people have lost all their old friends and comrades, been tortured and wounded, and are still fighting like we can win. Now it's cynicism that starts to feel embarrassing, not hope. I touch the tattoo on my neck that I got in memory of Anna, look at the pictures of other şehîds lining the walls, and stop myself the next time I go to add a self-effacing eye-roll onto the word 'revolution'. Our fallen comrades didn't fall for nihilism.

In leftist movements in the West, hope can be treated as an afterthought, as something that's nice if you have it, but if you don't you can plough on regardless. We continue marching, blockading, campaigning, petitioning, as if the motions of taking action will yield the same fruit even if they are not rooted in an insistence on hope. But action without hope is just complaining. The systems of power tolerate a certain level of dissent because it gives society a chance to blow off steam, and gives those in power a veneer of legitimacy and accountability. It is entirely in the interests of those in power that we rebel in some way without truly believing that we can achieve radical system change.

When we feed our rebellion with hope, with the belief that we will be victorious, it can become revolution. We can start building up the systems of democratic power that can take on systems of domination, and win. This is what it means to have a revolutionary approach to political organising – that you have the strength to sow seeds of freedom even when the world is still cold and dark, when it's hard to believe that anything will ever change.

Back home, it sometimes seemed we needed a protective shell of cynicism to engage in political organising. To be caught believing or even hoping we could succeed was embarrassing, showing you up as naive or childish. 'It's all doomed to fail, and we've probably got it wrong, but I guess we should do this anyway" was the most motivation I for one could come up with half the time. Was it just that we wanted to be able to say we told you so? Or was it that our consciences wouldn't quite let go? Was it that things were either *definitely* going down the tube if we did nothing, or only *probably*, perhaps even *maybe*, if we acted? And there it is. Hope isn't certainty or even optimism. It's just knowing that we don't actually *know*. Cynicism and nihilism are forms of arrogance. Hope accepts that we are tiny little parts of the cosmos who do not have an all-seeing wisdom that allows us to predict the future. We can only pedal and push in our own little corner, but who knows what ripples will spread? Or what ripples are already heading our way. Of course, when we admit that, we open ourselves up to disappointment and pain, and also ridicule. So we wrap hope up tightly and shove it deep down where it couldn't be touched any more.

Natalia

Another garden, this time in Rojava, so early in the morning that it's closer to night. We rise before the sun and walk a familiar path from our beds to the young orchard straining to take root in soil baking hard under the sun. It's still cool this early, but once the sun emerges the heat will be relentless, maxing out the thermometers and dragging moisture out of everything it touches. So we water the vegetable patches and the orchards in the evenings and early in the mornings, giving the roots a few hours to absorb water before the sun makes it impossible. My footsteps crunch on parched grass and thistles as I walk from tree to tree with a bucket of water in each hand. I measure the passing of time by the band of light moving across the mountains on the horizon, by the small shifts in the soundscape as night slips into day. I drink in the fresh air as the trees drink in the water — mornings are peaceful. In the daytimes, we move not just through stifling heat but the reality of imminent invasion, of the Turkish army and mercenaries gathering on the border, of the necessity to make preparations for war. But as the sun is still rising, we prepare for a different kind of future. A future in which the olive and fig and mulberry trees that we have planted bear fruit and cast shade for those who will make this place their home after we've gone.

In Kurdistan, when you ask people a question about the present, their answer often starts in the past. During the 2019 Turkish invasion of Rojava, a friend interviewed a resident in a village outside of a town that Turkish forces were drawing closer to every day. She asked about the situation of the war, how it was impacting village life. The man, no stranger to losing his home to war, started telling the history of the Ottoman Empire, and made his way towards the present by way of the mountains of Kurdistan and the previous year's invasion of Afrin. He understood how the history of a region gives form and momentum to its present, how our past shapes our future.

So when we look at the resistance brewing in Chile, in Lebanon, in Hong Kong, in Rojava, in Iraq, we see it as the bubbling up of an ancient struggle. When we see Black Lives Matter and Fridays for the Future and the Standing Rock resistance, we recognise Wounded Knee, the Black Panthers, the Diggers, and go even further back. We see it as part of a long history of humanity pushing back against the forces of oppression and exploitation. We see it as not just a reaction against a moment, but a dismantling of the categories that shape our world: dominating over dominated, human over nature, man over woman, rich over poor, state over subject.

And when we come up against obstacles and failures, when it's tempting to give up, we remind ourselves to step back and use a wider lens. Resistance is not an incident, it's a process, a line that we can trace back thousands of years. Knowing this gives us power, the ability to hold onto our hope as we are rocked by the tumultuous waters of struggle. The revolutionaries we met in Kurdistan feel the weight of that history not as a burden on their shoulders but as an anchor that steadies and strengthens them. We have done our best to learn to do the same, to feel ourselves part of a movement that spans millennia and crosses borders. To stand firmly and proudly, shoulder to shoulder with those around the world who fight with the patience of our elders and the insistence of youth, rooted in our history and reaching for the stars.

AFTERWORD

We wrote this book because we couldn't *not* write it. Because when things feel big, and bright, and important, you can't just shut them away inside yourself. Because the revolutionaries we had the honour to work alongside in Rojava asked us to, sharing stories in order to build bridges between their struggles and ours. None of the lessons we've tried to share here are unique. There are many people and organisations across the world already having these conversations. For lots of people, we are not bringing very much that's new. Not everyone had to go as far as we did to figure it out either! But it's a chorus, not a competition to be heard. What we've been lucky enough to experience, we should share.

As close friends, loved ones, comrades, acquaintances, and those who just can't resist a good edit took a look at early drafts of this book for us, a question kept coming up: what now? Where do we go with all of this?

Since we came back from Kurdistan that's exactly what we've been trying to figure out, and a lot of the time it feels like we're still just blundering around, taking dead ends and tripping over our own feet.

It would be misleading if we said that was the only reality though. Life will never be the same again and the lessons we learned are with us every day as we engage with community organising, bridge building, developing militancy, radical education, creating networks of rebellious love and care, discussing and questioning, always questioning. We're trying to not keep making the same mistakes, while making sure no one is left behind. Trying to broaden our networks and move the frame of possibility.

We sat down to work out what were the most important messages to get across, finding ourselves staring at a revolutionary shopping list: History and rooted struggle; belief and hope in ourselves and in society; gender liberation; collective care paired with passionate, unboundaried commitment; knowing who you are; always asking the big questions; criticism of the ideologies that are dominant in the world right now; relentless self reflection; education; militancy, joy and love.

There's a dozen other books we didn't write, pages and pages that just don't fit. Other people might have been able to tell you all this and more through theory and history. We tell stories, so we chose the stories we felt we needed to tell. We've woven the questions that we think we need to be asking — and even some of the answers — into the stories that we've written on these pages.

The Kurdistan Freedom Movement offers itself to anyone in the world who wants to be a part of it. Really a part of it, not just through solidarity actions or support initiatives that are disconnected from ourselves. Increasing numbers of internationalists across the world are finding ways to work with the movement and within its many different forms and organisations. You don't have to go far to do it. You could go all the way to Kurdistan, and you'd be welcomed with open arms. But there's a lot we can do from our homes, no matter where they are.

The movement offers itself also as an inspiration, a source of ideology and strength that many different movements can draw on. Anti-colonial movements, including Black feminism, Zapatismo, and the Kurdistan Freedom Movement, are not a side chapter in revolutionary history. They are at the forefront, opening the way for resistance to spread across the world.

Sometimes the road seems bumpy, long, and confusing. Where we go from here, what the next step is, right here and now, is always the hardest question. To ask these questions and seek the answers means to embark on a long, often daunting, journey. But whatever the answer is, we're not going to find it alone. We need to join forces, fall into step and walk side by side along the road. A long journey in company is a whole other story.

ACKNOWLEDGEMENTS

This book is a collective effort. From advice to patience; from encouragement to posing the all-important challenging questions; from morning cuppas to intense 2am chats, it really would be impossible to mention everyone who's been part of the process. Hopefully you all know who you are.

Still we'd like to give the thanks we can. To Anna F, Auntie Soup, Chloe, Dee, Em, Etzali, Gemma, Greg, Hannah, Jo, Joe, Leslie, Lizzie, Lotte, Maddy, Matt, Rhian, Rowan, Ta, Tijda and Zahra for your insightful comments and reflections, and meticulous proofreading. To Active for making it happen, Matt for the beautiful designs, and Craig for the enthusiastic support.

To Phe, Jono, and Sorcha for letting us take over their homes and cover them in weird post-its and the smell of takeaways on work weekends. To the workers at Wetherspoons and Greggs who ignored their bosses and left us in peace even though we didn't order anything as we set up a makeshift office around a table.

To the homes and families that have kept us fed, warm and well in heart and mind throughout this time: Green Wood and The Bog, and everywhere else we've laid our heads.

To the friends of the Andrea Wolf Institute, the 'hevpals' of home, and all our comrades near and far, past and present, for helping each other find the way along the bumpy paths of struggle.

To the Nest, for all the highs and lows.

Once more (and forever) to Anna Campbell, for lighting the way.

And the deepest gratitude and respect to all the comrades who have brought the struggle this far. We stand on your shoulders, and we swear to do our best to do you justice.

GLOSSARY

Abdullah Öcalan — One of the founders of and the leader of the Kurdistan Workers' Party (known by its Kurdish acronym PKK), and the thinker behind the ideology of the Kurdistan Freedom Movement. He has been held as a political prisoner by the Turkish state on a prison island for over 20 years. Also referred to as Reber Apo.

Azadî — Kurmanji for 'Freedom' or 'Liberation', always used in the political and collective sense. Often seen in the slogan 'Jin, Jiyan, Azadî', meaning 'Women, life, freedom'. This slogan was widely used during the uprisings across Iran in October 2022 by a wide range of groups, and has its roots in the revolutionary politics of the Kurdistan Freedom Movement.

Commune — The core political unit of democratic confederalism, meaning either a small organised neighbourhood, or a group living together collectively. Communes take decisions and deal with problems through discussion and direct democracy.

Democratic confederalism — The political system of the Kurdistan Freedom Movement, as proposed by Abdullah Öcalan. A structure built from the bottom up on core principles of direct, grass-roots democracy, ecology, and women's liberation.

Democratic modernity — The Kurdistan Freedom's Movement name for the future we are building, based on the principles of women's liberation, ecology and grass-roots democracy.

Ezidi — A minority religion within Kurdistan particularly targetted by state forces throughout history. Most recently the Islamic State committed genocide against the Ezidis, with many of the women kidnapped into sexual slavery. Sometimes spelled as Yezidi.

Hevaltî — Kurmanji for 'friendship', also carrying the meaning of 'comradeship', and understood as a way of revolutionary life and love that starts to model relationships beyond systems of oppression.

ISIS — The Islamic State in Iraq and Syria, also referred to as IS, ISIL, or its Arabic acronym DAESH. A global jihadist Islamic fundamentalist organisation that occupied swathes of land across Iraq and Syria to establish a so-called Islamic caliphate, in which extreme brutality and violence against women was widely practised.

Jineolojî — The 'Science of Women and Life' has been developed as an alternative scientific paradigm in the Women's Liberation Movement in Kurdistan. It criticises positivist sciences as a means of power and aims at connecting women's knowledge, wisdom and analysis to theoretical and practical efforts to liberate women and societies. The Jineolojî Academy is an autonomous women's institution composed of regional research centres, various institutes and committees.

Kurdistan — The region in the Middle East with an indigenous and majority Kurdish population, divided by the nation state borders of Turkey, Syria, Iraq and Iran.

Kurdistan Freedom Movement (KFM) — The social movement that broadly follows the ideology of Abdullah Öcalan, operating across Kurdistan, the Middle East, and globally.

Kurmanji — The dialect of Kurdish commonly spoken in Western and Northern Kurdistan (Rojava and Bakur).

Liberalism — The ideology supporting capitalism and the state that developed during the enlightenment. Characterised by fetishising the individual, denying society, co-opting narratives of freedom, and championing social structures based on laws rather than ethics.

North and East Syria — The area of Syria currently administered by the governance structures born out of the Rojava revolution, but extending beyond Rojava to include Arabic-majority areas.

Peşengtî *(peh-sheng-tee)* — The Kurdish revolutionary principle of being an example, leadership through embodying your values. Sometimes translated as 'vanguard'.

PKK – The Kurdistan Workers' Party, which began as a Marxist national liberation movement in the 1970s. Consists of guerilla forces and a political wing. Under the guidance of its leader Abdullah Öcalan the PKK has moved to an anti-state and anti-patriarchal position, playing a vanguard role in Kurdistan Freedom Movement ideology.

Rojava — The region of Kurdistan located within Syrian nation state borders, the Kurdish word for 'West'.

Rojava, Bakur, Başur, and Rojhilat — The Kurdish words for West, North, South and East, referring to the regions of Kurdistan within the nation state borders of Syria, Turkey, Iraq and Iran, respectively.

Syrian Democratic Forces (SDF) — The military force comprised of the YPG and YPJ as well as many other military units including Arabic-majority, Syriac-Assyrian and Armenian units, which has led the fight against ISIS in Syria. The SDF is accountable to the Syrian Democratic Council, a political body established through the Rojava revolution.

Şehîd *(sheh-heed)* — Those who have been lost in struggle, martyrs of the movement.

Tekmil and critic/self-critic — A method of collective personal development, attempting to dismantle internalised mechanisms of oppression. People analyse themselves and others in relation to systems of oppression and give reflection on how to develop beyond them.

Welatparêzî — Kurdish expression that means 'love and defence of the land'. It means to have a bond with the homeland and to defend your country, culture and language against colonialism, oppression and assimilation. In the Kurdish community, the term Welatparêzî is also used for Kurdish supporters of the anti-colonial liberation struggle.

YPG and YPJ — The People's Defence Units and Women's Defence Units, Kurdish led military units which spearheaded the fight against ISIS and other jihadist groups, including in the Battle of Kobane.

FURTHER LEARNING

This section is in no way comprehensive or it would be the length of another book. What's listed here is a combination of historical and political works that go deeper into the Kurdistan context; texts and other works put out by the movement itself; lessons from our movements closer to home; and some more of the thoughts, stories, and visions of the world that inspire us and are in the same spirit and direction as the movement and beliefs we talk about here. We're not necessarily completely aligned with everything we're sharing, but we see these works as parts of a rich chorus that is asking the right questions. We've intentionally mixed fiction with non-fiction, because we believe that's the way to truth, and included some audio and videos because there's different ways to learn.

Works of Abdullah Öcalan:
» *Prison Writings: The Roots of Civilisation*, Pluto
» *Prison Writings II: The PKK and the Kurdish Question in the 21st Century*, Transmedia
» *Prison Writings III: The Road Map to Negotiations*, International Initiative
» *Democratic Confederalism*, Transmedia
» *Liberating life: Women's Revolution*, International Initiative
» *The Political Thought of Abdullah Öcalan*, Pluto Press
» *Manifesto for a Democratic Civilization, Volume 1*, New Compass

» *Manifesto for a Democratic Civilization, Volume 2*, New Compass
» *The Sociology of Freedom: Manifesto of the Democratic Civilization, Volume III*, PM Press/Kairos
» *Beyond State, Power, And Violence*, PM Press

Writings on the Kurdistan Freedom Movement:

» *Revolution in Rojava: Democratic Autonomy and Women's Liberation in Syrian Kurdistan*, Ercan Ayboga, Anja Flach, and Michael Knapp; Pluto Press
» *Their Blood Got Mixed*, Janet Biehl; PM Press
» *My Whole Life Was A Struggle*, Sakine Cansiz; Pluto Press
» *The Kurdish Women's Movement: History, Theory and Practice*, Dilar Dirik; Pluto press
» *This Fire Never Dies*, Fréderike Geerdink; Leftword Books
» *Killing and transforming the dominant male, and Revolutionary Education*, from the Andrea Wolf Institute. Available free at jineoloji.org/en ⟹ publications ⟹ pamphlets.

Even more books!:

» *Natives: Race and class in the ruins of empire*, Akala; Two Roads
» *Emergent Strategy: Shaping Change, Changing Worlds*, Adrienne Maree Brown; AK Press
» *Parable of the Sower and Parable of the Talents*, Octavia Butler; Seven Stories Press
» *Caliban and the Witch: Women, the body, and primitive accumulation*, Sylvia Federici; Autonomedia
» *Capitalist Realism: Is there no alternative?* Mark Fisher; Zero Books
» *Our Word Is Our Weapon: Selected writings*, Subcommandante Galeano (Marcos); Serpent's Tail
» *Matriarchal Societies: Studies on indigenous cultures across the globe*, Heide Göttner-Abendroth; Peter Lang
» *The Hainish Cycle*, Ursula K. Le Guin; Various
» *The Carhullan Army*, Sarah Hall; Faber and Faber
» *Assata: An Autobiography*, Assata Shakur; Lawrence Hill Books

- » *The Will to Change: Men, masculinity, and love*, bell hooks; Simon and Schuster
- » *We Make the Road by Walking: Conversations on Education and Social Change*, Myles Horton and Paolo Freire; Temple University Press
- » *Chav Solidarity*, D. Hunter; Active
- » *The Song of the Lioness series*, Tamora Pierce; Atheneum Books
- » *We Want Freedom: a life in the Black Panther Party*, Mumia Abu Jamal: South End Press
- » *Wild Geese: selected poems*, Mary Oliver; Bloodaxe
- » *We Do This 'Til We Free Us: Abolitionist Organising and Transforming Justice*, Mariame Kaba; Haymarket Books
- » *Zami: A New Spelling of My Name*, Audre Lorde; Persephone Press
- » *Braiding Sweetgrass: Indigenous wisdom, scientific knowledge, and the teachings of plants*, Robin Wall Kimmerer; Penguin Books Ltd
- » *No Shortcuts: Organizing for Power in the New Gilded Age*, Jane McAlevey; Oxford University Press
- » *Soil and Soul: People versus Corporate Power*, Alistair McIntosh; Aurum
- » *The Witches Trilogy*, Terry Pratchett; Gollancz
- » *The Wolf Wilder*, Katherine Rundell; Bloomsbury Children's Books
- » *The Shepherd's Life*, James Rebanks; Allen Lane
- » *Now That We Have your Attention*, Jack Shenker; The Bodley Head
- » *The Bear and the Nightingale*, Katherine Arden; Del Ray

Websites, campaigns and solidarity networks:
- » Jineolojî: Jineoloji.org/en
- » Academy of Democratic Modernity: democraticmodernity.com
- » Kurdistan Solidarity Network: kurdistansolidarity.net
- » Scottish Solidarity with Kurdistan: facebook.com/ScottishSolidaritywithKurdistan
- » Rise Up For Rojava: riseup4rojava.org
- » Women Defend Rojava: womendefendrojava.net/en

Films:
- » *Three Roses of the Revolution* (2022) — Available on Youtube
- » *Commander Arian: A story of women, war and freedom* (2018

- » *Gulistan: Land of roses* (2016)
- » *Maxmûr: Blooming in the desert* (2020) Available on YouTube
- » *Kurdistan: Girls at War / La guerre des filles* (2016) — Available on YouTube
- » *Şoreşa Jin/Women's Revolution* (2017) — Available on YouTube
- » *Blooming in the Desert: Three women in Raqqa are rebuilding their future* (2021)

Podcasts:

- » Çay at the Women's Front: womensfront.com
- » Mother Country Radicals: crooked.com/podcast/mother-country-radicals

ABOUT THE AUTHORS

Jenni lives in the wet bit of Scotland surrounded by amazing people and semi-working vehicles, and supports herself to scheme revolution and write by doing care work. She's eternally grateful for lush woods, mountains, mischief, dogs, families of all kinds, comrades, physical activity, people telling her when she's wrong, good food and good company. Above all, she's grateful for the struggle. The Kurdistan Freedom Movement has already changed her life and she is still figuring out where the journey goes.

Natalia arrived in England via Poland and the USA and is now happy to call Yorkshire home. She's worked in community food projects and the agroecological movement for many years, which has allowed her to combine her love of spreadsheets, mulch and meeting facilitation. When she's not doing political organising she tries to squeeze in time for rollerskating, reading teen fantasy novels, growing flowers and deep frying things.